THE FIGURE OF THEATER

The Figure of Theater

SHAFTESBURY, DEFOE, ADAM SMITH,
and
GEORGE ELIOT

David Marshall

NEW YORK
Columbia University Press
1986

The Press wishes to acknowledge the assistance of the Frederick W. Hilles Publication Fund of Yale University in the preparation of this volume.

Columbia University Press
New York   Guildford, Surrey
Copyright © 1986 Columbia University Press

Printed in the United States of America

Library of Congress Cataloging in Publication Data

Marshall, David, 1953 Dec. 20–
   The figure of theater.

   Bibliography: p.
   Includes index.
   1. English prose literature—History and criticism.   2. Theater in literature.   I. Title.
PR756.T45M37   1985   828'.08   85-10967
ISBN 0-231-06084-X

This book is Smyth-sewn and printed on permanent and durable acid-free paper.

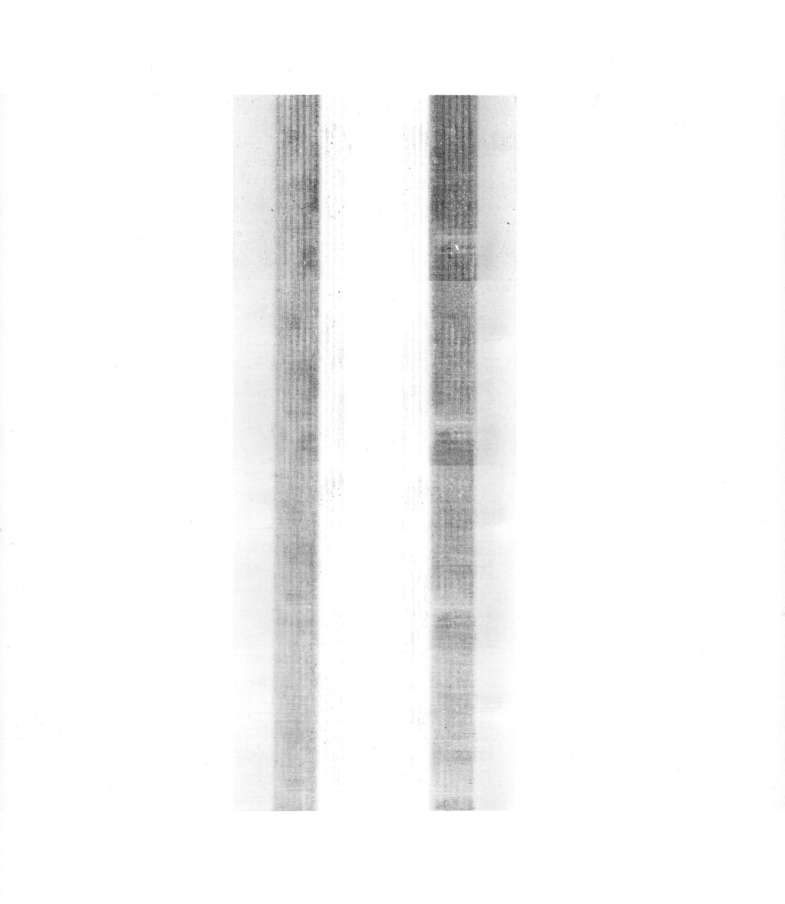

For my grandparents

Contents

Acknowledgments

IN *Soliloquy, or Advice to an Author,* Shaftesbury warns against "the coquetry of a modern author, whose epistles dedicatory, prefaces, and addresses to the reader are so many affected graces, designed to draw the attention from the subject towards himself, and make it be generally observed, not so much what he says, as what he appears, or is, and what figure he already makes, or hopes to make, in the fashionable world." Shaftesbury himself in his preface to the *Characteristics* disavows any "dedication, direct or indirect application for favour to the public, or to any private patron or party whatsoever." However, I suggest in the following pages that even Shaftesbury found it necessary to acknowledge the public and private readers inscribed in both his public and his private texts; and in an age in which authors more freely acknowledge their own authorship on title pages and elsewhere, I have looked forward to making some public acknowledgment of the communities of colleagues and friends in which and for which I wrote this book.

One difficulty in writing acknowledgments for *The Figure of Theater* is the extent to which the book seems to me a palimpsest of times and places, drafts and versions, dialogues with people and texts. Early versions of the manuscript benefited from the generous teaching and conversation of Hugh Kenner and Louis Marin. Many others allowed me to draw them into dialogue in and about the early stages of this work: especially, Richard Macksey, Vicki Dello Joio, Victoria Kahn, Robert Mankin, Timothy Murray, Bill Nemir, Neil Saccamano, Marilyn Sides, and Barry Weller. I would like to express my special gratitude to Michael Fried, whose own work has informed my understanding of some of the central issues in this book; his advice, confidence, and intellectual commitment have guided me from the outset of this project.

I am grateful for the support and encouragement I received while completing this book from my colleagues in The Literature Major and the English and Comparative Literature Departments at Yale University. Peter Brooks, Paul de Man, and J. Hillis Miller were particularly kind and generous in many ways; I am also grateful to Geoffrey Hartman, Thomas Greene, John Hollander, Ronald Paulson, Martin Price, Patricia Meyer Spacks, Alan Trachtenberg, and the Fellows of The Whitney Humanities Center for the interest they have taken in my work.

Margaret Ferguson and Jean-Christophe Agnew each played the role of sympathetic reader for me, offering serious responses to all the versions of this text. A course that I taught with Jean-Christophe Agnew allowed me to refine and deepen my interpretations of Smith, Eliot, and the theatrical perspective. I would like to thank the students in that seminar and in many other courses I have taught at Yale for helping me try out and work out my readings. I also would like to thank Norton Batkin, Jennifer Wicke, Kimberly Benston, Leslie Agnew, Cindy Marshall, Karen Marshall, and especially Candace Waid for conversations about my work and timely encouragement. My parents, who always believed in this book, provided every opportunity.

I would like to thank Jean Edmunds, who typed the manuscript with reassuring care and intelligence, and Jill Campbell, who proofread the text with all the skills of an acute critical reader. I am grateful to Leslie Bialler, my editor at Columbia University Press, for his understanding and efficiency in preparing the text for publication. Versions of chapters 7 and 8 were presented as lectures for the Humanities Center of The Johns Hopkins University in 1982. Chapter 7 appeared in a slightly different form in *Critical Inquiry*, June 1984. (Vol. 10, no. 4. Copyright © 1984 The University of Chicago.) I thank the various audiences who have entered (and will enter) into dialogue with this book.

THE FIGURE OF THEATER

Must all be vail'd, while he that reades, divines,
Catching the sense at two removes?

George Herbert,
"Jordan" (I)

Introduction

"L'homme est né spectateur."
L'Abbé Batteux

THIS book offers an interpretation of the figure of theater in the *Characteristics* and other texts by Shaftesbury, *Moll Flanders, Roxana,* and other texts by Daniel Defoe, Adam Smith's *The Theory of Moral Sentiments,* and George Eliot's *Daniel Deronda.* In the chapters that follow, I trace how theater appears and reappears in these texts as a figure for a range of interrelated concerns that cut across the disparate realms of book publishing, fiction writing, moral philosophy, epistemology, and aesthetics. Shaftesbury, Defoe, Smith, and Eliot, I will argue, all are concerned with the theater that exists outside of the playhouse: the theatrical relations formed between people who face each other from the positions of actor and spectator, and the play of characters created by a view of the self as a persona, a role, or a representation that can display or conceal or counterfeit the signs of inner feeling. Theater, for these authors, represents, creates, and responds to uncertainties about how to constitute, maintain, and represent a stable and authentic self; fears about exposing one's character before the world; and epistemological dilemmas about knowing or being known by other people. These concerns are staged in a variety of terms and contexts. For Smith and Eliot, for example, such fears and dilemmas take place within the context of investigations into the conditions of sympathy. Shaftesbury and Defoe are preoccupied with the theatrical status of the published book and the relation formed between authors and readers. Defoe's investment in theatrical impersonation can help make sense of both his anxieties about fiction and his obsession with disguise and deception. All of these authors use the terms of theater to reflect on, dramatize, and enact the multileveled problem of publishing characters before the eyes of the world.

I stress that Shaftesbury, Defoe, Smith, and Eliot use theater to dramatize and enact and not merely to reflect on various problems, just as I specified that theater creates and responds to uncertainties as well as representing them, because I am arguing that the figure of theater does more than simply "stand for" particular issues that in themselves have nothing to do with the theater. Obviously such issues as the status of the published book, eighteenth-century anxiety about fiction, philosophical debates about identity, and the conditions of sympathy have been discussed without any reference to theater. My claim is that for Shaftesbury, Defoe, Smith, and Eliot, all of the issues I have outlined are characterized by their theatrical aspects; the figure of theater appears because these problems were perceived in terms of theatrical acts and relations. Theater, then, for these authors, is a source of great ambivalence. Unlike the traditional *theatrum mundi* metaphor that pictured the world as a stage and people as players in a relatively unproblematic way, the figure of theater for Shaftesbury, Defoe, Smith, and Eliot dramatizes a recurrent dialectic between theater as problem and theater as solution. Throughout this book I will trace the interplay between the threat of the theatrical position of appearing as a spectacle before spectators; the protection of dramatic impersonations that would conceal the self from those who would see, name, or know it; and the dream of an act of sympathy that would allow those who face each other as actor and spectator to transcend theatrical distance through a transfer of parts and persons.

Some readers will be struck by the apparent incongruity of the authors whose names appear together on the title page of this book. I have chosen to place in juxtaposition authors and texts of rather distinctive characters: literary criticism, philosophical investigations, and autobiographical reflections by an aristocratic and eclectic man of letters; fiction and writing about fiction by a notorious literary hack credited by some with the invention of the English novel; a systematic book of moral philosophy by a professor known today primarily as an economist; and a carefully crafted nineteenth-century novel about Jews by a woman who wrote under the name of a man. In crossing boundaries between and even within fiction and philosophy, I have tried to suggest that through the figure of theater one can see fiction, aesthetics, moral philosophy, and epistemology addressing many of the same questions in analogous terms. For each of these authors, however—especially those who wrote before modern generic categories were institutionalized in the nineteenth century—genre itself is often in question. Shaftesbury, for example, who rejected philosophical systems, called *The Moralists* a "philosophical romance." He advocated the dramatic form of the dialogue and he wrote public letters, soliloquies, and Sternean commentaries on his own work that resist classification. Defoe neither thought nor claimed that he was writing novels and he was troubled by the theatrical aspects of his fictions. Smith and Eliot were more secure in their respective genres of "treatise" and "novel" yet I suggest that to some extent *The Theory of Moral Sentiments* can be read like a novel that offers a view of the world strangely similar to that presented by Defoe and Eliot; Smith is as concerned as a novelist with the fictions that we use to represent others and ourselves. It is almost a commonplace to consider Eliot's works as "philosophical novels." I will argue that *Daniel Deronda* can be seen as a dramatization of *The Theory of Moral Sentiments*. Eliot displays the correspondences between sympathy and theater that are suggested by Defoe and Shaftesbury and made explicit by Smith.

It is a presupposition of this study that *all* of the texts analyzed should be regarded as "philosophical novels." To say this is to make a claim about the importance of these texts; virtually all of them are in the strange position of being accounted for in the history of ideas yet somehow considered eccentric or even marginal. *Soliloquy, or Advice to an Author* and the *Miscellaneous Reflections* have been largely neglected by recent criticism while *The Theory of Moral Sentiments* is treated mostly as the province of sociologists and social psychologists. Defoe of course has received a great deal of attention (there has even been a revival of interest in *Roxana*) and Eliot's *Daniel Deronda* is certainly considered a major work by a mainstream novelist. At the same time, however, Defoe is not always taken seriously as a "literary" artist and a philosophical thinker; and many critics, agreeing with Henry James that Eliot became excessively involved with the "Jewish" part of the novel, have felt that *Daniel Deronda* lacked coherence. This book argues that in all of the works discussed the figure of theater acts as an organizing principle that brings together major philosophical issues crucial to the history of both the novel and the representation of the self. My characterization of these texts as "philosophical novels" is also meant to imply that they need to be read closely. Since I am not reading the texts of Shaftesbury, Defoe, Eliot, or even Smith as treatises that can be reduced to philosophical propositions or general assertions about theater, my interpretations will attempt to take their language seriously, even their colloquialisms or casual figures of speech; my readings will trace the figure of theater by attending to nuances of language, analogies, and narrative structure, proceeding in ways that a psychoanalytic approach might proceed. In considering these "philosophical romances" (to borrow Shaftesbury's phrase) I will focus on both characters and authors as they dramatize and enact theatrical situations and relations. The reader also plays a part in the textual scenarios I am examining.

By focusing on the figure of theater in texts of Shaftesbury, Defoe, Smith, and Eliot, this book will differ from studies primarily concerned with theater as a theme or a motif, dramatic conventions, or the influence of drama on the novel. I write in the context of discussions about how the novel supplanted theater as a popular genre in the eighteenth century,[1] and how novelists such as Richardson and Fielding borrowed dramatic forms and conventions,[2] but the scope of this book does not include specific plays (or considerations of their production or influence). I should also point out that although I will discuss theater as a problem for Shaftesbury, Defoe, Smith, and Eliot, and although I will discuss their negative attitudes toward the condition of theatricality, I am not suggesting that these authors should necessarily be considered as writing within an antitheatrical tradition. This tradition is entirely relevant to my readings, and I have found Jonas Barish's *The Antitheatrical Prejudice* to be an important point of reference, especially its analysis of what antitheatricalists have found so threatening about acting and the theater.[3] If I speak of the antitheatrical positions of the authors in question, however, I am not usually referring to their opposition to the stage or to the production of plays. My concern with a critique of theatricality in the works of these authors—a critical investigation of the literal or figurative position of appearing as a spectacle before spectators as opposed to a critique of the institution or practice of performing plays—is more specifically informed by Michael Fried's analyses of the spectacle-beholder relation in painting and sculpture[4] and Stanley Cavell's use of the terms of theater in his discussions of scepticism, tragedy, and film.[5] This book, however, focuses on the specifically literary aspects of the figure of theater for Shaftesbury, Defoe, Smith, and Eliot. For these authors the problem of theater invariably raises questions about publishing and representing characters, reading, and interpretation. Each of these authors is preoccupied with the necessity of reading and being read by other people.

This book makes a double claim: it argues that Shaftesbury, Defoe, Smith, and Eliot are deeply concerned, even obsessed, with the conditions of theater and that interpretations of their work that do not take this into account must remain blind to some of their texts' most important aspects. Theater is not an arbitrary theoretical category imposed on the texts; the relevance and the theoretical dimensions of the terms of theater are articulated through close readings which try to make sense of the problems that the authors themselves have set in play. My book also suggests, however, that the figure of theater provides a significant cultural paradigm for eighteenth-century English culture, that it represents a locus where crucial issues in fiction writing, moral philosophy, aesthetics, and epistemology are addressed and acted out by a surprising variety of influential authors. This last claim, of course, can only be suggested here; this book does not propose to be an exhaustive or systematic study of the figure of theater in English culture. I end the book with an interpretation of *Daniel Deronda* because I believe that Eliot's investigations into the conditions of theater and sympathy look back to the eighteenth-century texts and issues considered here, as if Eliot were declaring her novel to be a continuation of and a commentary upon those earlier discussions. *Daniel Deronda* can help us to understand how the problem of theater gets translated and transformed in the transition from the eighteenth- to the nineteenth-century novel; in my conclusion I suggest that the figure of theater itself played a role in this transition. More research and readings will be needed to understand the historical dimensions and transformations of the figure of theater.[6] In the chapters that follow, I explore certain historical and theoretical questions that I hope will open up new readings of both neglected and well-worn texts while delineating the characteristics, implications, and pervasiveness of what Shaftesbury (in a related context) called "a certain powerful figure of inward rhetoric."

PART I

Shaftesbury and the Theater of Characters

Of all the artificial Relations, formed between Mankind, the most capricious and variable is that of *Author* and *Reader.*

> Shaftesbury,
> *Miscellaneous Reflections*

All turns upon the nature of a character.

> Shaftesbury,
> *Philosophical Regimen*

Prologue

ON March 1, 1711, when *The Spectator* made its debut upon the London scene, the metaphor that pictured the world as a stage was reputedly thousands of years old. The Renaissance, which had reflected upon the concept of *theatrum mundi* to an unprecedented degree, still provided a view of the world; the playhouses, closed for a time by the Puritans, had been open again for fifty years. Thus in writing under the title of *The Spectator* and declaring, "I live in the World, rather as a Spectator of Mankind, than as one of the Species,"[1] Joseph Addison was situating himself within a familiar frame of reference. He was assuming an eighteenth-century version of a familiar pose when he announced in the prologue to his journal: "I have acted in all the Parts of my Life as a Looker-on, which is the Character I intend to preserve in this Paper."[2]

What was new for Addison's readers, however, was themselves: their own role as *readers* at the beginning of a century in which the rise of journalism and the rise of the novel would invent (or reinvent) the reading public. Addison characterizes these readers—whom he numbers, perhaps overoptimistically, at "Three-score thousand"—as a "Fraternity of Spectators . . . in short, every one that considers the World as a Theatre."[3] But it is their presence as a *public* that gives the *theatrum mundi* metaphor a new turn. For although these readers will look to the pages of *The Spectator* for representations of the scenes and characters of their society, they have become spectators of *The Spectator*. Addison acknowledges that his reading public is *his* "Audience";[4] and in his first observation as the Spectator he focuses on the reader in the act of examining a book and enquiring after the author. He resolves to withhold "my Name, my Age, and my Lodgings," satisfying the reader's

"Curiosity" with only a sketchy account of his life, since "communicating them to the Publick" would "draw me out of that Obscurity which I have enjoyed for many Years, and expose me in Publick Places." Although the author admits that he is "frequently seen in publick Places," he claims that not more than a half dozen friends "know" him; and the Spectator wishes to avoid "being stared at."[5] Surely a spy needs to preserve anonymity, whether in the Court or the Coffee-House; but the scene of these negotiations between author and reader might have been sketched by Henry James: the "Looker-on" finds himself the spectacle of those he would see without being seen. As the author addresses the public to invite them to see the world as a stage, he must acknowledge from the outset that his book as well as the world will be seen as theater.

In 1710, one year before Addison's first appearance as the Spectator, the Earl of Shaftesbury seemed less certain about how to negotiate a safe relation with that "Fraternity of Spectators" whose public view makes publishing a book seem like a theatrical act. Writing in his book, *Soliloquy, or Advice to an Author,* he complained about those authors who "exhibit on the stage of the world that practice which they should have kept to themselves."[6] Shaftesbury is referring in particular to authors of memoirs and essays who, despite the private character of their texts, insist on "appearing in public or before the world," publishing before the "eyes of mankind."[7] I would like to suggest, however, that Shaftesbury writes in a context in which the act of publishing itself—regardless of the character of the book—placed the author "on the stage of the world." In the course of the eighteenth century the public increasingly would abandon the playhouse and reconstitute itself around individual acts of reading; historically, spectators would give way to readers.[8] Figuratively, however, readers remained spectators: the assembling of a group of anonymous, isolated, unseen observers collectively known to authors as (and only as) the public in a sense reproduced the conditions of an audience. In literature and aesthetics, the *ut pictura poesis* tradition continued to picture readers as spectators, despite the attempts of Lessing and others to separate the arts; Kames' formulation was typical: "writers of genius, sensible that the eye is the best avenue to the heart, represent everything as passing in our sight; and from readers or hearers, transform us, as it were, into spectators."9 My point is that in the sphere of published books, *all* readers were transformed into spectators, as it were. The eyes of the world, to which all published books were inevitably addressed, in turn transformed the text to theater.

By the middle of the eighteenth century, when Dr. Johnson would define "To PUBLISH" first as "To discover to mankind; to make generally and openly known" and second as "To put forth a book into the world,"10 Fielding would begin a novel with the assertion: "An author ought to consider himself, not as a gentleman who gives a private or eleemosynary treat, but rather as one who keeps a public ordinary, at which all persons are welcome for their money."11 Writing in 1710, Shaftesbury is more troubled with the conditions that Fielding seems to embrace from the outset; Shaftesbury is troubled by the book's commodity status and especially by the public realm in which published books by definition were destined to appear. In the pages that follow I will examine Shaftesbury's view of the conditions of the book and the characters of authors and readers. My focus will be on the *theatricality* of these conditions and relations: what it means to publish a book before the eyes of the world, what it means to publish oneself before the world. I will consider the prospects that theater offers for knowing oneself and the threat that theater poses to the concept of the self. At stake, also, will be the character of philosophy for Shaftesbury.

CHAPTER 1

The Characters
of Books and Readers

TO begin, the book must face or efface the reader. The three volumes of *Characteristics of Men, Manners, Opinions, Times,* first published by Shaftesbury in 1711, begin with a "PREFACE" which stands in place of (as well as in the place of) "all prefatory or dedicatory discourse" (1:1). This brief text, written with no trace of a first person singular, refers the reader to *Soliloquy, or Advice to an Author,* where Shaftesbury scorns those authors who "in due form of preface and epistle dedicatory, solicited the public" or ventured to "address a work" to a great man, hoping to pass "for something considerable in the eyes of mankind" (1:197). Instead, this preface which is not a preface offers a citation, apparently provided for the printer by the Author, which declares: "That (according to his best judgment and authority) these presents ought to pass, and be received, construed, and taken, as satisfactory in full, for all preliminary composition, dedication, direct or indirect application for favour to the public, or to any private patron or party whatsoever . . ." (1:1). Then, as if a legal document, the text concludes, "Witness his hand, this fifth day of December, 1710" and is signed by sixteen printed characters ("A.A.C.A.N.A.AE.C./ M.D.C.L.X.X.I.") in which initially the suppressed name Anthony Ashley Cooper can be deciphered. If the reader is a witness, it is to the impersonal, typographical "hand" of the book which in a single gesture so to speak, appeals to its readers to witness that they are not appealed to. This book applies to no one, public or private; from the outset its readers are faced with their supposed absence from the text's address.

Upon turning the page, however, the reader will find a treatise entitled "A Letter Concerning Enthusiasm" addressed "To My Lord ⁎⁎⁎⁎⁎"—whose name can be pronounced by a printing press only. This title page placed within the borders of the book informs us that the "Letter" was "Printed first in the year MDCCVIII"; in the upper right corner of the next page one finds the date "*Sept.* 1707" followed on the next line by the epistolary "MY LORD." Shaftesbury thus begins the *Letter Concerning Enthusiasm* by imagining the end of his text: first, by inscribing the name of a *destinataire* at the head of the page; and then, by picturing that reader with the completed manuscript before him, awaiting his eyes. After appealing to "MY LORD" to "cast your eye slightly on what you have before you" for the sake of "amusement" or "to be entertained," Shaftesbury considers the necessary address which must precede entrance into a text. He reflects on the "established custom for poets, at the entrance of their work, to address themselves to some muse" (1:5). Allowing that it appeared natural for an ancient poet "to address himself in raptures of devotion to those acknowledged patronesses of wit and science" (1:6), Shaftesbury complains to his friend and patron that in their time such an address would lack verisimilitude. But if the modern writer would appear ridiculous in appealing to a muse, this does not mean that such an application is in itself out of date. The muse (as a character personated and invoked in the text) may have become an anachronism but the appeal and address the muse represents still seem necessary:

> How much the imagination of such a presence must exalt a genius we may observe merely from the influence which an ordinary presence has over men. Our modern wits are more or less raised by the opinion they have of their company, and the idea they form to themselves of the persons to whom they make their addresses. A common actor of the stage will inform us how much a full audience of the better sort exalts him above the common pitch. (1:8)

The muse, then, must be replaced, not abandoned. A new form of invocation and a new image to be addressed must be found, since exaltation seems to depend upon the image of the person to whom the writer inevitably speaks. Yet what is the meaning (to borrow Milton's phrase) of the names Shaftesbury must call in the invocation that begins his book?

From the imagined presence of what Shaftesbury has called "angelical company" (1:8), we have passed to the ordinary presence of the company of men, to the idea formed of actual persons addressed, and then finally to the audience that an actor faces from a stage. Shaftesbury earlier implied the presence of the writer's audience by considering whether the witnesses of a display of devotion to a muse could be moved or even credulous; but here the audience is the recipient of rather than the witness to an address. In being modernized, the muse has been placed at the end as well as at the beginning of the text. It stands not only before the text, in time and on the page; it now stands after the text as well—or before it in a new spatial sense, facing and receiving the text in its finished form. The muse has become the reader; and in becoming the reader, a (second) person whose idea and presence need to be imagined, it has become an audience. The writer is compared to the actor on the stage who seeks inspiration from the audience he imagines before him.

Once the figure of theater has been introduced, Shaftesbury applies it even to the person he imagines he addresses, asking:

> And you, my lord, who are the noblest actor, and of the noblest part assigned to any mortal on this earthly stage, when you are acting for liberty and mankind; does not the public presence, that of your friends, and the well-wishers to your cause, add something to your thought and genius? (1:8)

We see again that at least in part it is the presence of the public that casts a situation as theatrical. Shaftesbury wonders if his lord's "sublime of reason, and that power of eloquence, which you discover in public" are "no more than what you are equally master of in private, and can command at any time, alone, or with indifferent company" (1:8). According to Shaftesbury, such an attitude would be more "godlike" (1:8). Thus the lord's nobility—indeed his divinity—would consist of his independence from and indifference to the presence of the public, despite his role as an actor on the stage of the world. Shaftesbury admits that his own performance in private is less inspired:

> For my own part, my lord, I have really so much need of some considerable presence or company to raise my thoughts on any occasion, that when alone I must endeavour by strength of fancy to supply this want; and in default of a muse, must inquire out some great man . . . whose imagined presence may inspire me with more than what I feel at ordinary hours. And thus, my lord, have I chosen to address myself to your lordship. (1:8–9)

It would appear that the address to Lord ***** (who in this text plays the part of Shaftesbury's patron Lord Somers) and Shaftesbury's decision to write his essay on enthusiasm as a *Letter* have been dictated by a need for some modern version of the muse. In default of a muse, Lord ***** has assumed the role of that imaginary presence who is addressed and appealed to for inspiration—a role that is now personated by the reader. If Shaftesbury has refused to name him in a dedication, he is still addressed and applied to: the patron and the deity of the text in another sense. Most remarkably, however, Lord ***** appears to stand for that public presence which turns a text to theater. After declaring in the Preface to the *Characteristics* his desire to avoid any application "to the public, or to any private patron or party whatsoever" (1:1), Shaftesbury begins the first section with a confession of his own need for an audience. Ironically, the reader who stands for this audience also stands as the ideal actor who would have no need of audiences. What sense can we make of these positions? To understand the situation of theater that seems supposed and denied simultaneously, we need to look at Shaftesbury's characterizations of authors, readers, and books.

Toward the end of *Soliloquy, or Advice to an Author* (which forms the third essay in the *Characteristics*) Shaftesbury interrupts his text and begins a new section with the remark: "But here it may be convenient for me to quit myself awhile in favour of my reader, lest if he prove one of the uncourteous sort, he should raise a considerable objection in this place" (1:197). Then quitting himself in one sense, he introduces onto the scene the character of a reader: "He may asks perhaps 'why a writer for self-entertainment should not keep his writings to himself, without appearing in public or before the world'" (1:197). This imaginary reader whose lines Shaftesbury writes and speaks is neither named nor identified— except insofar as he is named and identified by his very anonymity. He is defined both by his facelessness and by the "here" and "in this place" which occasion the consideration of his objection: the time and place which have become the printed, published book before him. He is and he stands for the public. We have seen that Shaftesbury condemns in this text those authors who exhibit private meditations "on the stage of the world." Shaftesbury, therefore, might appear to be incriminating himself with remarks such as: "I hold it very indecent for any one to publish his meditations, occasional reflections, solitary thoughts, or other such exercises as come under the notion of this self-discoursing practice"—a practice of "privately conversing" with oneself which is both advocated and practiced throughout the essay (1:109).

However, after raising the objection of the reader, Shaftesbury maintains:

> In answer to this I shall only say that for appearing in public or before the world, I do not readily conceive what our worthy objector may understand by it. I can call to mind, indeed, among my acquaintance, certain merchant-adventurers in the letter-trade, who in correspondence with their factor-bookseller are entered into a notable commerce with the world. (1:197)

These are the "avowed authors" who solicit the public or address their works to patrons in order to look good in the eyes of the world. Shaftesbury, for this part, claims to have no concern for "what regard the public bestows on my amusements, or after what manner it comes acquainted with what I write for my private entertainment, or by way of advice to such of my acquaintance as are thus desperately embarked" (1:197). Evoking his imagined reader in order to dismiss him, Shaftesbury denies that he has used his bookseller as a postman to deliver his book to the world. Writing his reader into the

text in order to rule him out, Shaftesbury denies the public character of his published book. The reader faces him not as a second
person but rather as a third person who benefits from the fact that
"'Tis requisite that my friends who peruse these advices should read
them in better characters than those of my own hand-writing." The
printing press offers "a very fair hand . . . which may save me the
trouble of re-copying"; the printer is merely an "amanuensis" who is
allowed to make as many copies as he pleases. "And if it be worth
any one's purchasing," continues Shaftesbury, "much good may it
do the purchaser. 'Tis a traffic I have no share in, though I accidentally furnish the subject-matter" (1:198).

   Shaftesbury pictures himself as if he were a stowaway
on a trading ship who has sailed for transportation only, not for
speculation. If his book appears in the marketplace, as a book, it is
only a commercial byproduct of a private correspondence which
has taken a rather long detour in getting from a writer to his friends.
Shaftesbury denies his presence in "the world": where printed characters transpose a personal text into an unsigned commodity; where
the reader becomes an unknown representative of the public and
the writer becomes an author. Indeed, just as he denies his reader,
he refuses his own role as well:

> And thus am I nowise more an author for being in print. I am
> conscious of no additional virtue or dangerous quality from having
> lain at any time under the weight of that alphabetic engine called the
> Press. . . . I can hardly think that the quality of what is written can
> be altered by the manner of writing, or that there can be any harm in
> a quick way of copying fair and keeping copies alike. (1:198)

Printing would maintain the consistency and integrity of the text;
but somehow this passage to uniformity and multiplicity disrupts
the continuity normally expected between book and author.
Shaftesbury claims that his passage through the press has not
changed him, but what has happened between the metonymy by
which he pictures himself under "that alphabetic engine" and his
denial that the final product either stands for or belongs to him? He
insists that the manner of his writing—the printed characters that,
contrary to the etymology of "manner," have nothing to do with his

"hand"—has no relation to the character of the essay whose purpose is to "consider of the way and manner of advising" (1:104) within the covers of a book called *Characteristics of Men, Manners, Opinions, Times*. The book's bound and printed form would be simply its outward bearing, its style of address, its characteristic mode or aspect: "Why a man may not be permitted to write with iron as well as quill, I cannot conceive; or how a writer changes his capacity by this new dress, any more than by the wear of wove-stockings, after having worn no other manufacture than the knit" (1:198). The book is a costume, the author a role; the text returns by way of modern technology to its (etymological) origins as something woven. Underneath the covers of the book's public dress, the private character of the text would remain unchanged.

Shaftesbury ends his dialogue with the reader he claims to ignore with a somewhat wishful air of conclusion: "So much for my reader, if perchance I have any besides the friend or two above mentioned" (1:198). But has he really removed himself from the stage of the world by denying the public character of his book? By 1710 the technology of the book has reinvented readers, and even if Shaftesbury would limit the destination of his text (its *destinataire*, whom it is written to) he cannot control the destiny already inscribed within its form: that is, who will receive it, the public realm in which it is destined to appear. The objection of the reader—whose image suddenly appears on the horizon of the text as Shaftesbury's quill traces some reflections for his friends—is not so easily dismissed.

Could a private text be published and still be private; could a text be public and private at once? These questions recall the problems of audience and address that we saw Shaftesbury confronting in his *Letter Concerning Enthusiasm*. The published *Letter* is one response to the contradictory desires to publish texts and keep them private; and I suggest that the great popularity of this genre in the eighteenth century is in part a response to the ambivalence about the conditions of the book which we have been examining in Shaftesbury's work. In speaking of the published

Letter I do not mean the fictional narrative composed of personal correspondence—what we today call the epistolary novel—although its history is relevant to these issues. In the narrative of letters the *expéditeur* and *destinataire* are clearly labeled. Within the frame of its fiction it is certain that none of its texts were written by "authors" for public view; it represents a closed dialogue between individuals which appears to take place behind closed doors—within sealed envelopes, so to speak. The "open" or "public" *Letter* (names invented to explain the genre by an age less comfortable with the lie of fiction) aims for this sense of private exchange but quickly enters the paradox of the private text made public, if only because the fiction of correspondence is less credible. The *Letter* lacks the repeated addresses and signatures which punctuate the epistolary novel, as well as the narrative events which both occasion the letters and remove them to a time before the reader's present. Thus the *Letter* becomes a contradiction in terms, especially in regard to its audience and address. It is a private exchange made public for the world. Its address generalized and/or suppressed, its signature replaced by asterisks, it suspiciously resembles that mass of faceless, voiceless print exchanged between anonymous parties: the book.[1]

It is not surprising, then, that in the first book he publishes Shaftesbury should turn to that textual hybrid, the *Letter;* nor is it surprising that within the *Characteristics* he should worry about the resemblance of his *Letter Concerning Enthusiasm* to its companion forms, the *Essay* and the *Treatise.* We have seen that Shaftesbury claims for his treatise *Soliloquy, or Advice to an Author* the characteristics of a *Letter:* a private, personal text exchanged between friends, not intended for the public. Conversely, his *Letter,* addressed to "My Lord *****" and signed by no one, often seems to act like a *Treatise* or an *Essay.* Yet just as he assures us that in his treatise he has no regard for our regard, Shaftesbury feels called upon to insist that his *Letter* is genuine: that is to say, that it was really written as a letter. Writing in the *Miscellaneous Reflections* on the essays assembled in the *Characteristics* (published three years after the first publication of the *Letter*), he refutes critics' speculations about the condition, rank, and even the existence of the Lord to whom the *Letter* is ostensibly addressed.[2] Shaftesbury insists that "there was a real great man characterised and suitable measures of address and style preserved" (2:167). Although he admits that "'Tis become indeed so common a practice among authors to feign a correspondency, and give the title of a private letter to a piece addressed solely to the public, that it would not be strange" for a critic to see the characteristics of the letter "as things of form," he maintains that he wrote a "real letter . . . not a precise and formal treatise designed for public view" (2:167–168).

Shaftesbury's problem here is similar to the predicament of the "editor" who complains in the preface to the memoirs of one Moll Flanders: "The World is so taken up of late with Novels and Romances, that it will be hard for a private History to be taken for Genuine";[3] although this predicament is the fault of no one more than the forger of that preface and book, Daniel Defoe. Defoe had reason to claim for his fiction the status of history and "reality," but why should Shaftesbury, writing some years after the publication of his text—which, after all, contains a series of thoughts on society, religion, government, and philosophy and not a fictive narrative—need to insist on the *reality* of his *Letter*? As he continues, he reveals an investment not just in one *Letter* but in the epistolary frame and design in general. Claiming that we would find no pleasure in reading the *Letters* of "a Balsac or Voiture" if we should "take it into our heads that both the personages and correspondency itself were merely fictitious," Shaftesbury asserts: "Let the best of Tully's Epistles be read in such a narrow view as this, and they will certainly prove very insipid. If a real Brutus, a real Atticus be not supposed, there will be no real Cicero. The elegant writer will disappear" (2:168). Shaftesbury's claims might seem puzzling for the modern reader, who is less concerned with the fictive character of such texts. In addition, we as readers know almost nothing about Lord ***** from his address and characterization in the *Letter Concerning Enthusiasm*, aside from some references to his nobility of rank and character. Would it matter if we supposed that Lord ***** was "supposed" (in the sense of feigned or forged) rather than "real"?

This question, however, is almost beside the point since Shaftesbury has passed from defending the reality of a particular *Letter* to positing the need for *Letters* to be real; or rather, he maintains the need for us as readers to believe that the *Letters* are really letters, whether they are or not. What changes when we read the address of a *Letter* as a fiction? The ideas or content are no less "real" but the "things of form," the conditions of the presentation of the text, are altered. If the correspondence and correspondent disappear, then we appear: as readers. The text becomes addressed to us. Fiction in this case means "designed for public view." Shaftesbury criticizes cases where "the title of Epistle is improperly given to such works as were never writ in any other view than that of being made public" (2:169). In particular, he censures Seneca as the "corrupter of Roman eloquence" (2:169); although his *Letters* might have begun as a real correspondence, with Epistles "honestly signed and sealed . . . the author by degrees loses sight of his correspondent, and takes the world in general for his reader" (2:170). Thus the *Letter*, in maintaining the private character of a text, would remove the author from the stage of the world; by appointing a private individual to replace the general reader as recipient of the text, the *Letter* would counteract the theatricality of the book's inevitable public address. Lord *****, then, in the *Letter Concerning Enthusiasm*, would replace and displace the audience for whom Shaftesbury would appear as an actor on a stage. His presence before the text would rule the reader out, deflect the address that destines the text for the eyes of the world. His position is so important for Shaftesbury that when the *Letter Concerning Enthusiasm* is published a second time in the *Characteristics*—thereby underlining its original contradiction in terms—Shaftesbury feels called upon to insist retrospectively that his text was not designed for public view, that the epistolary form was not a fiction meant to disguise the author's regard for the world.

If one were to play the discourteous reader who is personated in the *Characteristics*, one might object that Shaftesbury protests too much—both in maintaining his treatise's disregard for its reading public and in defending the "reality" of his *Letter*. One might object also that in condemning the "style and manner" of Seneca, he is also condemning himself. Indeed, in his defense of the *Letter*'s reality, Shaftesbury inserts a footnote to explain: "If in this joint edition, with other works, the letter be made to pass under that general name of treatise, 'tis the bookseller must account for it. For the author's part, he considers it as no other than what it originally was" (2:168). The bookseller, in fact, seems to have been confused by the subtlety of Shaftesbury's distinctions: in the *Characteristics*, the *Letter Concerning Enthusiasm* does appear as "TREATISE I" just as "TREATISE II" is called *Sensus Communis; An Essay on the Freedom of Wit and Humor in a Letter to a Friend.*

    Let us suppose, however, that Shaftesbury's *Letter Concerning Enthusiasm* "originally" and "really" was a letter and that Lord ***** (according to reliable sources, Shaftesbury's friend and patron Lord Somers) not only existed but actually received the manuscript from its author. This would not mean that Shaftesbury had no design or purpose in choosing to write his reflections in letter form; nor would it necessarily imply that his sights went no further than his correspondent. Consider, for example, Shaftesbury's plans for the essays he was engaged in at the time of his death, which were to be published under the general title of *Second Characters, or The Language of Forms*. Writing to Sir John Cropley in 1712 (in what appears to be a real letter) he wonders whether to publish the English version of his essay *A Notion of the Historical Draught of Hercules* with or without its companion piece, which he originally wrote as a letter to Lord Somers—the "friend-lord, whose property this is, and to whom it is my chief delight to join myself, in these as in former thoughts and contemplations."

    "For my own part," writes Shaftesbury, "should that lord approve the thing, I am resolute enough to send both *Letter* and *Notion* without more ado to Darby (supressing names only), to be printed in the very same manner and character as the 'Letter of Enthusiasm' was." Here Shaftesbury combines an account of the private correspondence he enjoys with his friend with a concern with "the Grub Street translators and retailers" who might "vend" his essay "in their own guise"[4]—in other words, a concern with the "traffic" through which the public becomes acquainted with his texts. The friend-lord—not yet but once again destined to become Lord *****, a character created by the printing press—seems merely a stop along the road to the booksellers. What does it mean for the author who claimed that the manner of writing did not affect the character of a text to plan to print his book in the manner and character of the *Letter Concerning Enthusiasm?*

We can get a sense of Shaftesbury's notion of the manner and character of his *Letter* by looking at his notes for the unfinished treatise, *Plastics: An Epistolary Excursion in the Original Progress and Power of Designatory Art.* The scheme for this published *Letter* was apparently written in 1712,[5] one year after the defense of the "reality" of the *Letter Concerning Enthusiasm* appeared in the *Characteristics.* In Shaftesbury's personal draft and design for the work, the following resolution appears:

> Upon mature thought, . . . resolved to address wholly, or at least principally, and in a continued strain at the head of each great division, to the friend-Lord, My Lord *** as Letter of Enthusiasm and that of Design (the leading treatise of this work). And thus every new part or chapter will have a kind of preface, or renewal of the address and epistolary style (My Lord, etc.). And therefore the Treatise itself should be entitled *epistolary* as giving warning of this mixed manner, viz. half-general address, but (begging the public's pardon) more than one half to the friend, the Lord etc. (SC:5)

Like the title of the projected work, the description of the text's proposed style indicates that the *Letter* has become *explicitly* a contradiction in terms. It is indeed an "excursion" in the sense that it transgresses the limits of the forms that hold *Treatise* and *Letter* apart. I quote at length from Shaftesbury's plans because they express both his anxiety about the terms we have been considering— these instructions are written to himself—and his extensive premeditation of the manner and character of his text. He continues:

> Accordingly it will be a new and not odd or unseemly way to begin each great division as Book or Part (but rather Part, indeed, since Books would be too formal to divide into and contrary to the epistolary idea), to begin I say each Part with the title, My Lord, set (as at

the beginning of the Letter of Enthusiasm and every other Letter) a little way below the contents. And for the subdivisions, and mere chapters or sections, these may begin not directly with the title but taking it in, (as the newer and more fashionable way is, in familiar letters), indirectly and curiously, in the first sentence or period after a word or two, (as "Would you imagine My Lord" etc.). (SC:5)

We see Shaftesbury planning a careful imitation of the characteristics of a letter; whether or not the *Letter Concerning Enthusiasm* was "real," it is clear that Shaftesbury came to regard its epistolary form and address as a model. They are rhetorical devices: in another note he instructs himself to use "the letter-style and particular private address . . . as much as possible in way of apostrophe and prosopope" (SC:7). Shaftesbury is aware, in designing his work, that the language of its form will be determined by the form of its language. Reminding himself repeatedly of the manner of the *Letter Concerning Enthusiasm*, he envisions the situation of discourse which is to be constructed around carefully placed enunciative acts: epistolary elocutions. He realizes that the character and scope of the work will not permit it to be cast entirely as a letter, so he plans to maintain at least the basic signals of a letter—the *feel* of a letter—even though it is destined for publication and the public. Or to put it another way (and I have been suggesting this all along), Shaftesbury formulates this rhetorical strategy precisely *because* his text will appear before the eyes of the world. This is a prospect that Shaftesbury will not admit. While a book such as the *Characteristics* or *Soliloquy, or Advice to an Author* must assure readers that they are disregarded, the *Letter* provides a formula which by definition keeps readers in their place: outside of the text's address. If the book is written *for* them, it at least maintains the fiction that it is not written *to* them.

We now have a sense of what is at stake in Shaftesbury's claims for the status of his philosophical texts. We have seen how the epistolary form in particular serves to deny the public character of the book and remove the author from the stage of the world. However, we also remarked that Lord ***** in the *Letter Concerning Enthusiasm* both takes the place of "the world"—what Shaftesbury elsewhere calls "that body of men whom we call readers"

(1:214)—and plays the role of the "audience" whom the author faces like a "common actor of the stage." The *Characteristics* begins with the figure of theater and the author's confession that he needs to imagine the presence of an audience in order to write. How can we understand this apparent reinstatement of theatrical relations at the moment that Shaftesbury seeks to deny the conditions of the published book by limiting his readership to one? Shaftesbury suggests the character of the problem when he proclaims in the *Miscellaneous Reflections*: "Of all the artificial relations formed between mankind, the most capricious and variable is that of author and reader" (2:296).

In saying this, Shaftesbury aims to indict the commercial relations between professional authors and the reading public. "Our modern authors . . . are turned and modelled (as themselves confess) by the public relish," writes Shaftesbury, "In our days the audience makes the poet, and the bookseller the author" (1:172–73). Shaftesbury's censure, however, goes beyond a concern with the effect of the marketplace. The relation between authors and readers also seems corrupted by a narcissistic appeal on the author's part to the reader's own narcissism, an appeal for the reader's favor. In his *Advice to an Author*, Shaftesbury condemns the discourse that stands as an apology at the end of a book in terms similar to his attack on prefatory discourse. "'Tis the chief strategem by which he engages in personal conference with his reader, and can talk immoderately of himself," writes Shaftesbury, adding that once the author has ingratiated himself with the reader, the reader "is not a little raised by this submission of a confessing author, and is ready, on these terms, to give him absolution and receive him into his good grace and favour" (1:213). This egotism is not limited to a particular place in the book, a section that might be excised like a dedication or a preface. It seems to have its roots in the *ego* itself: the first person singular who appears as a character in the text.

> An author who writes in his own person has the advantage of being who or what he pleases. He is no certain man, nor has any certain or genuine character; but suits himself on every occasion to the fancy of his reader, whom, as the fashion is nowadays, he constantly caresses and cajoles. All turns upon their two persons. (1:131)

At issue here are the persons who face each other across and in a text: not the particular people who at a given moment enact the parts of author and reader—for instance an anonymous English nobleman and his friend-lord; or, for that matter, me and you—but rather the at once particular and general grammatical persons who name each other in discourse. The presence of the person of the reader seems to subvert the genuine character of the author: as if the character "I," once assumed, becomes a kind of dress or role. (I will have more to say about this in the next chapter.)

Shaftesbury continues in this passage to compare the relationship between the persons of author and reader to the relationship in "an amour or commerce of love-letters" where the author "has the privilege of talking eternally of himself, dressing and sprucing himself up, whilst he is making diligent court, and working upon the humour of the party to whom he addresses" (1:131). The intercourse between author and reader is cast as so much strutting, solicitation, seduction—what Shaftesbury calls "the coquetry of a modern author" (1:131). In case we are in doubt as to what this means, elsewhere in *Advice to an Author* Shaftesbury reverses his figures and characterizes the lover by comparing him to an author: "His case is like the author's who has begun his courtship to the public, and is embarked in an intrigue which sufficiently amuses and takes him out of himself. Whatever he meditates alone, is interrupted still by the imagined presence of the mistress he pursues" (1:116). The terms here are strikingly similar to the discussion prefacing the *Letter Concerning Enthusiasm* in which Shaftesbury posits the need for an "imagined presence" to replace the muse. We saw that the presence of "My Lord" was meant to discount courtship to the public; but how is Shaftesbury's need for an audience to witness his performance different from the desire of the author or the lover to "be witnessed by the party whose grace and favour he solicits"? (1:116). Only Lord *****, it appears, "the noblest actor . . . on this earthly stage," seems capable of indifference to the "public presence," capable of elevating his thoughts "in private, . . . alone, or with indifferent company" (1:8).

These theatrical relations are not just the province of the modern author, the writer of prefaces, dedications, apologies, or love-letters; they are implicit in the relation of persons contained within the book, the very characters of authors and readers. For Shaftesbury: "'Tis evident that an author's art and labour are for his reader's sake alone. 'Tis to his reader he makes his application, if not openly and avowedly, yet at least with implicit courtship" (2:296). Shaftesbury would abstain from this apparently unnatural intercourse by claiming a status for his texts that is different from the status of published books, by denying that he is in any way "an author, for being in print." It has become clear, however, that it is not merely the act of publishing a book which is seen as theatrical: it is writing itself, the relation with a reader which is entered when a writer begins a text. If not openly and avowedly then at least implicitly, the very act of writing—in its seemingly inevitable public destination, its solicitation, appeal, and application, its dependence on the imagined presence of a witness, its necessary address which posits an audience before the text—this act itself creates a theatrical situation analogous to the public arena Shaftesbury wishes to avoid.

Is the theatricality of books then unavoidable? Speaking of the reader in the third person (in other words, not addressing him) Shaftesbury boasts of the "little courtship I have paid him, comparatively with what is practiced in that kind by other modern authors" (2:306). Indeed, the reader personated by Shaftesbury in *Advice to an Author* is himself "of the uncourteous sort." Furthermore, Shaftesbury asserts that in the memoirs of the ancients, "even when they writ at any time concerning themselves, there was neither the *I* nor *thou* throughout the whole work. So that all this pretty amour and intercourse of caresses between author and reader was thus entirely taken away" (1:132). How could the ancients—or Shaftesbury—short of embracing silence, abstain from the enunciative acts that inevitably establish a relation between a first person and a second person: the persons implicit in all discourse? In his notes for the *Second Characters, or The Language of Forms*, Shaftesbury plans a strategy for dealing with the grammatical persons of his text. "The use of the ego banished in all but the epistolary kind" (SC:12), he instructs himself, conspiring to "speak always (without once failing) in the style of *we, us*, and *our*, for *I, me*, and *mine*. Also the author and the authors, keeping the *I* and *me* for the text: which the epistolary address may excuse" (SC:8). Thus we see another motivation for the epistolary design: the form of the letter excuses the use of *I* and *you*; it provides a framework which makes the occasional appearance of those persons acceptable. "The free use of the *ego* or *I* will be best near the beginning of each head or division . . . where the epistolary address is renewed and fresh in the ear" (SC:8). Shaftesbury vows, however, to use even the epistolary address "as little as possible: and to substitute in its room, the fashionable *one*, from the French *on*, viz. *on solitude, on voudroit, on est bien aise*" [sic] (SC:8). Shaftesbury seems determined to find a form that not only would avoid the roles of "author" and "reader" but would also remove any trace of their printed, personal, or grammatical characters.

Shaftesbury finds such a form in the dialogue.[6] Less awkward than that self-contradictory textual hybrid, the public *Letter*, the dialogue offers another alternative to the sort of book that sets into play the capricious and unnatural relation formed between authors and readers. *Soliloquy, or Advice to an Author* is in good part devoted to an endorsement and defense of the dialogue as an ideal form of philosophical thinking and writing. The dialogue displays the structure of the "self-discoursing practice" that Shaftesbury prescribes for philosophers and authors; and it also serves philosophy by acting as "mirror-writing" or "a kind of mirror or looking-glass to the age" (1:131). This original form of poetry and philosophy, however, is especially appealing to Shaftesbury because it presents the possibility of writing a text in which there appears "neither the *I* nor *thou* throughout the whole work"—that is, neither the *I* nor *thou* of the author and reader. After praising this characteristic of classical memoirs, Shaftesbury writes: "Much more is this the case in dialogue. For here the author is annihilated, and the reader, being no way applied to, stands for nobody. The self-interesting parties both vanish at once" (1:132). In the dialogue, the positions joining author and reader appear to disappear. With the authorial *I* reduced to nothing, the reader—unaddressed—is asked to take no one's position. No *you* stands for the reader. The dialogue represents the absence of both author and reader.

The text that Shaftesbury envisions resembles what Émile Benveniste calls the *récit historique*. Describing this modern type of historical narrative, Benveniste writes:

> L'historien ne dira jamais *je* ni *tu*, ni *ici*, ni *maintenant*, parce qu'il n'empruntera jamais l'appareil formel du discours, qui consiste d'abord dans la relation de personne *je : tu*. . . . A vrai dire, il n'y a même plus alors de narrateur. Les événements sont posés comme ils se sont produits à mesure qu'ils apparaissent à l'horizon de l'histoire. Personne ne parle ici; les événements semblent se raconter eux-mêmes.[7]

In the dialogue, of course, the *énonciation* of the text's discourse is displaced onto the characters who speak; but the illusion that Shaftesbury imagines for the dialogue is not so different from the illusion Benveniste describes in the historical narrative. The text seems to engender itself; in a sense there is no text at all—only "events" which seem to produce themselves independently, to which the "reader" is a spectator. In Shaftesbury's terms:

> The scene presents itself as by chance and undesigned. You are not only left to judge coolly and with indifference of the sense delivered, but of the character, genius, elocution, and manner of the persons who deliver it. These two are mere strangers, in whose favour you are no way engaged. (1:132)

In this description you are no longer a reader. Following the annihilation of the author, you witness persons—or rather personages, not grammatical persons—who deliver sense and don't pretend to converse across the impersonal book. If there is persuasion in the rhetoric of the dialogue, it does not (appear to) have the reader in mind. The commerce of a personal conference is absent; indifferent, you are ignored by strangers, left alone, rather than being courted by a seductive and appealing author.

It is on these grounds that Shaftesbury praises "the primitive poets," who wrote "mimes or characterised discourses"

and poetry which was "an imitation chiefly of men and manners."
Homer, "the father and prince of poets" is seen as "the great mim-
ographer." In his works, which are "an artful series or chain of
dialogues," he "describes no qualities or virtues; censures no manners; makes no encomiums, nor gives characters himself; but brings
his actors still in view. 'Tis they who show themselves" (1:129).
Drawing on Aristotle's praise of Homer in the *Poetics*,[8] Shaftesbury
explains that the poet "makes hardly any figure at all, and is scarce
discoverable in his poem. . . . He paints so as to need no inscription
over his figures to tell us what they are or what he intends by them"
(1:130). The figure of the artist gives way to the figures of the text,
which appear to speak for themselves. The writer of the dialogue
would be like the painter who must disappear behind the tableau
which must stand for and by itself.

In this context we can understand in a new light the
design of the epistolary form for Shaftesbury: the letter approxi-
mates the scene of the dialogue. Shaftesbury writes in the draft for
the *Second Characters:* "since dialogue-manner (whether diverse or
recitative) too ponderous and vast; endeavor though in the letter-
style and particular private address, (as O Theophilus! My Lord or
Reader!), to introduce scenes and machines of this sort in many a
chapter and everywhere in general" (SC:7). As a letter, the text
would constitute a dialogue between its first person and its specific
(fictional) *destinataire:* in principle, excluding the reader, turning
him into a witness to a scene which occurs accidentally, as it were,
before his eyes. The author would have the status of an actor in the
dialogue; the reader would be displaced by the character of the
reader personated in the text. However, like the relations between
author and reader that frame the *Letter Concerning Enthusiasm*,
these "scenes and machines" present us with a paradox: they turn
the text to theater. Resembling a staged drama, formally indistinguishable from a script, the dialogue is clearly a theatrical model.
After Homer, Shaftesbury contends, "There was no more left for
tragedy to do . . . than to erect a stage and draw his dialogues and
characters into scenes . . . with that regard to place and time which
was suitable to a real spectacle" (1:130).

The dialogue transforms the reader into a spectator to a theatrical scene—but, for Shaftesbury, its purpose in doing so would be to escape the situation of theater which characterizes the relation between author and reader. Or to put it another way: the dialogue breaks down the theatricality implicit in writing and reading books—the address which creates an audience facing the text, the appeal to a witness whose imagined presence seems necessary to the author's performance, the public appearance of the author on the stage of the world—by turning the text into a dramatic presentation whose scenes appear to enact themselves. The reader is a witness to a spectacle with this important difference from the Reader engaged in a textual relation with an Author: being unsupposed, he is neither posed for nor played to; although an audience, neither his approval nor applause is solicited. This audience cannot inspire; not a public presence, it makes no one less private or less alone, even in thought. Unimagined, it can not be addressed. Faced with the dialogue, the reader becomes an unknown witness: what Diderot would later describe as a "spectateur ignoré."[9]

In fact, Shaftesbury's vision of the dialogue, or the text which would act like a dialogue, describes essentially the same condition that Diderot would demand from painting and theater some fifty years after the publication of the *Characteristics*. Just as the epistolary narrative contains a closed set of dialogues (as distinguished from the formal *Letter* which is open to the public) in painting as in the theater: "La toile renferme tout l'espace, et il n'y a personne au délà."[10] Diderot writes in the *Salon de 1767*: "Une scène représentée sur la toile, ou sur les planches, ne suppose pas de témoins";[11] Shaftesbury wanted to apply this supposition to the scene of writing. The ideal represented by this sort of theater is figured in Diderot's *Discours de la poésie dramatique*: "Soit donc que vous composiez, soit que vous jouiez, ne pensez non plus au spectateur que s'il n'existait pas. Imaginez, sur le bord du théâtre, un grand mur qui vous sépare du parterre; jouez comme si la toile ne se levait pas."[12] This model of theater would defeat theatricality—or at least appear to do so. Paradoxically, the dialogue dramatized in a text would deny the dialogue which joins author and reader; theater would be used to negate its own conditions, to deny its own terms.

As the analogues, figures, and positions of theater return and turn against themselves, we can sense that theater—for both Shaftesbury and Diderot—is intolerable, desirable, a danger, a resource, inevitable, unavoidable, necessary. In the next chapter, I will discuss the risks and possibilities offered to Shaftesbury by his dramatic method of philosophy. The paradox we have encountered of theatricality defeated by theater points to what is at stake for Shaftesbury in being an author and a philosopher: it marks the problems of writing philosophy in published, printed characters; and, as we shall see, it reveals the problems of characterizing the self.

CHAPTER 2

The Characters
of Philosophy

WE have seen that Shaftesbury advocates the dialogue (both despite and because of the paradoxical relation it establishes with its reader) as the medium best suited for authors and philosophers. A look at the *Characteristics*, however, shows that only one of his books attempts to resemble a formal dialogue: *The Moralists, A Philosophical Rhapsody. Being a RECITAL of Certain Conversations on Natural and Moral Subjects*. Even in this work—first published in 1709, one year before *Soliloquy, or Advice to an Author*—Shaftesbury refrains from writing a strictly generic dialogue, choosing instead to combine narrative with quoted discourse in what he called in the Advertisement to the first edition "a philosophical romance" (2:334). *The Miscellaneous Reflections* assures us that *The Moralists* "aspires to dialogue" and is written with "those poetic features of the pieces anciently called mimes" (2:333–34). Its author is said to be "a poet in due form, and by a more apparent claim than if he had writ a play or dramatic piece in as regular a manner, at least, as any known at present on our stage" (2:334). These claims, however, appear in an account of the tensions, limitations, and failings of form of the piece—problems which are, in fact, suggested from the outset in *The Moralists*. In the first pages of the book, Shaftesbury sets up an epistolary, narrative frame that establishes the fiction that one "PHILOCLES" is writing "to" one "PALEMON" in response to the latter's request for a written recitation of a conversation which had occurred the day before. The narrator must preface his recital by explaining to his reader the difficulties of writing a philosophical dialogue.

The problem, according to Philocles, is that philosophy itself is in such ill repute that its images, its "representations," "picture," and "portraitures" (2:7), are scarcely believable. Philosophy "is no longer active in the world, nor can hardly, with any advantage, be brought upon the public stage" (1:4). The theater of philosophy must be unconvincing since moderns would appear ridiculous using the roles, characters, and manners of the interlocutors of classical dialogues; and if philosophy were to present the age with its own reflection, it would present a disagreeable image to its disfigured and postlapsarian readers. The modern author, then, faced with the absence of an adequate subject for representation, finds himself in a dilemma: "This is the plain dilemma against that ancient manner of writing which we can neither well imitate nor translate" (1:134), writes Shaftesbury in *Soliloquy, or Advice to an Author*. The philosopher is faced with a crisis of modernity: "dialogue is at an end. The ancients could see their own faces, but we cannot" (1:134). [1] Thus the author who would try to use the dialogue in order to negotiate a position on the stage of the world finds that philosophy is out of place on that public stage. The reader seems disengaged as well as unengaged; the modern philosopher, it would seem, must turn to mixed, hybrid, disguised, and self-contradictory forms of writing in order to avoid the theatricality of the book while still engaging his reader.

If the dialogue has reached an end, however, it nonetheless plays a key role in Shaftesbury's thought. While it negotiates relations with the reader and turns theater against its own conditions, the dramatic method of the dialogue also provides a way of coming to terms with the self. According to Shaftesbury, the dialogue provides not just the medium but also a structure for philosophical thinking. If offers a private "looking-glass" in which we might "discover ourselves, and see our minutest features nicely delineated, and suited to our own apprehension and cognizance" (1:128). The form of writing used by poets and philosophers is advocated as a form of thinking, a "pocket-mirror" (1:128) of the mind in which "we should, by virtue of the double reflection, distinguish ourselves into two different parties" (1:128–9). This "work of self-inspection" is what Shaftesbury calls the "dramatic method" (1:129) of philosophy. The reflection provided by this dramatic method is double because "two faces . . . present themselves to our view" (1:128): we face ourselves divided into two parts, playing or personating two different interlocutors. However, in order to become a spectator to this double reflection of ourselves in dialogue, we must first divide ourselves. The division into two parts effected by the dialogic method is itself doubled: one is divided to face an image of oneself divided in two; one becomes an audience to oneself playing two different parts. This double and doubling reflection is the image and enactment of the message which, according to Shaftesbury, comes to us from the Greeks, "that celebrated Delphic inscription" which Shaftesbury renders as: "Recognize yourself; which was as much as to say, divide yourself, or be two" (1:113). Having condemned the narcissism of authors who reveal themselves to readers, Shaftesbury advocates a sort of private narcissism that depends on a double reflection. In a sense, he reworks the story of Narcissus found in the *Metamorphoses* in which Tiresias prophesizes that Narcissus will live long "si se non noverint"—if he never "knows" or "recognizes" himself. For Narcissus, ironically, self-knowledge means self-destruction because he doesn't recognize himself when, divided in two, he sees his reflection in a looking-glass of water. Taking himself for someone else, his moment of self-recognition comes too late; it makes knowing himself impossible since it irrevocably cuts him off from himself, denies him the self. The ambiguous prophesy of Tiresias also points to Oedipus, who becomes king because he can recognize himself (that is, as "man") in the riddle of the Sphinx, but who loses all because he can not recognize himself in the stories that people tell in Thebes. He discovers his identity only when he uncovers his doubleness and duplicity, his double roles as father-brother and husband-son. Like Narcissus, he recognizes himself too late; self-destruction comes when he realizes that he and someone else are one. Shaftesbury asserts that self-knowledge depends on self-recognition: which means the self must be doubled *and* divided. By translating the Delphic oracle as "recognize yourself" Shaftesbury insists on the double, reflexive, and repeated act which characterizes self-knowledge. Philosophy offers a mirror through which "we could discover a certain duplicity of soul, and divide ourselves into two parties" (1:112). It allows us to look back at ourselves and know ourselves again. The dialogue is itself a double of this *dédoublement*: a reflection, representation, and enactment of the act of self-division through which an identity is established.

Paradoxically, this "self-examining practice and method of inward colloquy" (1:211) both allows and denies the philosopher the possibility of being "by himself"—a condition which Shaftesbury rules out for "lover, author, mystic," and "conjuror" and reserves for "the man of sense, the sage, or philosopher" (1:116). We saw Shaftesbury's characterization of those "public-spirited" authors who, "though they are often retired, . . . are never by themselves. The world is ever of the party" (1:109). In contrast, the philosopher is supposed to be independent of any real or imagined presence to whom his thoughts would be addressed—like Lord *****, the noblest actor on the stage of the world. Shaftesbury's formulation of this possibility is both explained and contradicted by the claim that philosophers, "able to hold themselves in talk," are "never less alone than when by themselves" (1:113). Shaftesbury's "home-dialect of soliloquy" (1:113), based on a dialectical "doctrine of two persons in one individual self" (1:121), establishes an "inspector or auditor . . . within us" (1:122). Thus the dialogist is independent of an other because he internalizes an other within himself; or externalizes a part of himself to play the role of inspector (from *spectare*: to look) or auditor. We witness again a movement which would appear to escape theatricality but which creates theater in another sense. In the *dédoublement* of the dialogue, one is turned into one's own witness; in addition, one becomes an audience to the dialogue itself. One doubles oneself to divide oneself, and in the process one creates a representation of one's own dialogue; one becomes a spectator to oneself as spectator to oneself. The model of theater, then, would seem to be contained in the structure of the philosophical method, as Shaftesbury defines and designs it. The act of soliloquy allows one to be by oneself because it sets up a scene of theater within the self.

In fact, the dialogic method is presented in theatrical terms from the outset of *Soliloquy, or Advice to an Author*—as the first half of the title itself suggests. In the first pages of the essay, Shaftesbury characterizes a reader to object: "who can thus multiply himself into two persons and be his own subject?" (1:105). The narrator of the treatise advises the reader to look to the poets who offer many instances of a person who "comes alone upon the stage" and "carries on the business of self-dissection. By virtue of this soliloquy he becomes two distinct persons" (1:105). Shaftesbury concludes that "had I nothing else to plead in behalf of our modern dramatic poets, I should defend them still against their accusers for the sake of this very practice" (1:106). The reader (that is, the interlocutor Shaftesbury has divided from himself—a reader, perhaps of Jeremy Collier's attacks on the theater) complains: "'Are we to go therefore to the stage for edification? Must we learn our catechism from the poets? And, like the players, speak aloud what we debate at any time with ourselves alone?" (1:106). The point, however, is that the stage in Shaftesbury's description is only occasionally literal; it is created by the "dramatic method" by which a "person of profound parts" (1:105), acting as if he were alone, divides himself into actor and audience and gives his thoughts "voice and accent" (1:113). Here we see the philosopher as Hamlet, the soliloquist who played the parts of actor, playwright, and director in the play which, according to Shaftesbury, "has only one character or principal part" and "is almost one continued moral: a series of deep reflections drawn from one mouth, upon the subject of one single accident" (1:180). (According to one critic, this perception marked a turning point in literary criticism from seeing *Hamlet* as a "tragedy of action" to seeing it as "an inward and subjective revelation."[2]) Like Hamlet, Shaftesbury's philosopher acts like a "madman" as well as an actor; he talks to himself "in different persons, and under different characters" (1:207). By himself, he is also beside himself when, in the "method of soliloquy,"

> by a certain powerful figure of inward rhetoric, the mind apostrophises its own fancies, raises them in their proper shapes and personages, and addresses them familiarly. . . . By this means it will soon happen that two formed parties will erect themselves within.

> For the imaginations or fancies being thus roundly treated are forced
> to declare themselves and take party. (1:123)

Philosophy, in these terms, turns the mind into a sort of play: into a dramatization of itself. A person gives rise to different persons (grammatical and dramatic) who act out points of view and represent their interactions. In this manner, writes Shaftesbury, we are instructed "to personate ourselves" (1:114). What does it mean, however, that the method that Shaftesbury posits as necessary for self-knowledge instructs one to *personate* oneself? Shaftesbury's terms have set the scene for this assertion; personate, from the Latin *personāre* (to represent, bear the character of) and originally from *persōna* (mask), means to act or play a part, presumably the part of a character in a drama. To act, play, represent or exhibit dramatically, to assume the character of—this is what we must learn to do for ourselves. The dramatic method of soliloquy—in its dialogic mode—would teach us to dramatize our own characters.[3]

It appears that a new set of problems is before us. If philosophy is to teach us how to know ourselves by playing or characterizing ourselves, transforming ourselves into personages which must be acted or represented, it must risk undermining the notion of the self itself—at least the notion of a self that could be differentiated from its characterization, representation, or personation. If the self is a role to be played, a mask to be assumed, then how can we recognize it as a stable entity: what Shaftesbury at various moments insists on calling the "true and native self" (1:182), the "real and genuine self," the "genuine, true, and natural self" (1:183), the "real character and true self" (2:271)? At one point in *Soliloquy*, Shaftesbury complains that "we are seldom taught to comprehend this self by placing it in a distinct view from its representative or counterfeit" (1:183). But *personate*, in addition to signifying a representation, also means to masquerade, to counterfeit or assume the person of someone else, to feign or imitate or mimic; *personate* and *impersonate* appear as synonyms in the dictionary. How can we comprehend the difference between the self and what authentically or inauthentically stands for it; or does the self become itself in being represented, formed into personages, given voice and enacted? There is evidently a radical instability in this dramatic or theatrical notion of the self.

"All turns upon the nature of a character," as Shaftesbury says in another context. Throughout the *Characteristics* and the *Second Characters*, character—as word and concept—stands and acts as a seminal figure. *Character* embodies the ambiguity and contradiction which are in question in Shaftesbury's notion of the self: for *character* means at once the aggregate of the distinctive features of something, its essential peculiarity or nature, the moral or mental qualities which distinguish one as an individual, individuality itself; *and* the face or features of something or someone, a personality invented by a novelist or a dramatist, the part assumed and played by an actor on the stage. *Character* is also writing itself: from its Greek etymology meaning to mark, stamp, or engrave to an alphabetic mark, a graphic symbol or sign, a figure, an expression, or direct representation. Is the character of a person something essential and individual or a role to be enacted, a figure that represents a self? Could it be all of these, and if so, could a self exist apart from its representation, before its enactment? What would be the difference between a representation of the self and a counterfeit or false representation, between the self's essence and its status as a fictive role? These are questions Shaftesbury must confront in characterizing the self.

Shaftesbury tells us that an "author who writes in his own person has the advantage of being who or what he pleases. He is no certain man, nor has any certain or genuine character" (1:131). However, even if *character* didn't itself undermine the concept of a genuine character, even if we understood how by writing in one's own person one loses one's own personality, how the assumption of *I* would dissolve or negate the *ego*; it is still uncertain how the writer of the dialogue (who is here contrasted with the "author") can be a certain man with a genuine character as he multiples and divides himself, personates his conflicting thoughts, raises shapes and personages out of his fancies, talks under different characters, and contains within himself a duplicity and multiplicity of persons. Where is the genuine character, the true and native self, in this proliferation of dramatic and grammatical persons who supposedly annihilate the "I" of the author? Does the dialectic of soliloquy represent synthesis or schizophrenia? How can philosophy, which "teaches me to distinguish between her person and her likeness, and shows me her immediate and real self, by that sole privilege of teaching me to know myself and what belongs to me" (1:193–94) first teach us to distinguish between these different versions of a persona-tion and a character, between an immediate and real self and its representation or counterfeit, between a proper sense and a figura-tive sense? How could we learn this by personating ourselves?

The determination to discover a real or genuine self combined with such ambiguous means of ascertaining it—acts and terms which appear to undermine Shaftesbury's very goals—pro-duce in Shaftesbury's texts a recurrent anxiety about identifying the self. "How am I myself?" (1:209) asks the author of *Soliloquy* while describing a dialogue between the self and its fancies. The self must be located, designated, distinguished from its outward features, manner, or expression. Can we understand it apart from the charac-teristics it manifests? According to Shaftesbury, philosophy instructs us how "to make us comprehensible to ourselves, and knowable by other features than those of a bare countenance. For 'tis not cer-tainly by virtue of our face merely that we are ourselves. 'Tis not we who change when our complexion or shape changes." However, continues Shaftesbury, "there is *that*, which being wholly meta-morphosed and converted, we are thereby in reality transformed and lost" (1:184). *That* is what is different from a countenance, a face, a complexion or shape; it is what is essential in the features and characteristics that somehow preserve, outline, and define us. We are faced with the question of how to understand this *that*, which can be designated only by a gesture of language—"mit Wor-ten und Fingerzeigen," in Rilke's words—a gesture which carries only the most specific and momentary or the most general of indi-cations: a name that fixes nothing, ascertains nothing, only points to a blind spot we must see already at the end of *that* in order for *that* to have any meaning or reference at all. Shaftesbury's problem here is not only a failure of language; he must determine the point at which the reflection taught to us by the philosopher's "vocal looking-glass" (1:114) ceases being named by *ourselves*. When (and how) does *that* in an instant of metamorphosis and conversion stop being *us*? What or who is named by *myself* and who or what is represented by the *that* I no longer represent or personate?

Shaftesbury describes the transformation of a person who returns from an absence so changed that we think him "another creature, and not the friend whom we once knew familiarly" (1:185). In this situation, he writes, or when "a revolution of this kind, though not so total, happens at any time in a character . . . 'tis to philosophy we then appeal" (1:185). We appeal to philosophy in the face of change, for it is "the known province of philosophy to teach us ourselves, keep us the self-same persons" (1:184). Philosophy, for Shaftesbury, seeks to fix the self, to recognize *that* and make it certain. In fact, it is by virtue of philosophy, which teaches us to know ourselves, that we can ascertain certainty itself, since "we can in reality be assured of nothing till we are first assured of what we are ourselves. For by this alone we can know what certainty and assurance is" (2:274–75). How we can be assured of anything before we know what assurance is, Shaftesbury does not explain. But the possibility of certainty and the ability of philosophy to regulate and conserve the self are essential to each other because the specter of change—what would transform and lose the self—seems inscribed within the problem of identity itself. In discussing metaphysical speculations about identity in the *Miscellaneous Reflections*, Shaftesbury wonders how a subject "is continued one and the same," with thoughts that continue in "the same relation still to one single and self-same person" (2:275). Asserting that the "self-examiners or searchers after truth and certainty" can't easily answer such questions, he ridicules Descartes' *cogito* and insists that the question of being must be posed both as "What constitutes the We or I?" and as "whether the I of this instant be the same with that of any instant preceding or to come?" (2:275). To know oneself, then, one must be able to recognize oneself: to know oneself again as the self is constituted over time. For Shaftesbury, philosophy, which would teach us to keep us ourselves by teaching us to double and divide ourselves, must stand opposed to metamorphosis.

Shaftesbury tries to change the terms of the problem of identity by declaring, "for my own part, I take my being upon trust" (2:276), and then asking not what he is but what he should be. But the threat that change poses to the self is not so easily dismissed by this act of faith. Frequently in the essays we read about the concern to "continue a day in the same will" (1:122), to "be warranted one and the same person to-day as yesterday, and to-morrow as to-day" (1:123), to "ascertain my ideas, and keep my opinion, liking, and esteem of things the same" (1:194). *Soliloquy* contains an allegorical story about a lover who claims in the face of temptation that he is "myself still" and is told: "keep yourself so. Be ever the same man" (1:119). In *The Moralists* Theocles remarks that "'Tis good fortune if a man be one and the same only for a day or two. A year makes more revolutions than can be numbered." He wonders how "there is a strange simplicity in this you and me, that in reality they should be still one and the same, when neither one atom of body, one passion, nor one thought remains the same" (2:101). The fate of the friend who became unrecognizable after that *that* which made him seem wholly metamorphosed seems again and again to threaten the person who would stay the same, preserve an original character. In the context of this need to keep characters the same we might understand in a new light Shaftesbury's investment in defending the printing press: he emphasizes the alphabetic engine's "quick way of copying fair, and keeping copies alike" at the same time he insists that the character of his work is not altered by the outward character or dress of printed characters.

This dilemma of identity is present throughout the *Characteristics*—either explicitly or just below the text's surface. We have seen that it is activated by the dramatic method which both forms the fundamental structure of the search for self-knowledge and itself undermines any stable or fixed notion of the self. The theatrical terms of the dialogue threaten to turn a character into a role, self-realization into acting; and they pose the problem that the multiplication and division of the self into different characters and persons must be the method through which a stable and consistent self is maintained. Theater is thus necessary and yet doubly dangerous to the real and genuine self. If the notion of acting is itself threatening, so much more so is the notion of dividing the self into a variety of roles or characters to be played successively or played off against one another. The transformation of the self into different parties, shapes, and personages must keep one the self-same person yet it acts by metamorphosing the self. How can the division and doubling of the "I" posit its permanence? Where is identity in the practice of turning the self into a cast of characters who converse and debate with themselves? The dialogic method—which in writing removes the "I" of the author from the work—challenges the assumption of a first person singular.

Shaftesbury attempts to resolve the dilemma of identity by means of a paradox: he suggests that one must become two in order to remain one. When one is beside oneself with abnormal or disordered perceptions, for instance, one is prevented from going mad by an internalized other within oneself, a "correctrice by whose means I am in my wits, and without whom I am no longer myself" (1:208). In such an internal dispute, Shaftesbury explains, "Fancy and I are not all one. The disagreement makes me my own" (1:209). The lover in the allegorical story stays himself by learning the doctrine of two persons in one: that he has a good soul that must win out over a bad soul. Thus the narcissism of philosophy's looking-glass focuses on self-mastery rather than self-love. It is not at all clear, however, how this attempt to control and fix the self through self-division can counteract the radical disruption of the self which appears to take place in the dialogic mode. Nowhere is this more apparent than in the *dédoublement* through which Shaftesbury plays critic to himself in the *Characteristics*. I have not yet had occasion to remark that the voice and person of the author of the *Miscellaneous Reflections*—the work that originally stood as the third volume of the *Characteristics*—are different from the voice

and person of the author of the first two volumes. The author of the
third volume speaks of the author of the first volumes in the third
person, as if he were someone else; and in the passage I quoted
earlier in which Shaftesbury writes of the problem of understanding
how one remains "one single and self-same person," Shaftesbury is
not only writing in the character of someone else, the author of the
Miscellaneous Reflections; but the character of the *Miscellaneous
Reflections* author is imitating and impersonating the author of the
first treatises. In other words, Shaftesbury—if we can call him
that—is personating someone else who personates Shaftesbury in
order to soliloquize about what constitutes the "I." Who is speaking
here?

   *The Miscellaneous Reflections on the preceding Trea-
tises, and other Critical Subjects* was first published in the joint
edition of the *Characteristics*. Unlike (at least the pose of) the essays
it follows, it is unmistakably a book designed to be printed and
published. To some extent it is a parody of the genre that Shaftesbury ridicules and condemns elsewhere, a book which exploits the
form of its own formlessness with chapter headings, labeled divi-
sions and subdivisions, titles, marginal notations, and extensive
cross-references—those characteristics of the modern book that
helped invent the modern reader. Here the mechanical voice of the
printing press speaks to convey the voice of an author to the reading
public. However, the first Miscellany proceeds for several pages
before an "I" appears on the scene of the text; and it is not until a
long paragraph later that the reader learns that the "chief intention"
of this first person singular "in the following sheets is to descant
cursorily upon some late pieces of a British author" (2:160); at which
point the probably confused reader only begins to suspect that the
"I" of the *Reflections*—a book as anonymous as the rest of the
Characteristics—is not supposed to be the "I" who wrote or spoke
the first five treatises. For the hundreds of pages that constitute the
rest of the volume, an author explains, comments on, discusses,
critiques, elaborates, judges, and defends the unnamed author of
the treatises we (on the basis of reliable historical documents) assign
to Shaftesbury, alias Anthony Ashley Cooper, the third Earl of
Shaftesbury.

It is not difficult to speculate about why Shaftesbury would have written the *Miscellaneous Reflections* in the guise of someone else. By speaking of himself in the third person he avoids assuming the "I" of confessions, defenses, and epilogues: the mark of the soliciting public author. The method also allows him to stand outside of his books, beside himself, as it were; to become his own first reader, examiner, or witness. Through a delayed *dédoublement* which repeats the structure of the dialogue, Shaftesbury is able to examine and criticize himself as if he were someone else, and to create a dialogue between the different parts of the book. But who is this "I" who speaks for Shaftesbury as he takes him for a subject? He defines his role as that of "critic and interpreter to this new writer" (2:161), his "part" as an "airy assistant and humourous paraphrast" (2:244), his activity as serving in a "commentator capacity" (2:273). Reading along, as it were, with the reader of the essays, he will also at a given moment accompany the author "at a distance, keep him in sight, and convoy him, the best I am able, through the dangerous seas he is about to pass" (2:272). However, the fictions surrounding this strange version of Dante's Vergil go beyond the poses of guide or commentator. At certain points the author of the Miscellanies announces he will "imitate our Author" (2:202), prefacing a monologue, for instance, with: "And thus in his proper manner of soliloquy or self-discourse, we may imagine him running on" (2:269). At such moments the "I" and the voice of the text become identical to the "I" and the voice of *Soliloquy* or the *Letter Concerning Enthusiasm*. The author states that "as his interpreter or paraphrast, I have proposed to imitate and accompany him, as far as my miscellaneous character will permit" (2:257), but the difference between accompaniment and imitation, the boundaries which keep one character from becoming another, seem destined to become blurred. Finally, after preparing us to "imagine our author speaking" (2:274), the text produces the reflections about identity that we have considered; for several pages we read a voice and manner indistinguishable from the author of *Soliloquy* until an "I" interrupts to say: "But I forget, it seems, that I am now speaking in the person of our grave inquirer" (2:283). It seems that an example was out of character and a moment later we are again asked to "at this instant imagine our grave inquirer taking pains to show us" (2:283–4) something else. The temporal markers in these state-ments—the "now" and "at this instant"—further challenge us to tell the difference between these (first) persons. Who and when am I when I say I am now speaking in the voice of another person; when and where does my first person transform itself when I ask you to imagine at this instant that I am someone else? These roles within roles that supposedly personate a "real" self evoke the vertigo of the playhouse. We must wonder whether we are witness to Shaftesbury's personation or impersonation of himself.

In the fourth Miscellany, after paraphrasing the "British author's" ideas about virtue and nature, the author of the *Reflections* declares, "These are our author's formal and grave sentiments, which if they were not truly his and sincerely espoused by him as the real result of his best judgment and understanding, he would be guilty of a more than common degree of imposture" (2:295). This paragraph is labeled "Serious Countenance of the Author" but what's in a countenance? As we wonder whose character this coun-tenance contains, maintains, or represents, the question of impos-ture is highly relevant. Shaftesbury continues to remark that "an affected gravity and feigned seriousness carried on . . . in such manner as to leave no insight into the fiction or intended raillery, is in truth no raillery or wit at all" but rather an immoral abuse, "foreign to the character of a good writer" (2:295). It is not surpris-ing, perhaps, since this chapter of the fourth Miscellany follows the chapter in which Shaftesbury personates himself to talk about iden-tity and change, that the subject of the *Reflections* should feel com-pelled to own his sentiments, to insist (under another countenance) that the countenance he displayed is really attributable to him. Nor is it surprising that in the manner of Defoe he should suggest that an impostor who allowed an insight into his fiction and feigning would not be guilty of imposture. In the same chapter Shaftesbury says that the metaphysical reflections he engaged in during the preced-ing chapter "may be looked on in philosophy as worse than a mere Egyptian imposition" (2:287). He is referring to the solipsism of scepticism but it seems clear that the realm of Egyptian imposi-tion—the world of counterfeiting, disguise, and imposture represented to early-eighteenth-century England by those analogues of actors, the gypsies—would encompass the form as well as the content of his speculations. Indeed, at the beginning of the same chapter about the self our Protean author refers us back to that treatise about recognizing, doubling, and dividing the self and the use of the authorial "I": he mentions that in the preface to the first edition of *Soliloquy*, the author "took occasion there, in a line or two, under the name of his printer, or (as he otherwise calls him) his amanuensis, to prepare us for a more elaborate and methodical piece which was to follow" (2:273). If we look back at that preface, which was not reprinted in the *Characteristics*, we do find such a claim; however, this message entitled "THE PRINTER TO THE READER" begins: "'Twou'd be in vain for me to protest to You, that it is *I*, *my self* (the true and lawful *Printer* of these papers) who, by these Presents, address You, in my own proper *Sense* and *Words*. You will neither believe I write what I write, or think what I think." Under the name of his printer, Shaftesbury—at least I believe that it is Shaftesbury—laments: "'tis the Misfortune of Us *Printers*: that having so freely accommodated our Authors with our *Name* and *Person*, we have neither left us for our private Use, nor are suppos'd to have any *Speech*, or *Utterance* of our own."4 Perhaps this is only a common degree of imposture. It would be easy to believe that Shaftesbury called in Defoe to be his amanuensis for this impersonation.

In fact, we do have an insight into Shaftesbury's fictions—into the character of the author—from the moment we decide to accept the character of the *Miscellaneous Reflections* as a pose. If the work represents a degree of imposture, it is not a counterfeit in the same manner as *The Life and Strange Surprizing Adventures of Robinson Crusoe, of York, Mariner, by Himself,* published a few years after the *Characteristics*; and surely Shaftesbury did not expect readers to believe that the *Reflections* were written by someone other than the author of the "preceding Treatises." However, this does not dismiss the question of imposture; for the recognition of the fiction of that impersonation must retroactively and retrospectively change the way one reads the *Characteristics*. By playing the part of an author playing the part of the author of the preceding treatises, Shaftesbury *doubly* turns the author of all and each of the essays into a role. Each "I" of each essay ultimately has the same status: the author of the *Letter Concerning Enthusiasm* who writes to Lord ✳✳✳✳, the author of *Sensus Communis* who writes to a friend, the author of *Soliloquy* who advises an author, the more formal author of *An Inquiry Concerning Virtue and Merit*, the personage Philocles who recounts a dialogue for Palemon in *The Moralists*, a text composed of dramatized voices—each first person is no more or less a role, disguise, impersonation, or pose than the character of the *Miscellaneous* author. Shaftesbury turns himself into a role to be imitated, mimicked, counterfeited, and personated both by portraying himself as a role and by showing that any textual "I" might be a persona or a mask. The outlines of a real and true self, the character of a self-same person, seem less and less distinct as Shaftesbury performs his dramatic method on himself.

Furthermore, this method turns Shaftesbury into an actor—as well as a role—in a double sense by making him spectator as well as personator of himself. Although, he writes, "we seldom see the character of writer and that of critic united in the same person" (2:324), Shaftesbury divides his double character to play critic to himself: for instance, to praise himself for having taken on the dialogue form after advocating it as an ideal genre, to have "come afterwards as a grave actor upon the stage, and expose himself to criticism in his turn" (2:333). By becoming his own critic, Shaftesbury also exposes himself as an actor on the stage. As reader, he acts as his own spectator; and as the author of the *Miscellaneous Reflections*, he helps to create the public audience which places the rest of his work on the stage of the world. The *Miscellaneous Reflections* plays its part in turning Shaftesbury's texts into theater. The *Characteristics* as a whole acts out the philosopher's dialogic practice by becoming a play of characters which contains its own dramatization and audience, its own self-addressing and self-regarding reading.

Characteristically, the *Miscellaneous Reflections* ends (and thus ends Shaftesbury's book) by becoming a play: a theatrical dialogue written in "the form or manner of our dialogue author"

(2:353) which is ostensibly a brief sequel to *The Moralists*. Further-more, as the author changes the scene of his text to assume the parts and characters of a conversation, the personages who are drama-tized in turn become actors who assume characters and parts. The author of the *Reflections* imitates the author of *The Moralists* in his dramatic method of "taking the person of a sceptic" (2:351) and as he delivers a discourse to his "zealot auditors" (2:355) the voice of the narrator interrupts his own monologue to remark: "The reader may here . . . remark a certain air of studied discourse and declamation, not so very proper or natural in the mouth of a mere gentleman" (2:357). Offended by a sense of rehearsal in "the delivery of these words," the auditors accuse the gentleman of carrying "lectures about with him to repeat by rote" (2:357). He in turn admits that "the words you have heard repeated are not my own" (2:358), allow-ing that he has been speaking the lines of Bishop Taylor. (The footnotes, instruments the printed book uses to speak in different voices, permit Jeremy Taylor simultaneously to accompany the text in his own voice and texts.) The gentleman, who excuses himself for not including "an intermission during my recital" (2:364), even-tually makes "his final bow in form" (2:369) and the curtain comes down on the *Characteristics*. We have witnessed another play within a play. Theater seems to generate theater: in a public book an author (personating someone who is imitating himself personating someone else) takes on the person of someone who, as if an actor, speaks as if by rote someone else's lines to a group of auditors. If we are to assume that the sentiments that the sceptical gentleman ex-presses in reality belong to Shaftesbury, we must recognize them at (at least) five removes. Shaftesbury explains the need "to raise parti-cular machines" such as this, by which his characters in *The Moral-ists* "feign" characters and resort to "personating" (2:335), by stressing the lack of verisimilitude in having contemporary gentle-men philosophize. Since the philosophical dialogue is out of place on the stage of the world, its dramatic characters must resort to play-acting in order "to carry a better face" and avoid "the appearance of pedantry" (2:335). However, the proliferation of parts and charac-ters is already inscribed within the dramatic method that generates both play-acting and mimes of play-acting throughout Shaftesbury's work. It is the dividend and product of the manner of writing in which the self becomes a role and the author a playwright who divides and multiplies himself into a cast of characters who act out the dramatization and personation of himself.

Where, then, is a genuine self in the kaleidoscope of roles and characters that the mirror-writing of philosophy has become? The situation we find outselves in might be figured by a scene that Shaftesbury describes in *An Essay on the Freedom of Wit and Humor*:

> If a native of Ethiopia were on a sudden transported into Europe, and placed either at Paris or Venice at a time of carnival, when the general face of mankind was disguised, and almost every creature wore a mask, 'tis probable he would for some time be at a stand, before he discovered the cheat; not imagining that a whole people could be so fantastical as upon agreement, at an appointed time, to transform themselves by a variety of habits, and make it a solemn practice to impose on one another, by this universal confusion of characters and persons. (1:57)

This, in a sense, is the scene of Shaftesbury's writing: a universal confusion of characters and persons (grammatical and dramatic, genuine and personated) set into play by a method that would reflect, discover, and preserve the single, real, and genuine shape of the self. As readers, we presumably are not as confused as the spectator in Shaftesbury's story—who, upon discovering the cheat, would find the scene so ridiculous "it would be hardly possible for him to hold his countenance"; but who, according to Shaftesbury, would himself become ridiculous "should it so happen that in the transport of ridicule . . . having his head still running upon masks, and knowing nothing of the fair complexion and common dress of the Europeans, [he] should upon the sight of a natural face and habit, laugh just as heartily as before" (1:57). However, do we not also risk taking a real face for a counterfeit, or a face for a self, or a costume for an identity? What, in Shaftesbury's terms, is the difference? Unlike the character of the eighteenth-century Ethiopian, the *less* naïve we become, the more we are faced with a confusion of characters and persons. There is finally no sense that we could come face to face with a natural, true, or authentic self, that we could recognize a self separate from its outward representation. The escape from theatricality seems to be an escape into theater: a realm which both underwrites and undermines Shaftesbury's philosophy. This is finally our problem not only as readers of Shaftesbury's texts but also as spectators and actors in the world of identities that Shaftesbury's texts add up to and represent.

Of course Shaftesbury never expects us to see beyond his characters—even if we are able to recognize them as such. Although his writing tells a story about its own conditions, puts forth its own problems, and refers to its own character, Shaftesbury is not engaged in autobiography. We have been examining the dramatic method Shaftesbury's texts advocate and act out in order to question the grounds of Shaftesbury's suppositions about self-knowledge. We must acknowledge, however, that his philosophical search to know and recognize the self is not directed at us, not undertaken for our benefit; the soliloquies of the *Characteristics* are not meant to end in revelation. But if the book is designed to refuse us and deny us knowledge, this is not to say that our presence is really ignored or that our problems in reading are unrelated to the positions and impositions that Shaftesbury must enact in his texts. We, as readers, are inevitably implicated in this scene of theater. This is because the scene of theater defines our interactions with Shaftesbury and his books; and also, because it is our world.

CHAPTER 3

Reading Characters

HAVING examined Shaftesbury's strategies for avoiding a theatrical relation with the reader of his books, and having examined how the dialogue's reintroduction of the terms of theater affects both the ends of Shaftesbury's philosophy and the position in which we must read the characters of the *Characteristics*, I now will focus on two notebooks in which Shaftesbury discoursed with himself about the character of the self and the role that the self must play on the stage of the world. These texts were not meant for us: found among Shaftesbury's papers after his death and not published for almost two hundred years (in 1900) these private memorandums were not intended for public view. The editor who brought the manuscripts to print named them the *Philosophical Regimen*; Shaftesbury named them with the Greek word for "exercises," and this is what they appear to have been: essays into philosophical problems, commonplace books for self-improvement, investigations that practiced the self-discoursing method of soliloquy. "Go on, then," writes Shaftesbury in one of these dialogues with himself, "exercise and write, but remember . . . for yourself and not for others"; he defines his "business" as "to improve by these, not publish them, profess, or teach them" (PR:242).

Shaftesbury writes these reflections only for the conversant, witness, and spectator produced within himself by the doubling and dividing of the internal dialogue. "Why writing? why this flourishing, drawing, figuring, over and over, the same still? what for?—What, but for the art? Not for show; but for exercise, practice, improvement.—Writing and then burning. Drawing and rubbing out" (PR:241). Written as if in invisible ink, this writing would withdraw from reading. This is part of its meaning, as is the fact that we read it. Since these texts were not burned, since their characters were not erased, they have everything to do with us. Indeed, the exercises describe Shaftesbury trying to come to terms with us: that is, with the public, the world. In entries such as "Reputation," "Self," "Artificial or Economical Self," "Natural Self," "Character and Conduct," and "Character," Shaftesbury seeks to understand the self and its relation to the world, to define the self in terms of its place before the eyes of the public. What is at stake is how one realizes oneself in and out of relation to others; *how* one must publish oneself—or renounce becoming public.

We can trace in the notebooks the same anxious investigations of what constitutes the self that we saw in the *Characteristics*. "What am I? what is this self?" asks Shaftesbury in "Natural Self" (PR:139). "Who am I?" he demands in "Character and Conduct" after declaring: "All turns upon the nature of a *Character*" (PR:189). Shaftesbury's attempts to point to *that* which defines the bounds and terms of identity reiterate the ambiguities the dictionary inscribes within the word *character*. He would divide the character into an inner and an outer character, the self into a natural self and an artificial or economical self. The outer character consists of the bearing and role one assumes in the world, the self one constructs and acts for the world; it is economical in the sense that it attempts to regulate the loss and preservation of the natural self in its public transactions. "Strive to find a character" (PR:192), writes Shaftesbury, "seek a character, a personage, manner, genius, style, voice, action. . . . This the study, performance, and music of life" (PR:195). The outer character seems necessary to protect and preserve the inner character. "If at any time the inward character suffer," writes Shaftesbury, "keep at least the outward. Keep it within reach and recovery." Calling it folly to "publish thy wisdom and strength in the preservation of inward character," Shaftesbury considers it greater folly to "expose thy loss of character, and show thy own weakness" (PR:200–201). The outward character would seem to shield the self from the eyes of the world, to screen it from public view. However, precisely because the outer character finds its place before the world, its position also appears to be dangerous. In the entry on "Shame" Shaftesbury asks: "What is the ground for all this anxiety? What is this stir about an outward character? . . . either I have a part still, or no part" (PR:63). The anxiety, he seems to answer himself in "Self," seems to result from the risk that the appeal to the world represented by the public aspect of an outer character would destroy rather than protect the self. "If others are courted and cultivated, self is forgot" (PR:118).

The outer character, as a role designed for others, would place one upon the stage of the world where one would forget one's "true" part and keep the regard of spectators in view. " 'Must I have nothing better to act?' And thus thou becomest one of those seditious and quarrelsome actors that mutiny against the master of the stage. For it is plain, whilst thou art thus affected, thy aim is towards spectators, not towards Him of whose approbation alone thou hast need" (PR:119). The noblest actor on the stage of the world would not aim toward spectators; the sin suggested here is not disobedience to God—Shaftesbury is speaking vaguely of "Providence"—but rather slavishness before an audience. The theatricality of the outward character is seen as incompatible with a genuine character. "Wilt thou never have done with that fancy of a name and character in the world?" interrogates Shaftesbury, "What is this more than a face or dress? . . . How impossible is it to preserve any *real character*, whilst that other fancy is in existence concerning *a character in the world?*" (PR:191).

The outward character takes its place on the stage of the world as a mask or costume that would threaten the existence of the real or inward self. We can see, then, that the self is defined not only by its nontheatrical aspect; in Shaftesbury's terms, the self seems anti-theatrical. Paradoxically, this is why the sense of affectation and exposure set in play by the outward character seems threatening at the same time that the pose of the outward character seems necessary. What Shaftesbury calls the "sacred recesses of the mind" (PR:117) must be kept *"a reserve"* (PR:113). "Turn thy eyes inward" (PR:124), he instructs himself. We saw that Shaftesbury considers it folly to "publish" the inward character when it is strong; accordingly, to call others "to be witnesses to this thy *regimen* and treatment in thy sick state" (PR:199) would be, in effect, "as a spectacle or beggar-like to move pity" (PR:201). The self-dispute and examination of the philosophical regimen—in which the self is constituted and discovered—must be kept private, removed from the regard of spectators. "Alas! what am I?" writes Shaftesbury in "Character," "If this be inwardly spoken and not aloud, if this be in the closet or study, in retiring time . . . it is excellent, and to be promoted, encouraged, aggravated" (PR:202). If this regimen leaves the closet or study and appears in the world, publishes itself and plays to others, it becomes theatrical: "Why tell thy tale, why sing thy ditty (wretch!) thus mournfully? Why tragedy? Why a stage? Why witnesses? What is this unbosoming? Wouldst thou have no bosom? no reserve?" (PR:203–204). Part of the danger here for Shaftesbury is that the heart, "thus prostituted," will be made "*common* and laid open"; but it is the sense of becoming "public" more than the sense of becoming "common" that is troubling here. In "seeking the applause" of others, the self itself is threatened: "Will not all character, both inward and outward, be thus overthrown?" (PR:204). To publish one's internal soliloquies—whether in the dress of a book's printed characters or behind the countenance of a character in the world—would be to create a stage, to appeal to witnesses. For Shaftesbury, the inner character should have no role in this public theater.

The alternative to presenting and personating the self on the stage of the world would be to keep the self private: "no show of inward work; no hint; no glance" (PR:205). Shaftesbury calls upon himself to renounce theatrical and published characters; instead, he would embrace a form of silence, choose a language that would be for the self alone. In "Character," he invokes *Ecclesiastes:* "If thou hast heard a word let it die with thee; and be bold it will not burst thee" (PR:205). This injunction to "be silent" (PR:243) does not announce a total renunciation of language: only language in its public characters. This sentence of silence would not be a condemnation to wordlessness but rather a gospel (so to speak) of an unutterable word. "Take therefore *the* Word in a higher sense, and as used in Scripture, for discipline, knowledge, message, εὐαγγέλιον, but *not to be preached* as that other" (PR:205). Shaftesbury's mission would stop short of communication, his philosophy would be a private school for the self alone. Although his meditations might lead to acts and deeds, the covers of his notebooks would seal off the space of both his internal dialogues and his self: "Not a word, not a syllable besides: but all within thyself, and to thyself alone, and this to be as sacred with thee, never to be transgressed" (PR:239).[1] Writing and indeed the very assumption of a self or character in the world institute situations of theater; therefore, the traditional acts of the philosopher—including preaching, teaching, writing and speaking to others, appearing in an exemplary character—must be seen as theatrical. Shaftesbury instructs himself to let "others speak magnificently of virtue, not thou. It is enough if thou act thy part silently and quietly, keeping thy rules and principles to thyself; and not hoping ever to make these understood by others" (PR:118). Shaftesbury suggests that even Socrates and Epictetus, "before such a world as this . . . would act a different part, according to the difference of times" (PR:118). Unable to escape the terms and situation of theater, the philosopher would have to act his part as if there were no audience, renouncing both instruction and communication. Shaftesbury would choose Marcus Aurelius as a role model, thus choosing himself only as an interlocutor in the private theater of the dialogue: the text that would represent words held in, shown only to oneself. The stage of the world, the real or imagined presence of witnesses, the shared language that when spoken would inevitably posit an other in relation to one's first person singular, a public character—all must be rejected in order to perserve *that* which constitutes a self.

Still, there is the book: that public place and forum that Shaftesbury's private notebooks have become. Moreover, there is still that printed, published collection of "personal" manuscripts turned treatises called the *Characteristics*. Shaftesbury doesn't burn his private writing, nor does he erase his printed characters; he doesn't finally keep his "word" unpublished and unpreached. Al-

though he lives for a time in Amsterdam under a fictitious name—
like a character created by Defoe—unlike Marcus Aurelius he cannot stay retired from the stage of the world. Unlike Socrates and
Epictetus, Shaftesbury becomes an author—despite his printed assurances to the contrary. In the "Maxims" which appear in the
Philosophical Regimen, Shaftesbury resolves next to the word
"SILENCE": "Let only what is necessary be said" (PR:224). But
what writing is necessary? Furthermore, if speaking before others or
writing in printed characters creates a theatrical condition which
must be shunned, how could one speak in a manner that would not
expose the self and fatally reveal the inner character? Is there an
alternative to silence which would not provide a show, hint, or
glance of inward work?

Shaftesbury proposes a response which might approxi-
mate a silent speech, a manner of speaking which would keep the
word within. This is what he describes as "the involution, the
shadow, the veil, the curtain" (PR:205): a language that acts as a
screen, keeps a curtain in front of the self instead of inscribing
the self before the world. It is, in Shaftesbury's terms, a "soft irony"
(PR:192), a manner of speaking that speaks but doesn't say what
it means; it maintains a silence, presents a private meaning in a
public guise.[2] In the *Essay on the Freedom of Wit and Humour*
Shaftesbury speaks of the need "for wise men to speak in parables,
and with a double meaning, that the enemy may be amused, and
they only who have ears to hear may hear" (1:45); but the double
language Shaftesbury suggests in his meditations applies to more
than this specific form of "railery" or ironic political discourse. The
"shadow" Shaftesbury imagines is also the character of a dialogue
who speaks the words of an author he both stands for and veils—
ensuring that when the curtain of the book is opened at the beginning of the performance, another curtain will remain in place. It is
finally an outward character—printed or personated—which allows
one a public presentation and representation without any show or
glance of inner work. "Remember, therefore, in manner and degree, the same involution, shadow, curtain, the same soft irony; and
strive to find a character in this kind according to proportion both in

respect of self and times" (PR:192). A character "in this kind" would allow Shaftesbury a manner, style, and voice; it would provide him also with a personage through which he could negotiate a safe relation with the world. This character would be a persona which masked rather than exposed the self—or even an actor for whom the curtain never rose. Designed to oppose spectators rather than appeal to them, this stance would allow the philosopher to stand beside himself, so to speak; his double meaning would be as much a play of characters as a play of words.

The *Characteristics*, then, represents both Shaftesbury's attempt to resolve the anxious investigations revealed in the *Philosophical Regimen* and his failure to do so. It displays his desire to make a place for philosophy on the stage of the world and his desire to define silence as saying only what it necessary. We see in the *Characteristics* Shaftesbury's strategies to speak in public characters while denying or renegotiating the inevitably theatrical conditions of publication. His textual fictions and impersonations, his narrative scenes and machines, and his meta-narrative polemics all seem accompanied by both irony and anxiety; but ultimately, Shaftesbury succeeds in appearing to us only as a series of textual characters. His character formulates, articulates, enacts, personates, presents, and conceals itself only through the characters that silently speak his books. At this point we should acknowledge the paradox that although Shaftesbury's dramatic method is meant to protect the self from the eyes of the world, and although this method seems to undermine the stability of the self it seeks to know, in Shaftesbury's terms, this mode of presenting the self in fact represents the "true" nature of the self. This is because it is the self's true nature to be represented. Shaftesbury's characterization of the outward character as a pose and posture which theatricalize the self or as a mask which conceals the self creates an illusion that there really is a genuine, authentic self hidden behind the disguise of a character in the world. The description of the confusion of the Ethiopian is followed with the reassurance: "Nor is the face of Truth less fair and beautiful, for all the counterfeit vizards which have been put upon her" (1:58). In the realm of characters, however, there is no reassurance that one could come face to face with a "true" *person* underneath or behind a *persona*. Just as the self we see in the *Characteristics* is finally reduced to a series of fictive roles or personated characters divided within a self, the nature of a character— as it is traced in the *Philosophical Regimen*—is finally no more than a textual creation: that which is figured by speech. Indeed, Shaftesbury's obsession with hiding and screening the self might itself be a screen to prevent him from recognizing that the self, in his terms, is not really there.

Reading the *Philosophical Regimen*, we witness Shaftesbury's attempts to reduce the self to its lowest terms. Beginning with the character that must appear in the world, he sees it as "a certain estate, body, circumstance" (PR:129) and then as a series of "appellations and better titles: a creature, subject, citizen" (PR:131). He pushes further and further the question "who am I":

> —Such a one, the son of such a one, of such a name?—No.—But what? who?—A man, a rational creature, of such a descent, of such a habitation? . . . But this is imaginary.—How imaginary? Was it my native country (as I call it) that gave me my being? . . . Consider: thou art a man. Does this signify anything or nothing? (PR:190)

Working his way through titles and honors, flesh and bones, Shaftesbury tries to find "the system of self" (PR:128) that contains or points to identity. Again and again it seems an artificial system, a fabricated construct with no more substance than "a pile of timber, brick, or stone"—whose perishing would be analogous to "the defacing of this or that structure, or of the imaginary and full as perishing structure of a character in the world" (PR:127). In the relentless dialogues which occur within the covers of Shaftesbury's notebooks, the self is reduced to a series of names set in relation to other names by the system of society that gives them meaning and authority. A face that can be defaced, a structure or frame whose only investment with self seems imaginary, an image or term whose signification is arbitrarily assigned—the character seems less and less real the more it is questioned and pursued. "Take up the clue," instructs Shaftesbury in "Artificial Self," "continue the thread, and see that it break off no more; no more unravelling; but wind thyself up; collect thyself with all thy might within thyself" (PR:128). But how is the following soliloquy anything but an unravelling of the imaginary texture of a character?

> What am I? who? whence? whose?—And to what or whom belonging? with what or whom belonging to me, about me, under me?—Quality, rank, birth, of what sort? what character, what dignity, and what born to?—An estate, title, name, figure? With whom the figure? Where? in country? or in town?—No, but in the nation, in the world.—Excellent: but how? Is it magnitude or curiosity only? Is it a figure according to art and masterly skill? Where are the judges, the masters in this kind? Or is it a figure as in a sum? What sum? the great sum? the whole? Which is the greater figure and which the less in this sum? What is a little figure? How little or great? Or what though great? What though the biggest unit? How long before a blank, a cypher only? Or though still a figure, what difference from a cypher? In these sums what are cyphers set either before or after? How increase the figure, how add or multiply in these numbers? Consider then what are the right numbers, proportions, and arithmetic; what really makes a figure; what a figure is; what a cypher only.
>
> Again, what am I? (PR:128)

Like the multiplication and division of the self we witnessed in the *Characteristics*, this dazzling accounting reduces the self through its different senses. "I" becomes a title, name, a figure in the world, and then suddenly a numerical figure whose value is canceled out as it becomes a blank, a cypher; and in becoming a cypher, "I" is not merely reduced to nothing; it becomes a hieroglyph, a coded mark whose meaning is not apparent, a character in a writing which hides its significations, a mysterious sign which stands for an unknown quantity or referent. "I" becomes a character itself, the most simple mark of writing, writing itself. Having passed from an individual and essential character to a character that stands as an imaginary personage or a fictive role, the self finally becomes writing itself. What can its figure stand for at this point? What value can it have or confer? As a mark that stands for nothing or as a mark that stands for something—thus denoting what can't be pointed to or seen directly—the figure of the self in Shaftesbury's terms seems to condemn one to end where one began: by asking, "Again, what am I?"

"Is it possible that self is measured or weighed out?" asks Shaftesbury in "Natural Self." "Where is this self then? where lies the man?" (PR:137). Whether speaking of the artificial or the natural self, the outer or the inner character, Shaftesbury's attempts to locate the self repeatedly draw a blank. To think oneself in one's body would represent a loss of self: "When I think I am hurt by any of these accidents that happen to a carcase, or to anything without my mind and real self, I am then out of my reason, and am not myself" (PR:136). Instead, Shaftesbury would think himself in certain judgments and beliefs: "If those thoughts and that purpose are taken from me, and the *I* remain, then may I indeed be said to be lost, or to have lost myself" (PR:138). But could one lose oneself and still call oneself *I*? Where are these thoughts that constitute the *I* who thinks them, these opinions that keep the self the same? The closer that Shaftesbury gets to the natural self in peeling off the layers of the outward character, the more he seems threatened with the loss of what he hopes to find. He asks himself: "what art thou afraid of losing? *Thyself?*" (PR:134). He reassures himself that each layer of character that can be pointed to does not represent the true self. Yet: "there is a real losing of self. There is that which, if lost, will be missed and sighed for. Take thou care of that loss" (PR:134). The loss that Shaftesbury speaks of, the absence that here would designate the self, is again the loss of that *that* which, when wholly metamorphosed and converted, means that *we* are in reality transformed and lost. Is there a self which lies outside of this most casual and most desperate of verbal gestures? Can it be seen as anything other than a textual indicator whose name has no value in itself but whose reference never can be ascertained?

Shaftesbury finally attempts to locate and identify the self by suggesting the notion of a mind "that acts upon a body" (PR:138), a "particular mind, an acting principle" (PR:137) that is analogous to a general mind or the "self" of nature (PR:138). The *I* becomes "part of this general mind, of a piece with it, of like substance . . . alike active upon body, original to motion and order; alike simple, uncompounded, ONE, *individual*; of like energy, effect, and operation" (PR:139). Shaftesbury's characterization appears in response to the Epicurean who would reduce the universe to "chaos, and a play of atoms" (PR:139). But we do not need to live in an age of scepticism to see that Shaftesbury's terms and reasoning turn the self into an object of faith.[3] Such a principle of self can not be known; it only can be imagined and believed in. Its only authority can be judgment, thought, opinion—whose only foundations are themselves. Only faith can determine—and only faith can see itself as determination—what lies beyond that *that*. What are the "*Me* and *I*"? "A property still kept in this body, a self still; an imaginary I; a secret link, union, sympathy" (PR:134). For Shaftesbury the self is finally a secret, what is kept from knowledge or observation. Or: an imaginary I, a fiction. Its order is the play of parts and persons, the written and personated characters that we witness as symbolic structures, as texts and in texts. Therefore, if I suggested that for Shaftesbury it is the true nature of the self to be represented, I did not mean that Shaftesbury believed that the self *could* be represented. I meant rather that we can know the self only as a representation; for Shaftesbury, the self finally is a representation. We might believe in the unknown meaning and reference of the self but we cannot leave the realm in which the *I* must imagine itself and others.

      The characterization of the self at which we have arrived has been inscribed from the outset in the sense and dynamics of Shaftesbury's portrayal of character. Numerous forces have been formulating this figure of the self—from the very first word that both stands before and stands for his book: *Characteristics*. Because of the conflicts between the realms of public and private, and the situation of writing a *book* of philosophy, the self in Shaftesbury's system must reconstitute itself in a form that will bear publication. It must find the guise of an outer character, a face to present to the world that is no more than the mask of a fictive role; or a manner of writing that will preserve a curtain or a veil, both speak and remain silent. These public manifestations (designed to face and deflect readers) turn character into personated characters or written, allusive characters: cryptic marks which indicate something that can't be said in so many words. Furthermore, the dialogic structure of philosophy turns the self into a character to be personated or a series of multiplied and divided personages. Despite its pursuit of an authentic and genuine self, Shaftesbury's philosophy never gets beyond a notion of self as a fictive role that must be imagined and acted out: destined to be realized and recognized only in the vertiginous drama of the dialogue. What is left behind these representations is finally, by virtue of its utter privacy and unutterability, unknowable. As thought which must somehow think itself, it is a representation to itself: a figure that imagination creates for itself from a character of language.

At this point we can recognize the interrelation and interdependency of the two aspects of theater and dialogue we have examined: a dialectic of theater as exposure and theater as mask. In these dynamics, one situation of theater necessitates another. In the world of books the theatricality of the relation between authors and readers and the exposure of appearing before the eyes of mankind necessitate a form that will speak in characters and figures that are capable of withstanding publication. Paradoxically, writing must turn to theater through the dialogue or present itself in the guise of a private text in order to deny its position before its audience of readers; authors must play roles and adopt personas in order to deny the role in which they actually appear. In philosophy, the self depends on the dramatic method to personate, dramatize, and recognize itself; yet this play of parts and characters undermines the stable, authentic self philosophy wants to posit. For the self, the unbearable prospect of appearing before the eyes of the world necessitates an outward character to protect and conceal that part of the self which could not survive its publication. Yet the outward character, in placing the self upon the stage of the world and depending on the regard of others, threatens to destroy the inner self. The inner self must flee from theatricality by fleeing to theater—which offers protection and exposure. Theatricality—the intolerable position of appearing as a spectacle before spectators—calls for the instatement of theater: the protective play of masks and screens that would deny the view of the spectators it positions and poses for. Theater is the realm against which and in which the self must define itself. Threatening loss and offering protection, theater finally provides the figures of speech and imagination that allow one to know the only self that can be known: representations or fictions which require faith, characters gestured to by the *that* of language.

This world of theater is the realm of Shaftesbury's texts: the realm figured by his texts and the realm we must enter in reading his texts. I have suggested that Shaftesbury's anxieties about publishing books both parallel and figure his anxieties about making the self public before the eyes of the world. In this sense I would like to suggest that the conditions of reading Shaftesbury's texts—conditions which inscribe us as readers and spectators—both parallel and figure the way we face each other in what we call the world. Shaftesbury's texts dramatize and cause us to enact our roles as readers and spectators; in this sense they don't so much figure or represent the world (in the manner of a realist novel) as they stand as a literal instance of the world in which we face the risks and uncertainties of personating ourselves and knowing each other through representations, reading, faith, and interpretation. Our position in reading those texts signed or not signed by "Shaftesbury" also places us in the realm in which we must appear before each other, design ourselves, act ourselves out: in which we must engage ourselves and each other in dialogue with the hope that we can mean something when we enter language and say *I*.

The failure of language represented by the polysemic *that*; the necessity of faith; the status of the self as fiction; the undermining of a notion of an identifiable, original, authentic, and true self; the necessity of interpretation—all of these problems are at play in the dialogue that ends the books of the *Characteristics*. It is no coincidence that this dialogue—which argues for freedom of thought and the impossibility of forcing people to be of one mind in matters of religion[4]—closes Shaftesbury's work with a discussion about faith, the impossibility of ascertaining the true, original, absolute meaning of a text, and reading. The sceptic gentleman (impersonated by the *Miscellaneous Reflections* author in imitation of Shaftesbury's impersonation) argues that religious toleration must exist because if dogma is to be based on "holy literature" (2:356) it can never be anything but one interpretation among many, not absolute truth.

> "There are," said he, "innumerable places that contain (no doubt) great mysteries, but so wrapped in clouds or hid in umbrages, so heightened with expressions, or so covered with allegories and garments of rhetoric . . . that they may seem to have been left as trials of our industry. . . . For when there are found in the explications of these writings so many commentaries, so many senses and interpretations, so many volumes in all ages, and all like men's faces, no one exactly like another: either this difference is absolutely no fault at all, or if it be, it is excusable." (2:356)

The "variety of readings" and "variety of senses" (2:356), along with corruptions in texts and imperfect copies, undermine the determination of a single, authentic meaning—the accessibility of a "very original, or a perfectly true copy of these books" (2:362). Even if an authoritative text could be established, there is "no certain mark to determine whether the sense of these passages should be taken as literal or figurative. There is nothing in the nature of the thing to determine the sense or meaning" (2:357). Shaftesbury and his sceptic are paraphasing a passage from Bishop Taylor's *Discourse of the Liberty of Prophesying*, which concludes "that it is almost impossible to know the proper interpretation" (2:358n) of these texts of holy literature. Since there is no authoritative reading, each additional new reading only lessens the possibility of a certain understanding: "since variety of readings is crept in, every reading takes a degree of certainty from any proposition derivative from those places so read."[5]

Holy literature is no different in these respects from secular literature, or the literature of philosophy; nor is it different from the realm in which Shaftesbury constitutes the self. In each case a text, make up of inevitably figurative language, can have no knowable original, absolute, certain sense; its sense is that which is gestured to by its language, stood for by the representation that finally refers to itself: what the reader must read *into* the text. In Shaftesbury's terms, to know the self one must read or decipher a text—a book, a character, an imaginary *I*. Knowledge, finally, can be no more than interpretation, or faith in what can't be ascertained through the language in which the self must be defined and ex- pressed. Like the world of the sceptic—where everything has the status of fiction, and subjective reading and faith in the fictions of others are the only foundations of what we call knowledge— Shaftesbury's world is also a realm of textual meaning and inter- pretation. And paradoxically, as such, it invents and necessitates readers: readers who must read both themselves and the selves of others. The reader who threatens the self is assigned a necessary role from the moment an "I" is spoken and assumed.

This is to suggest not only that Shaftesbury expects readers, but what he expects from them: he writes in the *Mis- cellaneous Reflections* (his defense of criticism and critical reading) that for him, *to read* is "to examine, construe, and remark with understanding" (2:306). The first term suggests the insight, the self- dissection and analysis, the weighing of conflicting forces enacted by the dialogue. The last part of the formulation asks us to notice while entering knowledge and comprehension, and also to mark again, to recognize or write or characterize. It is the word *construe*, however, that is at the center of Shaftesbury's definition. *Construe* (from the Latin *construere*: to pile together, build up, construct) means to form by putting materials together. It also means to con- struct in the sense of combining words or parts of speech or sen- tences grammatically. One construes when one analyzes or traces the grammatical construction of a sentence, when one takes its words in such an order as to show the sentence's meaning; this is also the case in the study of a foreign language where one adds a word-for-word translation, or translates orally a passage of an an- cient author—accompanying a text with one's own voice. To con- strue is to give the sense or meaning of, to explain, expound, or interpret; it is also to give a meaning to, put a construction on actions or persons in an interpretation that might be apart from the real sense. (How calmly the dictionary contains and allows this particular risk among its glosses.) To construe is to deduce by interpretation, to judge by inference, to infer, to inform by way of explanation. This is the way Shaftesbury asks to be read, this is how we must understand the composition of his texts and the self we can know only through its various textual manifestations. This realm of interpretation is made necessary by that which we call the self; at the same time it names and defines the conditions of the self's possibility.

PART II

Acts of Solitude:
Theater in the Narratives of Defoe

I have frequently looked back, you may be sure, and that with different thoughts, upon the notions of a long tedious life of solitude, which I have represented to the world, and of which you must have formed some ideas, from the life of a man in an island. Sometimes I have wondered how it could be supported, especially for the first years, when the change was violent and imposed, and nature unacquainted with anything like it. Sometimes I have as much wondered why it should be any grievance or affliction, seeing upon the whole view of the stage of life which we act upon in this world it seems to me that life in general is, or ought to be, but one universal act of solitude.

Daniel Defoe,
Serious Reflections of Robinson Crusoe

Nothing is more free than the imagination of man; and though it cannot exceed that original stock of ideas furnished by the internal and external senses, it has unlimited powers of mixing, compounding, separating, and dividing these ideas, in all the varieties of fiction and vision. It can feign a train of events, with all the appearance of reality, ascribe to them a particular time and place, conceive them as existent, and paint them out to itself with every circumstance, that belongs to any historical fact, which it believes with the greatest certainty. Wherein, therefore, consists the difference between such a fiction and belief?

David Hume,
An Enquiry Concerning Human Understanding

A Charm invests a face
Imperfectly beheld —
The Lady dare not lift her Veil
For fear it be dispelled —

But peers beyond her mesh —
And wishes — and denies —
Lest Interview — annul a want
That Image — satisfies —

Emily Dickinson

Prologue

IN 1704, Defoe began the preface to *The Storm* with this depiction of the position in which an author faces his readers:

> Preaching of sermons is speaking to a few of mankind: printing of books is talking to the whole world. The parson prescribes himself, and addresses to the particular auditory with the appelation of *My brethren*; but he that prints a book, ought to preface it with a *Noverint Universi*, Know all men by these presents.[1]

One year later, Defoe began a preface to his *Review* with a different image of the author's stance: "When Authors present their Works to the World, like a Thief at the Gallows; they make a Speech to the People."[2] Each of these contradictory poses will be familiar to readers of Defoe: on the one hand, Defoe the Puritan moralist, who continues in his preface to argue that "he that prints and publishes to all the world" has a greater responsibility to be truthful than "he that preaches from the pulpit";[3] and on the other hand, Defoe the author of various criminal autobiographies, who was locked in Newgate himself and sentenced to stand in the pillory in 1703. Yet in one sense Defoe's comparisons are not really contradictory; both prefaces picture the author speaking to the world, presenting himself to the public. The thief "at the gallows" (where, for instance, Colonel Jack's brother "made his Exit")[4] and the parson at the pulpit (from the Latin *persōna*: mask; and *pulpitum*: scaffold, platform, stage) both address their audiences from a sort of scaffold or stage. The design of both comparisons figures the theatrical position in which the author of a book "publishes to all the world," the "exposing to public view"[5] (as Defoe calls it) which Shaftesbury calls "exhibit[ing] on the stage of the world" (*Characteristics*, 1:109).

Defoe made one of these analogies explicit in a mock sermon that he published in *The Review* in 1706, criticizing a church's plan to raise money with a play: "as if there were not farce enough acted upon that stage, the pulpit, but the hearers must be sent to the theatre to make it up."[6] One of Defoe's critics complained in *Remarks on the Review*: "tis plain he has an Inbred Spleen against all Churches, by his Ridiculing all Preachers as Actors, and saying, that all Preaching is theatrical, and a Trade for Money; and puts them on the same Foot with the Stage."[7] The author, however, in Defoe's terms is finally more theatrical than the parson: while the parson prescribes himself, delivers the text he has written to an audience he sees and knows, the author inscribes himself before a public audience which must stand for the world; his public address by definition inscribes an audience before the book. In his prefaces, Defoe must confront the book's theatrical aspect. Like the author we saw characterized by Addison, the only "brethren" he faces form a "Fraternity of Spectators."

Yet if Defoe shares Shaftesbury's sense that his readers face him as spectators, this is also because Defoe faces his readers as an actor. In reading Defoe, we find ourselves again in the position of Shaftesbury's eighteenth-century Ethiopian at carnival time "when the general face of mankind was disguised, and almost every creature wore a mask"—except that the "confusion of characters and persons" which leaves our minds "still running upon masks" (*Characteristics*, 1:57) is likely to be greater. Defoe himself wrote in 1727: "we live in a general Disguise, and like the Masquerades, every Man dresses himself up in a particular Habit."[8] Many readers have recognized that such characterizations describe Defoe's manner of acting in the world as well as his world view. Maximillian E. Novak, for example, aptly remarks that Defoe's description of a contemporary as "a Man, whose Life has been to act in a Mask" more accurately applies to Defoe himself.[9] John Robert Moore has identified "eighty-seven different fictitious personalities"[10] assumed by Defoe in his texts, comparing Defoe's adoption of a "specific *persona*" in a given text to "an actor in a Greek tragedy" who speaks "through a mask."[11] In a book entitled *Daniel Defoe's Many Voices*,

E. Anthony James has tried to delineate the variety of "authorial masks," roles, and voices that Defoe used to costume his many "first-person" narrators.[12] Indeed, even before Defoe performed the great fictive impersonations we know him for today—from *Robinson Crusoe* to *Roxana*—he was recognized by his contemporaries as a master of disguise and imposture. When, in 1719, Charles Gildon wrote of "those various Shapes and Changes which [Defoe] has pass'd without the least Blush" he was summing up a notorious career as well as prophesying Defoe's role as an author of fictive autobiographies: "The Fabulous *Proteus* of the Ancient Mythologist was but a very faint Type of our Hero, whose Changes are much more numerous, and he far more difficult to be constrain'd to his own Shape."[13] It is not necessary to rehearse the many roles and masks that earned Defoe this reputation: the changing of his name from Foe to Defoe, the too realistic impersonation of *The Shortest Way with the Dissenters*, the forged memoirs of Mesnager, writing on both sides of issues, acting as a spy—these are only a few of the most well-known examples. Defoe has been recognized as a masterful actor who obsessively used masks, disguises, pseudonyms, voices, costumes, roles, characters, personae, impersonations, impostures, fictions.[14] Furthermore, many of the characters that Defoe personates are themselves obsessed with changing identities, disguises, masks, and impostures. To read Defoe—his printed or personated characters—is to enter the theater.

Readers have differed in their responses to this theater. In his own time, Defoe's fake memoirs of Mesnager were called "the most notorious and grossest Piece of Forgery that ever was fobb'd upon the Publick";[15] and we like to believe there were readers who took *The Life and Strange Surprizing Adventures of Robinson Crusoe, of York, Mariner . . . Written by Himself* or *A Journal of the Plague Year . . . Written by a Citizen who continued all the while in London* as genuine historical accounts, at least for a time. The nineteenth century, particularly anxious about delineating the lines between history, fiction, and lying, was disconcerted by the deceptive character of Defoe's impersonations. Complaining that Defoe rarely issued his books as "works of imagination, but as narratives actually intended to deceive the public," Edmund Gosse wrote in 1888: "These artifices matter little to the reader, who now would rather that Defoe should have written fiction than reported fact."[16] A biographer called Defoe "perhaps the greatest liar that ever lived."[17] It may be that the characterization of Defoe as the ultimate realist (which for so long dominated critical attitudes toward his work) was an attempt to domesticate the skills that one contemporary referred to as "the little Art he is truly master of, of forging a Story, and imposing it on the World for Truth . . . with all the little embellishments of Lies that are contriv'd to set it off. . . ."[18] The same terms that *Read's Journal* used in 1718 to condemn Defoe's forgery—one year before he began to write the texts that we call novels—were later used to praise his verisimilitude.

Today, with the relative security of bibliographical evidence and generic categories inherited from the nineteenth century, we are likely to look at Defoe and say, as Novak does, that the "ability to argue through a mask or a persona was precisely Defoe's genius"—and then, to seek "to reach behind the mask . . . in an effort to ascertain what particular interest or idea Defoe is seeking to advance."[19] Through various efforts to "establish what he actually believed"[20] critics and scholars have replaced Defoe the liar, hypocrite, and political hack with Defoe the Christian moralist, Defoe the economist, Defoe the social critic, Defoe the journalist, Defoe the artist. Indeed, with these and other characterizations, we have fulfilled Gildon's prediction that if Defoe's "Works should happen to live to the next Age, there would in all probability be a greater Strife among the several Parties, whose he really was, than among the seven *Graecian* Cities, to which of them Homer belong'd."[21] These different approaches, of course, have contributed to our understanding of the ideas and issues at play in Defoe's work and world. Yet is it possible to reach behind Defoe's masks and find a "real" or "actual" Defoe? "This, Sir, is an Age of Plot and Deceit, of *Contradiction* and *Paradox*," wrote Defoe in 1709, "It is very hard under all these Masks to see the true Countenance of any Man."[22] Can we find a person beneath the persona, a self that is less fictitious than the guises and disguises that are displayed to the world?

In his study of the aesthetics of fraud, Hugh Kenner remarks about *Robinson Crusoe*: "The reader is meant to respond to Crusoe's book exactly as Crusoe responded to Friday's footprint."[23] For us the footprints in the sand are the printed characters that stand for Defoe's personated characters, the traces we must reason back from—at two removes—in order to construe the character of Defoe. We have been warned not to reason back to Robinson Crusoe; he is only another character, behind whose forged signature we must posit another man. But how do we know when we reach Defoe— that actor whose identity has seemed so protean, so masked, from the outset?

I do not mean to be disingenuous: like many other authors, I intend to construe a Defoe with desires, anxieties, designs, ambivalences, points of view, a social context, a past, a present, and a future. In particular, I will posit a Defoe who repeatedly reflects on his own activities of writing, fiction-making, and imposture. My point is that in an age which no longer deplores Defoe's theatrical deceptions we should not be too quick to look behind Defoe's masks; we should neither merely catalogue his masks nor dismiss them as means to ends which sometimes make it difficult to know what Defoe really thought. These masks may inform us about the only Defoe we can hope to know. They might identify Defoe— not by revealing the self behind the role but rather by displaying Defoe as an actor, and thereby allowing us to construe the makeup of the self as it is acted out in Defoe's texts. My design, then, is to examine the role of theater in Defoe's works: to show how the theater (and the situations it presents and represents) is continually figured, enacted, and rehearsed. It has been noted that the Restoration stage lent some of its conventions to the eighteenth-century novel as the two gradually exchanged places, so to speak, on the English scene.[24] Such discussions usually center on Fielding and Richardson: the former, writing as both a playwright and a novelist, inscribed his work within the *theatrum mundi* tradition; the latter, first praised by Diderot for his *tableaux*, has been described as a dramatic novelist who often modeled his character's gestures, dialogue, and scenes on the conventions of the stage. Defoe, however, is usually excluded from these characterizations—and he is, of course, different in major respects. Yet I will argue that the figure of theater both frames and informs Defoe's work. Whereas Richardson and Fielding may seem *dramatic*, Defoe is concerned with the *theatrical* aspects of his texts. Richardson and Fielding embrace the dramatic aspects of their fictions and present their characters as if they were characters in a play; Defoe above all saw his characters as actors who acted out his own position as a spectacle and his own activity of play-acting. I hope to show that Defoe's sensibilities regarding the theatricality of characters and books were like Shaftesbury's; for Defoe, as for Shaftesbury, the situation of theater meant a problematic relation formed between a spectacle and a spectator that both responded to and created problems for the self. Reading Defoe in this light, we will need to reflect on our own role as spectators: how our presence as readers plays a part in motivating Defoe's poses and in turning his texts to theater.

CHAPTER 4

Fictions and Impersonations:
The Double Imposture

IN a scene near the end of his *Life and Strange Surprizing Adventures*, Robinson Crusoe and his newly formed allies perform a ruse to transform themselves into an imposing army which can defeat the English mutineers. Together they stage a dramatic fiction to convince their enemy that they have fifty men instead of eight. The Captain makes up "a Fiction of his own"[1] about the designs of the "Commander" of the island (RC:208) and Robinson Crusoe, who has described himself as "Generalissimo" and Friday as "my Lieutenant-General" (RC:207), plays the part of "Governour" by hiding in the dark while the loyal sailors are directed to speak the proper dialogue for the scene: "one of the Men was order'd to speak again, and say to the Captain, *Captain, the Commander calls for you*; and presently the Captain reply'd, *Tell his Excellency, I am just a coming*: This more perfectly amused them; and they all believed that the Commander was just by with his fifty Men" (RC:209). Throughout his narrative, Crusoe has been portrayed as a fabulous artificer whose skill at forging objects and playing roles allows him to turn his solitary life on an island into a fiction of life in the world. He calls his hut a country house and plays king to his animals; with its details and artifacts of everyday life, its imitations of the things and customs of the England he left behind, the fantastically realistic counterfeit world that Crusoe constructs for himself is, as it were, his novel. In this scene, however, the pretence and play are directed toward others; after the first theatrical illusion succeeds in capturing some prisoners, Crusoe adds a new character to the cast by personating his own representative: "When I shew'd my self to the two Hostages, it was with the Captain, who told them, I was the Person the Governour had order'd to look after them . . . so that as we never suffered them to see me as Governour, so I now appear'd as another Person" (RC:210).

After the final victory Crusoe receives some English clothes from the Captain and appears before the men in a new guise: "I came thither dress'd in my new Habit, and now I was call'd Governour again" (RC:213); but this is only after Crusoe has described how the Captain "brought me to my self," how he comforted him "to compose me and bring me to my self" (RC:212). He is referring to the shock he experiences at the prospect of being rescued but characteristically, the context Defoe elaborates here adds a figurative dimension to the idiomatic "plain style" that Crusoe writes. We must take these colloquial expressions at face value, as it were, and wonder what it means for Crusoe to be composed and brought to his self between appearing as another person and resuming a role in a new guise.

This confusion of parts and persons is underlined by a brief yet strange incident in Crusoe's story of his counterfeit army. As the loyal sailors advance to persuade the mutineers to surrender, we learn (as if by chance) that one of the sailors is named "Robinson."

> We came upon them indeed in the Dark, so that they could not see our Number; and I made the Man we had left in the Boat, who was now one of us, call to them by Name, to try if I could bring them to a Parley, and so might perhaps reduce them to Terms . . . so he calls out as loud as he could, to one of them, *Tom Smith, Tom Smith; Tom Smith* answered immediately, *Who's that*, Robinson? for it seems he knew his voice. (RC:207)

There are two more casual references to this sailor named Robinson and then we never hear from him again. A man, previously an adversary, "now one of us," names the other sailors to "reduce them to Terms" and his voice calling out names him (to Tom Smith and consequently to the reader) as Robinson; yet Robinson Crusoe, who earlier has described the uncanny experience of hearing "a Voice calling me by my Name" (RC:112), does not seem to notice that this man has been reduced to his "Term." Are we to believe that Robinson is merely a common English name which Defoe, as the master of realism, knew would turn up a couple of times in any group of men, even on a desert island; or is this coincidence merely one of Defoe's famous oversights? What is strange is that it makes sense at this moment for Robinson Crusoe to lend his name, as if obliviously, to another sailor. Crusoe, who begins his life story by mapping the etymology and metamorphosis of his name, hears his name doubled in the scene in which he calls out as if he were another person—as names, titles, and roles are being exchanged at a rapid pace. After this comedy of impersonations and ruses in which he appears as other persons and appears not to recognize his name, it is only appropriate that Crusoe should need to be composed and brought to himself. Appropriately, also, a few pages later Crusoe describes how when he returned to England, "I was as perfect a Stranger to all the World, as if I had never been known there" (*RC*: 216); when he goes to reclaim his fortune he must recall himself from "Civil Death" and take an "Oath that I was alive, and that I was the same Person" (*RC*:220).[2]

These losses, transformations, multiplications, and restorations of identity can be explained within the context of autobiography—especially religious autobiography. It is no coincidence that upon returning to the world Crusoe finds that his income has been donated to "the Monastary of St. Augustine . . . for the Conversion of the Indians" (*RC*:217). Later in this book, in a chapter on *Moll Flanders*, I will consider how the structure of autobiography plays a part in Defoe's portrayal of versions and conversions of the self. In this discussion, however, I have been emphasizing the dramatic method at play in Crusoe's ruses and personations of himself—all of which occur in the context of Defoe's impersonation of the character of Robinson Crusoe. We might better understand the theatrical character of these scenes from *Robinson Crusoe* and their relation to Defoe's position in appearing as another person if we recognize that they can be seen as a dress rehearsal for a similar scene in *A Journal of the Plague Year*, published three years after *Robinson Crusoe*. This scene, the longest single episode in the book, portrays another military ruse performed by three men trying to escape London and the plague.

Although A *Journal of the Plague Year*, like most of Defoe's narratives, is "spoken" by a first-person narrator, the character that Defoe personates to tell the story reports mostly as an "eyewitness."[3] With an obsessive curiosity that would be at home in a novel by Henry James, he acts as an observer; even when constrained within his house, he is a spectator as "many dismal spectacles represented themselves in my view, out of my own windows" (PY:189–190). The *Journal*, which the title page tells us was "Never made public before," is not a private history in the manner of *Robinson Crusoe* or *Colonel Jack*; supposedly based on "memorandums" or "private meditations" which the narrator tells us are "reserve[d] for private use" and not to be "made public on any account whatever" (PY:94), the book is mostly made up of other people's stories: the narrator's "observations without doors" (PY:94) and the accounts for which he acts as an anthologist. This Journal, then, has a public character; framed like the narrator's windows, it positions us as witnesses to the sights and stories that have been presented and represented to the narrator. The story of the three men who attempt to flee London is one such account in which the narrator does not initially play a part. He states his intention to provide the reader with the story of the men "if the reader will be content to have me give it in their own persons" (PY:77), although it turns out that he has "much more to say before I quit my own part" (PY:77).

The purpose of these coming attractions, followed by other scenes and reflections, is not explained; but they define the terms of the narrator's method in representing the men's adventures: when he returns to the story he indeed attempts to quit his own part—his role as first-person narrator—and turn the text over to the parts and persons of the men. A narrated story is transformed into a series of first-person statements; after the introductory phrase, "And thus they began to talk of it beforehand" (PY:137), the text takes on the form in which each character speaks his own part, in his own person: a dialogue. Not content to relate the story, the narrator attempts to dramatize the scene, causing it to be enacted on the page. As it gives voice to a dialogue, the text of the narrative becomes like the text of a play. The mediating presence of "he said" disappears and for a time the reader is presented with blocks of speech, prefaced and vocalized by the silent names that stand for the characters who are supposed to speak them. Like a play, the dialogue appears in the present tense, as if it were occurring before our eyes. Like the text of a play, it also has a prospective sense: as speech we are to imagine spoken by actors in a future present.

Dialogues, of course, appear elsewhere in Defoe's work and are common in eighteenth-century literature. What is remarkable here, however, is the considerable effort displayed by the narrator (that is, Defoe playing the part of the narrator) to keep this theatrical form before our eyes. The demands of exposition force him to interrupt the dialogue repeatedly. Surely, simply relating the story in a third-person narrative would be easier; but he returns to the dialogue again and again. At one point, in the space of three pages, the narrator is compelled to provide four footnotes in order to explain the action represented by a dialogue between the characters of John and a constable. Rather than interrupting the format of the page to remind us of the difference between what John says, how the scene looks to the constable, and what is really going on, the narrator resorts to footnotes for the effect of dramatic irony. Such technical and textual devices may remind us that we are reading a book, but they provide us with the point of view that an audience to a play would have; and they show the extent to which the narrator is trying to maintain the dialogue form. Dramatic narrative—a text which acts like a play—is clearly desired in these pages.

Furthermore, the central scene of the narrative, occurring at the moment when footnotes both mark and preserve the dramatic form, contains what might be called a play within the play. Having used dissembling and a "little fraud" (PY:144) to make their way through the environs of London, the men and some other travelers respond to a blockade with a ruse that calls for dramatic fiction, play-acting, visual illusions, and stage props. John forges a scheme to convince townspeople who are frightened of being contaminated by carriers of the plague that standing before them is an army of desperate soldiers rather than a small group of destitute travelers. He directs Richard

> to cut some poles out of the trees and shape them as like guns as he could, and in a little time he had five or six fair muskets, which at a distance would not be known . . . and all this while the rest of them sat under the trees by his direction, in two or three bodies, where they made fires at a good distance from one another. (PY:150)

When seen up close these props would be recognized as poles, but when viewed from a distance, disguised with cloth and colored with mud, they appear to be guns. The people are positioned to create a theatrical illusion so that "such a sight as this" will convince and deceive their spectators, who, "by all that they could see, could not but suppose that they were a great many in company" (PY:150). John talks to them "as if he had been the sentinel placed there upon the guard by some officer that was his superior" (PY:151)—according to the retrospective stage directions provided by a footnote. Speaking "in the language of soldiers" (PY:157), John is the author, director, and leading actor in this imposture, which we see not as spectators to the theatrical illusion but as witnesses to the production of the spectacle. Although we witness the dialogue on the page, the footnotes offer us a back-stage view of the action: "Here he called to one of his men, and bade him order Captain Richard and his people to march the lower way on the side of the marches, and meet them in the forest; which was all a sham, for they had no Captain Richard, or any such company" (PY:153). The sham has such verisimilitude for the townspeople that the travelers soon encounter "several parties of horsemen and footmen also about, in pursuit of three companies of men, armed, as they said, with muskets" (PY:154). For the reader, however, Defoe portrays his characters in these scenes as if they were a company of actors. It makes sense at this point to recall that John and Thomas worry that they will be arrested as vagrants: the vagrancy laws they discuss were aimed at actors, among others; and antitheatrical tracts in the Renaissance not only labeled actors as vagrants but also accused them of spreading the plague.[4]

Theater, then, provides a frame in which to see these scenes from Defoe's narratives. In particular, it helps us to understand why, as the episode from *Plague Year* dramatizes the production of theatrical illusions, Defoe's text itself becomes theater for an extended period of time. (No other episode in the book is presented in dialogue form.) The impersonations and fictions used in the ruses of Robinson Crusoe, John, and their companions are specifically theatrical in character; and implicit in this assertion (and my readings) is the assumption that as these characters metamorphose themselves into different parts and persons and stage realistic illusions that are taken for reality, they can be seen as figures for Daniel Defoe—who is himself engaged in appearing as another person or quitting his own part to give a story in the persons of other people. These characters act out Defoe's acting; their fictions and impersonations reflect and repeat Defoe's fictions and impersonations.

These parallels lead us to another characterization: the theatrical performances enacted in the texts we have been examining are specifically scenes of deception. Addressed to unwitting spectators who don't know they're being drawn into a drama, these performances are made up of fraud, imposture, and dissembling. It is perhaps not surprising, then, that Defoe, speaking in the person of H. F., prefaces his dramatization of the travelers in *Plague Year* with the warning that he writes "without taking upon me to either vouch the particulars or answer for any mistakes" (PY:77); he defends the story "whether my account be exactly according to fact or no" (PY:137). He claims that his story is history, but at the same time—as if worried that he might be accused of presenting a fiction for the truth—he insists that the "story has a moral in every part of it, and their whole conduct, and that of some whom they joined with, is a pattern for all poor men to follow, or women either, if ever such a time comes again" (PY:137).

The stories, of course, are a pattern for play-acting more than anything else. But readers of Defoe will recognize appended to this narrative within the narrative one of Defoe's prefaces in miniature. A moral justification, a claim of historical truth or a vague hint of fiction, and an almost legalistic denial of responsibility appear together as if formulaically before practically all of

Defoe's fictional narratives. I suggest that these prefaces reflect Defoe's anxieties about his own activities of imposture, dissembling, and fiction-making as he presents fictions that claim to be history about imposture, dissembling, and fiction.

Defoe, according to Hugh Kenner, "wrote *Robinson Crusoe* but forged a book 'by' Robinson Crusoe and counterfeited Robinson Crusoe himself. The counterfeiting went on all the time he was writing the book; the forgery occurred on the moment when he elected to omit his own name from the title-page."[5] It is the preface to Defoe's narrative fiction that usually authorizes this moment, testifies to the signature that turns novels into lies. If the nineteenth-century novel is like a playhouse with clearly marked entrances and exits, enabling its readers to consign fiction to a carefully delineated space, the eighteenth-century novel is more like a carnival that continually transgresses its own borders, insisting that its readers take its fiction as part of the real world.[6] Standing "outside" of the text, the preface is the scene of this transgression; it is the place where one voice (usually editorial, sincere, rational) asks us to believe in the authority of another voice, ignoring the possibility that its own authority and authorship might be equally in question. We are informed, for example, in the preface to *The Life and Strange Surprizing Adventures of Robinson Crusoe . . . Written by Himself* that the "Editor believes the thing to be a just History of Fact; neither is there any Appearance of Fiction in it" (RC:3). In such affidavits for authenticity we are told the complicated story of the discovery of a manuscript (such as the *Memoirs of a Cavalier*) or, as in the preface to the life story of Moll Flanders, "Written from her own MEMORANDUMS," presented with the predicament: "The World is so taken up of late with Novels and Romances, that it will be hard for a private History to be taken for Genuine."[7] At times Defoe allows that his story might not be history in the strictest sense, as in his warning about the episodes we considered from *A Journal of the Plague Year* or in the preface to the *Farther Adventures* of Robinson Crusoe where he refers to "the part that may be called invention or parable in the story."⁸ At such moments we find a defense of the morality and utility of the story; but in general, and even where Defoe comes close to conceding the fictive status of his texts, the prefaces display a deep investment in the fiction of history: the fiction that there is no fiction.⁹

Defoe's need to dissemble in order to deny the presence of dissembling in his book—to try to deceive his readers rather than presenting them, as later novelists would do, with a convention-governed counterfeit which they voluntarily would pretend to believe—must be seen within the context of the anxiety about fiction that all English authors had to face in the beginning of the eighteenth century. Literature, it is well known, on the defensive in the western world since *The Republic*, sustained a multifaceted attack in Puritan England.¹⁰ Puritan doctrine maintained that to create imaginary people, events, and places was to enter into a sort of rivalry with God, to usurp his role as creator. As J. Paul Hunter has written, the Puritans who helped to shape Defoe's England were suspicious of "anything fictional—a suspicion deriving from the Puritan conception of the world and events as emblematic. For the Puritanism of the late seventeenth century, fiction simply falsified the detailed world of fact and event—and thereby obscured the clear message that God wrote for men in 'real' happenings."¹¹ Fiction, made up of false statements, was not seen as being significantly different from lying. In addition, as mere amusement, it was considered an inducement to idleness; and in portraying the passions and various forms of new life, it was supposed to encourage immorality. It would seem, then, that Defoe had good reason not only to defend his fiction but to insist that it wasn't fiction at all.

Accordingly, many readers have explained Defoe's fictions of history as a conformation to "the booksellers' working idea that stories supposed to be true will be more readily approved and will sell better."¹² Others have seen Defoe as genuinely struggling to be an artist in the Puritan tradition;¹³ although most readers throughout the eighteenth and nineteenth centuries seem to have shared the doubts Charles Gildon expressed in 1719 about Defoe's sincerity: "the Design of the Publication of this Book was not suffi-

cient to justify and make Truth of what you allow to be Fiction and
Fable; what you mean by *Legitimating, Invention,* and *Parable,* I
know not; unless you would have us think, that the manner of your
telling a Lie will make it a Truth."[14] In recent years Defoe has been
rehabilitated as a Puritan moralist and spiritual allegorist;[15] at the
same time he is also recognized as taking "private delight in deception" and "mere dissembling."[16] One critic argues that Defoe gradually grew accustomed to writing fiction;[17] while another argues that
narrative fiction became so problematic for Defoe that he abruptly
had to stop writing it with the end of *Roxana.*[18] It is generally
agreed, however, that religious and social interdictions presented
problems for Defoe—whether he believed in their validity or just
pretended to or repeatedly contradicted in practice what he believed
in theory. I have suggested that most authors at the beginning of the
eighteenth century felt called upon to justify the publication of
their books. Defoe is no exception; and the anxiety he manifests at
the prospect of publishing fiction seems to add to the problematic
character of the published book. Defoe must defend or deny his
fictions—and sometimes he does both simultaneously. Throughout
his work, he must not only justify his fiction but resort to fiction to
insist that he is telling the truth. What is at stake in Defoe's impostures?

Even in the preface to *The Storm,* published fifteen
years before the first of Defoe's romances, Defoe seems obsessed
with the supposed dangers of telling a lie in print. We have seen
already that in the preface to his book—a collection of personal
reflections and eyewitness accounts of a great storm that Defoe
solicited in newspaper advertisements—Defoe asserts that an author
has a greater responsibility to be truthful than a parson does. He
admits that in a work "in which I must tell a great many stories . . .
a great part of mankind will question the sincerity of the relator" but
he claims to have taken seriously "the proper duty of an historian
. . . to be very wary what he conveys to posterity."[19] Complaining
about writers of the past in whom "the little regard to truth, and the
fondness of telling a strange story, has dwindled a great many valuable pieces of ancient history into mere romance,"[20] he expresses a

kind of horror at the thought of a lie which is preserved in a book, locked into perpetual deception: "if a book printed obtrudes a falsehood, if a man tells a lie in print, he abuses mankind, and imposes upon the whole world, he causes our children to tell lies after us, and their children after them, to the end of the world."[21] Defoe claims to set the highest standards for himself so that the world can not "charge him with a forgery"[22] and he vows to "keep exactly within the bounds of truth,"[23] to present stories that are "dressed in the desirable, though unfashionable garb of truth."[24] It is characteristic of Defoe that even truth should be figured as a garb; and one can't help wondering if the sincere and moralistic author of this preface is just another role played by the man who easily would have gained a reputation as a notorious imposter and master of forgery even if he had never written a novel.

Prefacing a journalistic compilation of other people's stories, Defoe protests too much, it seems. Indeed, one paragraph from the preface seems to acknowledge Defoe's peculiar position in preaching this particular sermon:

And while I pretend to a thing so solemn, I cannot but premise I should stand convicted of a double imposture, to forge a story, and then preach repentance to the reader from a crime greater than that I would have him repent of: endeavouring by a lie to correct the reader's vices, and sin against truth to bring the reader off from sinning against sense.[25]

Defoe may or may not impose upon the world in *The Storm*, but in looking at his career as a whole it seems clear that his pretending— that is, both his dissembling and his moral claims—convicts him of just such a double imposture. Given Defoe's fictions and fictions of history (not to mention works such as the forged historical memoirs of Mesnager, faked by Defoe to prove that Harley was not guilty of treason)[26] it is difficult to know whether the conviction Defoe expresses in the paragraphs quoted above is the product of his unconscious or his audaciousness.

Part of the problem in considering Defoe's conflicts about religious or social interdictions and fiction writing is that

Defoe's own contributions to the "moral literature" on literature are made up of contradictions and paradoxes. Defoe writes in the preface to *Moll Flanders* that "this Work is chiefly recommended to those who know how to Read it."[27] Yet repeatedly, we are faced with not knowing how to read Defoe's statements. Fulfilling Gildon's prophesy about Defoe's protean legacy, critics have characterized Defoe both as a practitioner of the "plain style" and as a dissembler and ironist.[28] In *The Complete English Tradesman*, after asserting that "the end of Speech is that men might understand one another's meaning," Defoe claims that "a perfect stile, or language" would be "that in which a man speaking to five hundred people, of all common and various capacities, Ideots and Lunaticks excepted, should be understood by them all, in the same manner with one another, and in the same sense which the speaker intended to be understood."[29] But after repeating in his pamphlets on the Hanoverian Succession the mistake of *The Shortest Way with the Dissenters*— that is, writing a satire that was so convincing that it was taken for a genuine example of what it set out to satirize—Defoe objected to his accusers that he had written with the "Strongest Irony," insisting: "Nor is this Irony concealed, *as has been suggested formerly*; but it is express'd plainly, and explicitly, in words at length."[30]

　　Perhaps Defoe's pamphlets fell short of his perfect style; but what does he intend to be understood by plain and explicit irony? How could irony be explicit and expressed plainly in words— or if explicit, when would it cease being ironic and begin saying what it meant rather than what it appeared to say? Is Defoe being ironic here? As we consider Defoe's statements about fiction and deception—how he responds to the problem of lying—we must acknowledge that we often have the sense that Defoe doesn't mean what he says. What happens if, when reading an apparently serious condemnation of speaking falsely or writing romances, we think we realize that the author of the statement is not telling the truth? Would we mean by this that he is not sincere, or that he doesn't believe what he's saying even if he thinks he does, or that he hypocritically doesn't practice what he preaches, or that our knowledge of other texts he has written makes us search for irony or ambivalence or a double standard? One critic has written of Defoe: "It is obvious that his use of terms like 'allegoric,' 'emblem,' 'allusive,' 'history,' 'fable,' and 'parable' are somewhat careless."[31] Another suggests that Defoe's religious interpretations for his fictions are "handled so carelessly that the results are meaningless when at their best, and farcical when at their worst." He concludes we should be "thankful that these queer little tails that hang down from such completely amoral stories as *Moll Flanders* and *Roxana* allowed Defoe to deceive himself about what he was doing, for without such self-deception he could not have written them."[32] Yet it is the sense that Defoe tries to deceive his readers, not himself, that has been found most disconcerting. Is he really careless and confused?

George A. Starr has argued that Defoe's contradictions concerning fiction and mendacity can be given some coherence within a system of casuistry.[33] He refers to the famous letter Defoe wrote to Harley claiming that hypocrisy and dissimulation could be a virtue: "But as a Lye Does Not Consist in the Indirect Position of words, but in the Design by False Speaking, to Deciev and Injure my Neighbour, So Dissembling does Not Consist in Putting a Different Face Upon Our Actions, but in the further Applying that Concealment to the Prejudice of the Person." Defoe continues with a story about gently tricking a man who is subject to convulsions and does not know that his house is on fire to go outside; and concludes: "Will any Man Tax me with Hypocrisye and Dissimulation?"[34] The "Design," then—what Defoe feels compelled to justify in the prefaces to his fiction—is what authorizes one to put a different face upon one's actions. Defoe uses this defense in a dialogue that might come closest to convicting him of a double imposture, since it deals directly with the writing of fiction: the discussion between the brother and sister in *A New Family Instructor*, published in 1727, three years after the end of the prolific years in which Defoe produced his famous romances. In this best-selling guidebook for moral education and reformation, a sister claims that "Reading Romances, or fictitious Stories" is a sin which can not be justified since such stories are "what the Scripture meant by *making a Lie*." She insists that "the writing or publishing a Romance, was a

Lie."[35] The brother's definition of a romance reads like numerous characterizations of Defoe's own fiction: "a formal made Story in Print, raised out of the Invention of the Author, and put upon the World to cheat the Readers, in the Shape or Appearance of Historical Truth."[36] Yet although he agrees with his sister that a romance is criminal if "told only with Design to deceive the Reader" and "bring him to believe, that the Fact related was true," he insists that "where the Moral of the Tale is duly annex'd and the End directed right . . . in such Cases, Fables, feigned Histories, invented Tales, and even such as we call Romances, have always been allow'd as the most pungent Way of writing." In this sense romances can be compared to "the Parables or Historical Relations, left upon Record by our Saviour himself."[37]

Depending on whether or not one believes Defoe's various claims for a moral design that will justify his fables, the dialogue's defense of romances will either acquit or convict Defoe of imposture and deception. (The reader of the dialogue presumably agrees with the brother since the righteous Puritan who accepted the sister's point of view would be compelled to throw down the dialogue itself; although one could agree with Defoe in principle and still not be convinced by the moral of *Roxana*, for example, or other fables masquerading as histories.) Defoe, perhaps retrospectively, tries to inscribe his work within the general framework of religious allegory which, with its less literal and less factual notion of truth, gradually was allowing narrative fiction to coexist with Puritan prohibitions.[38] This position, and the concept of a morally justifiable deception which would admit fiction but claim that it provided moral instruction, would seem to arm Defoe with substantial defenses of his fictions—or at least of his romances.[39]

We must acknowledge, however, that Defoe does not finally take refuge in these defenses of fiction. He is not satisfied with the path of Puritan allegories which, as Hunter has shown, "circumvented the charge of 'feigned history'" by not pretending to "correspond to 'real' names or places."[40] He is not satisfied with the rationalizations, discussed by Starr, that sought to justify fiction that served a moral purpose. In spite of his possible defenses, Defoe keeps returning to the fiction that his fictions are true. In the voice of a feigned historical personage, he claims to be writing about real people, places, and events; like Dante, he claims that his allegory is history—which is not to say that it isn't allegorical.[41] In Defoe's writings, the fiction of history appears where a moral design seems lacking; and, as if gratuitously, it often appears together with a moral justification and a hint that all the particulars of the story can't be vouched for. The fiction of history, like the preface that frames it, stands outside of the fiction of the narrative. It has no allegorical truth; it sins against literal truth; in itself, it says nothing about good or evil. What does this deception represent?

The fiction of history shifts the question of truth from the specific events of the narrative to the author who supposedly speaks the text. The text would represent more than a story: it would stand for a person. Not content with the "once upon a time" of a parable or the "what might have been" that Aristotle called the province of poetry,[42] Defoe's texts evoke the authority of the first person singular. The prefaces usually present one printed voice to vouch for the authenticity of the voice that speaks the narrative; often another character such as an editor, relator, or witness is added. Such are the powers of illusions in black and white to authorize themselves. One lie is denied by replacing it with a larger lie—a lie that is less defensible, morally speaking, but which gambles on total conviction. I am suggesting, then, that Defoe's conversion of fiction into fraud indicates that Defoe's investment in fiction (and thus in the fiction of history) lies in an act of impersonation as much as in the telling of a story. Those long, breathless narratives that allude to "scenes" but never break for chapters, books, or sections are, in effect, dramatic monologues; they would refer to a character as much as to specific events which may or may not have occurred.

To say this by no means resolves the contradictions inherent in Defoe's positions. Indeed, although Starr and Hunter have taught us a great deal about how to reconcile Defoe's seemingly contradictory statements about fiction by reading them within their social and religious contexts, in this discussion I am less interested in reconciling Defoe's contradictions than in speculating about what necessitates them. I am arguing that Defoe's anxieties about fiction and deception focus less on the act of writing fiction than on the act of impersonation—which both denies his fiction and undermines his fiction's defense. Defoe's predicament in writing first-person fiction is no longer the lie of fabricating a story but rather the lie that gives fiction authenticity and authority. This lie is the deception of imposture and it imposes upon the world in a different manner than the fiction it presents. The lie of fiction becomes the lie of theater: the *trompe-l'oeil* of an impersonation "putting a different face upon our actions" that has no apparent moral design in its "concealment." Defoe's lie as an author is personal misrepresentation: representing himself as another person, speaking in the person of someone else. If he is convicted of a double imposture, he stands condemned for the sin of play-acting.

By beginning this discussion of Defoe and fiction with readings of episodes from *Robinson Crusoe* and *A Journal of the Plague Year*, I wanted to suggest that to make sense of Defoe's anxieties about fiction we need to consider how such preoccupations are acted out in the fictions themselves, not just in his statements about fiction. *Robinson Crusoe* and *Plague Year*, for example, provide miniature allegories for the acts of theatrical and deceptive fiction that Defoe himself is engaged in—acts which I have argued contribute the most to his predicament in writing fiction. Defoe's second sequel to *Robinson Crusoe*—the *Serious Reflections During the Life and Surprising Adventures of Robinson Crusoe with His Vision of the Angelic World*—is a particularly interesting example of the way Defoe figures and reflects upon his situation in writing since it is located somewhere between narrative fiction and polemical discourse. It reveals the extent to which Defoe is invested in his impostures as well as the potential for anxiety in an impersonation that won't stop at the borders of narrative fiction. The *Serious Reflections* are also revealing in this context since they are presented in the voice and character of Defoe's earliest and most morally justifiable impersonation. Not a Newgate criminal, a lawless pirate, or an immoral mistress, Robinson Crusoe is no worse than the archetypal prodigal son. He speaks to us as a sincere, penitent, and honest man who retrospectively casts his spiritual autobiography in the framework of religious typology and providential patterns.

In the sequel to *Robinson Crusoe*, an even more explicitly (if less subtly) Christian book, Defoe disguised as an "editor" seems secure enough about the moral instruction of the first and additional adventures to acknowledge the claim that "the author has supplied the story out of his invention," protesting only about the pirate editions that strip the story of the religious reflections that provide "the improvement which alone recommends that invention to wise and good men." The fiction of history which prefaces the original narrative is not abandoned here (the preface denies the book is a "romance") but it seems relatively unimportant.[43] However, in the following year, 1720, after the publication of more adventure stories, pseudobiographies, and romances, Defoe published a bizarre series of spiritual meditations and reflections under the signature of Robinson Crusoe. In this book the problem of Crusoe's historical or fictional status, a problem which one might have assumed to be rationalized or defused, is again activated.

It is easy to assume that Defoe's revival of Robinson Crusoe was an attempt to cash in on the previous success of the name he had made famous. But could this be the motivation for the continuation of the impersonation? It is not inconsistent, perhaps, for the character of Crusoe to engage in moral meditations, yet with the exception of a few comments, the book is without reference or relevance to the life or adventures of Robinson Crusoe. Defoe's claim, in the first paragraph of the preface supposedly written by Crusoe himself, that the *Serious Reflections* provide the moral for the fable of the first two books,[44] suggests a further need to justify the fictions that have preceded and to secure their place in the category of virtuous deception advocated in *A New Family Instructor*. It is doubtful, however, that this anxiety could be cured by reintroducing the fiction that prompted it. The claim for a moral design is made, after all, by Robinson Crusoe—not by an editor or novel writer. One is reminded of the conclusion to *Captain Singleton*, the pirate romance Defoe completed just before he wrote the *Serious Reflections*. Here the narrator becomes obsessed with a disguise he has adopted and insists that neither he nor his companion will abandon their foreign costumes and disguising beards, or even speak their native English in public—in short, that they live an unending impersonation.[45]

What is remarkable (if entirely characteristic) about Defoe's imposture, however, is that he puts on the mask of Robinson Crusoe to address the very question of Robinson Crusoe's reality, as well as problems of truth and deception. In the preface he writes while "putting a different face upon his actions," Defoe attempts both to assert and to explain the fiction of his character's historical existence. This leads him into an incredibly complicated series of paradoxical positions—which, I believe, need to be taken seriously in all their contradictions. Most immediately, we are presented with the problem of how to read the reflections of a "man" (in fact, a fiction) who at the moment he says "I, Robinson Crusoe" asserts the truth of his existence and perpetuates a lie in the same text in which he admits his fictional status—in the voice and authority of that fiction.

The text is thus ruled by a paradox. Recommending his reflections for "the just and only good end of all parable or allegoric history," that is, for "moral and religious improvement," the voice of Robinson Crusoe speaks of his earlier narratives as an "imaginary story" that has "its just allusion to a real story" (SR:xi–xii). In a passage often quoted by critics to show Defoe's intentions as an allegorist, Crusoe insists:

> All these reflections are just history of a state of forced confinement, which in my real history is represented by a confined retreat in an island; and it is as reasonable to represent one kind of imprisonment by another, as it is to represent anything that really exists by that which exists not. The story of my fright with something on my bed was word for word a history of what happened, and indeed all those things received very little alteration, except what necessarily attends removing the scene from one place to another. (SR:xii)

This voice of reason explains that "Facts that are formed to touch the mind must be done a great way off, and by somebody never heard of" (SR:xiii), suggesting that the "life of a man you knew . . . would have yielded no diversion, and perhaps scarce have obtained a reading" (SR:xiii). As we read such arguments, it seems reasonable to excuse the former deception of a man who seems to hint that he is Daniel Defoe; although we might need to overlook such eccentric uses of language as "facts that are formed."

However, the preface to the *Serious Reflections* almost simultaneously confronts and denies the accusation that Robinson Crusoe and his books are fakes. Defoe speaking in the person of Crusoe recounts the charges against the first two volumes that "the story is feigned, that the names are borrowed, and that it is all a romance; that there never were any such man or place, or circumstances in any man's life; that it is all formed and embellished by invention to impose upon the world" (SR:ix). In response to these accusations, which not only recall Gildon's attack but also sound like the *Read's Journal* characterization of Defoe published one year before *Robinson Crusoe*, the preface proceeds with the rhetoric of a legal document to claim that the accusers are themselves guilty of falsehood and invention: "I, Robinson Crusoe, being at this time in perfect and sound mind and memory, thanks be to God therefor, do hereby declare their objection is an invention scandalous in design, and false in fact; and do affirm that the story, though allegorical, is also historical" (SR:ix). As if writing a last will and testament in which the legacy of his own reality is at stake, with a willful performative speech act Robinson Crusoe declares himself to exist: I declare myself to be, therefore I am.

Hunter has reminded us that it would be consistent for a text to purport to be both allegorical and historical, since for Puritans history itself was emblematic and allegorical.[46] Yet Defoe's defense that his story is allegorical—his explanation that it is reasonable to "represent anything that really exists by that which exists not"—is undermined by his insistence that the episodes of the first two volumes "are all historical and true in fact" (SR:xi). He refuses to abandon his claim that the text is literally and factually true: "It is most real that I had a parrot and taught it to call me by my name; such a servant a savage, and afterwards a Christian, and that his name was called Friday, and that he was ravished from me by force, and died in the hands that took him, which I represent by being killed; this is all literally true" (SR:xi).

In the next paragraph Defoe again returns to hints that would encourage an allegorical and autobiographical application of his fiction. But either there really was a footprint in the sand—real sand, on a real island—or there wasn't. The problem is not how to reconcile allegory and history; Defoe wants to say that his fiction is literally true but not literally true. He wants to allow that Robinson Crusoe might not really exist—but only in the voice and character of a real Robinson Crusoe.

In his essay "A Plea for Excuses" J. L. Austin describes two types of defenses that can respond to an accusation: "In the one defence, briefly, we accept responsibility but deny that it was bad: in the other, we admit that it was bad but don't accept full, or even any, responsibility."⁴⁷ Defoe has chosen both of these options simultaneously: justification and denial. Each excuse is in itself a defense against the accusation that he wrote fiction, or lied. Even when the deception of fiction can be morally justified, Defoe cannot let down his mask. He wants to stand both inside and outside of the fiction. He can admit the fiction but not the imposture; he will abandon and explain the lie of fiction but he needs the lie of theater. Defoe is thus caught between two contradictory impulses (two needs, two anxieties) which can't be reconciled. The result is a preface constructed of logical contortions and paradoxes, and a command performance in which Defoe plays the role of Robinson Crusoe for one last time.

It is appropriate that in the preface Defoe allows a comparison of Robinson Crusoe's history with the "History of Don Quixote" (which he claims to be an "emblematic history" of a certain Duke de Medina Sidonia). Such a comparison evokes the confusion of fact and fiction played out by a narrative which claims to be history and by characters who construct fictional identities for themselves; in the sequel to *Don Quixote*, characters from books seem to acquire real existence as they move through the landscape and meet their readers. In the *Serious Reflections*, Defoe might be seen as a Don Quixote who has been taken in by his own books; and if Don Quixote is cured of madness, Defoe, too, seems to be able to stand beside himself in a sane sense—as in his serious reflections on "Talking Falsely" where he refers to morally justifiable parables: "Such are the historical parables in the Holy Scripture, such 'The Pilgrim's Progress,' and such, in a word, the adventures of your fugitive friend, 'Robinson Crusoe'" (SR:107).

A world is changed in the gesture those inverted commas make as they frame the name of Robinson Crusoe, the name that stands without quotation marks at the end of the preface, as did *By Himself* on an earlier title page. (In the same year, Alexander Selkirk—the misanthropic celebrity who returned from his famous shipwreck to live in a cave in Scotland and dance with his cats—was buried at sea.) Yet Defoe's investment in his impersonation of Robinson Crusoe prevents him from divesting himself of his costume, even if he is willing to acknowledge his role in an almost Brechtian manner. In the *Serious Reflections* Defoe again puts on the costume of Robinson Crusoe in order to address the guilt generated by his imposture.

Defoe enacts the serious reflections that seem to have prompted him to resume his impersonation—his reflections on the very act of misrepresenting himself as Robinson Crusoe—beyond the border of the preface to the book. The *Serious Reflections* include meditations in addition to "Of Talking Falsely" such as: "An Essay upon Honesty," "Of Atheistical and Profane Discourse," "Of the Immorality of Conversation," and "Of Listening to the Voice of Providence." Alongside of meditations on religion and morality, these discussions dwell specifically on problems of honesty and deception, sincerity and hypocrisy, lying, fiction, language, truth, and the recognition of voices. In the section on "Talking Falsely," after the passage cited above in which Robinson Crusoe's adventures are compared to biblical parables and *The Pilgrim's Progress*, Defoe continues to brood on the "spreading evil in telling a false story as true" (SR:108). Such lies, says Robinson Crusoe, continue "a brooding forgery to the end of time"; the "fraud goes unto the world's end" (SR:108). Defoe thus returns to the image of the printed lie which he contemplated in the preface to *The Storm* sixteen years earlier: "if a man tells a lie in print, he abuses mankind, and imposes upon the whole world, he causes our children to tell lies after us, and their children after them, to the end of the world."[48] And just as he followed that reflection with the fear that he should "stand convicted of a double imposture," in the *Serious Reflections* Defoe follows his image of an endless fraud with the fear that his defense of his fictions might lead to the same sort of conviction:

> If any man object here that the preceding volumes of this work seem to be hereby condemned, and the history which I have therein published of myself censured, I demand in justice such objector stay his censure till he sees the end of the scene, when all that mystery shall discover itself, and I doubt not but the work shall abundantly justify the design, and the design abundantly justify the work. (SR:109)

Defoe assures his readers that his forgeries will have a less apocalyptic end: he promises a revealed purpose and design which presumably would acquit him of a double imposture where his other defenses seem to have failed. What sort of end could change the last judgment Defoe fears for his impersonation?

One might expect the *Serious Reflections* to end with the "vision of the Angelic world" which follows Defoe's spiritual meditations. However, after describing a bizarre, imaginary voyage above the earth, the author continues: "I have a mind to conclude this work with a short history of some atheists, which I met with many years ago, and whether the facts are testified or not, may be equally useful in the application" (SR:306–307). We can recognize this disclaiming preface as a signal that we are entering the realm of fiction—not that we ever left it. The book will end with a parable, whose complicated narrative is briefly this: an atheist knocking on the door of an atheist friend is answered by what he thinks is his friend's voice telling him that there is a God and that he should repent. However, unknown to the visiting atheist, the voice belongs not to his friend but to a religious man who "not very distinctly seen . . . spoke aloud in the person of his friend" (SR:311). The atheist next meets a student who speaks the same admonition and persuades him to repent; then returning to the house of the friend (who has also repented, by the way) the men are amazed to hear the friend (truthfully) deny that he had said anything to the atheist that day. (The religious man has removed himself from the scene.) They conclude that the atheist must have heard "some voice from heaven" (SR:323) and are thoroughly converted. This is the bare outline of the parable, but I hope that its design will begin to take shape: Defoe, speaking in the voice of his famous impersonation, tells a story concerned with voices, an impersonation, and a mistake—and belief in the existence of an unseen authority. The reader is called upon to conclude, "Here is a visible evidence of God" (SR: 324), since only Divine Providence could have arranged the complicated circumstances that led the men to repent. According to the story, however, the men—who lack the reader's omniscient point of view—become believers for a different reason:

> Yet even in this we see how the power of imagination may be worked up by the secret agency of an unknown hand, how many things concurred to make this man believe he had seen an apparition, and heard a voice; and yet there was nothing in it but the voice of a man unseen and mistaken. . . . here was neither vision or voice, but that of an ordinary person, and one who meant well and said well. (SR:324)

The moral of Defoe's fable seems clear: an instance of mistaken identity and an act of impersonation lie behind a man's religious instruction and improvement—his salvation. Taking advantage of the power of imagination to make us see shapes and hear voices that aren't quite there, an unknown gentleman (a secret agent) speaks "in the person" of someone he is not; just as Robinson Crusoe "appear'd as another person" and played an unseen authority in his military masquerade; just as Defoe, the unknown hand and unseen authority behind the text, speaks in the person of Robinson Crusoe.

If the hidden gentleman is guilty of imposture in winning an in-
credulous man's belief, surely he "meant well and said well." Who
would tax him with hypocrisy and dissimulation? The story, then,
works as an allegory and apology for the impersonation Defoe
would like to see as virtuous deception. Simply because there has
been a "serious mistake," he writes, "should not at all hinder us
from making a very good use of such things; for many a voice may
be directed from heaven that is not immediately spoken from
thence" (SR:324–25). The story's allusive meaning implies that in
assigning authority for Crusoe's words, in looking behind his mask
for the source of his voice, we should not stop at Defoe. This is a
more respectable admission (not to mention justification) of ven-
triloquy.

A final note: Defoe's parable about the virtues of speaking "in the person" of someone else dwells on voices: in their debate
on religion the student and the atheist speak of a "secret voice"
(SR:315), "the voice of conscience" (SR:316), "the voice of His
providence" (SR:319), "the voice of God, and the voice of the devil"
(SR:320), a "voice" spoken "to my understanding" (SR:322), and a
"voice from heaven" (SR:323). It is appropriate, then, that their
conversation adopt the textual form that is designed to represent
voices: the dialogue. The page begins to resemble the text of a
play—with labeled character parts and bracketed stage directions—
at the moment when the student claims to come across a "dialogue"
(SR:313) in a book; at which point he asks the atheist to read aloud
some lines written on the back of the title page. As the atheist gives
voice to the lines—the student refers to his "performance" (SR:
313)—the text of the dialogue indents to render the lines as they
appeared on the page:

> "But if it should fall out, as who can tell,
> That there may be a God, a heaven, and hell,
> Had I not best consider well, for fear
> 'T should be too late when my mistakes appear?"
>   (SR:313)

As the dialogue continues, these verses occasion a strange textual event: a few pages later, the student refers to the lines but when he recites them, they read:

> "*You'd* best consider well, for fear
> 'T should be too late when *your* mistakes appear."
>
> (SR:316, my emphasis)

Why and how have the pronouns been transposed here? One could assume that the student changes the words to suit his audience, but the indented and typographically distinct citation on the page indicates that he is reading, not paraphrasing. When the atheist next refers to the lines, they appear again in the first person: "It's all TOO LATE, now my mistakes appear" (SR:319). I don't want to make too much of these textual transformations since Defoe has a reputation for carelessness and haste; yet in speculating about the appearance of the verses here we need to recall further that they also appeared in the preface to *The Storm*. There, they are written in the third person:

> If it should so fall out, as who can tell,
> But that there is a God, a Heaven, and Hell,
> Mankind had best consider well for fear,
> 'T should be too late when his mistakes appear.[49]

This citation indicates more than another example of the verses' shifting pronouns; it forms another point in the constellation of associations we can see taking shape at the end of Robinson Crusoe's last performance.

I want to suggest that the instability of pronominal reference displayed by Defoe's verses is inscribed within the confusion of parts and persons that informs the parable about impersonation and the attribution of voices; as well as the book written in the voice of Robinson Crusoe that the parable ends. Furthermore, this confusion is a part of the process and form of the dramatic dialogue that presents a written text as speech to be imagined as vocalized by different characters; and it is no coincidence that Defoe's text should turn to dialogue at the end of Robinson Crusoe's imposture nor that a confusion of speakers should occur when the characters in the dialogue themselves read aloud from a book that contains a dialogue. Finally, it makes sense that this protean citation should return us to the preface Defoe wrote sixteen years earlier about the consequences of deceiving in print, the problem of identifying the voice of God, and the risks of presenting other people's first-person narratives. After having supposedly silenced the problem of fiction with defenses of allegory and moral instruction, Defoe is still troubled by the lie of play-acting. The final allegorical defense of impersonation with which he ends Robinson Crusoe's monologue paradoxically takes on a dramatic form which destabilizes the assignment of voices to persons and returns to a scene of anxiety in which he pictured the theatrical position in which an author faces his readers and worried about the deception of romances masquerading as histories. The ending of the *Serious Reflections* recapitulates the contradictory motivations, anxieties, and responses that we saw at play in generating the book's dramatic monologue and meditations. Consequently, despite the wishful allegory that presents Defoe's imposture in the best of lights, the last words of Robinson Crusoe betray a stubborn insecurity: "I hope I have said nothing of it to misguide anybody, or to assist them to delude themselves, having spoken of it with the utmost seriousness in my design, and with a sincere desire for a general good" (SR:325). To the end, "Robinson Crusoe" worries about how his play may have deluded his readers. It is one of the ironies of fiction and history that the *Oxford English Dictionary* quotes from *Robinson Crusoe* by Daniel Defoe to illustrate this definition of the word *design*: "in a bad sense: crafty contrivance, hypocritical scheming."

CHAPTER 5

Moll Flanders:
Portrait of the Artist
as a Play-Actor

ROBINSON Crusoe's *Serious Reflections* illustrate how the pulpit in which Defoe plays the parson can double as a scaffold on which he stands convicted of imposture. We saw how sermons he delivers about fiction, history, and allegory can turn from defenses to monologues of self-incrimination. It is not surprising, then, that Defoe's next major impersonation, published within a year of the *Serious Reflections*, begins by asserting the fiction of its history and then aligns the defense of fiction with the defense of theater. Writing in the preface to *The Fortunes and Misfortunes of the Famous Moll Flanders* in order to "Justifie the Publication" of the book—in particular, "our Design in publishing it"—an editorial voice proclaims:

> The Advocates for the Stage have in all Ages made this the great Argument to persuade People that their Plays are useful, and that they ought to be allow'd in the most civiliz'd, and in the most religious Government; Namely, That they are applyed to virtuous Purposes, and that by the most lively Representations, they fail not to recommend Virtue and generous Principles, and to discourage and expose all sorts of Vice and Corruption of Manners; and were it true that they did so, and that they constantly adhered to that Rule, as the Test of their acting on the *Theatre*, much might be said in their Favour.[1]

This is the same argument that Defoe uses to defend Moll's Newgate autobiography about immorality and illegality; although he seems to remember by the end of the sentence that associating the book with the stage is more likely to suggest guilt than innocence. Defoe continues, however, in speaking of his book, to boast that "There is not a superlative Villain brought upon the Stage, but either he is brought to an unhappy End, or brought to be a Penitent" (5). Whether because Defoe shared Shaftesbury's sense that publishing oneself or one's book was a theatrical act that placed one before the eyes of the world, or because the theatrical lie of imposture (appearing as another person) was on his mind as he began a new fictive impersonation, or both, Defoe prefaces his book by entering the controversy surrounding the theater. Indeed, I suggest that *Moll Flanders* itself enters the theater: for Defoe, the text is a stage and all its characters are players—some of whom figure Defoe's own activity of play-acting. In this chapter I will argue that more explicitly and consistently than Defoe's previous work, *Moll Flanders* reflects upon the conditions of theater and rehearses theater's possibilities. Following the impersonations and defenses of Robinson Crusoe, Defoe begins *Moll Flanders* by acknowledging the attack on the stage as well as the attack on fiction; yet if the antitheatrical indictment informs and characterizes Defoe's text, this does not mean that *Moll Flanders* is entirely defensive. In many ways it can be seen as a celebration of the deceptive, theatrical activity that elsewhere causes problems for Defoe. It can also help us to understand theater as a response to anxieties about presenting and representing a self in the world.

Although the Restoration unlocked the doors to the playhouses during Defoe's lifetime, the debate on the morality of the theater continued. Puritan antitheatrical sentiment at this point in history was less likely to appear with the hysterical horror of William Prynne, whose *Histrio-mastix* (published in 1633) objected to the very essence of theater. Instead, attacks were directed at particular manifestations of theater and the social context in which theater took place; but suspicion of the stage, like distrust of fiction, remained. In the years preceding Defoe's romances, Jeremy Collier placed himself at the center of the debate with his *A Short View of the Immorality and Profaneness of the English Stage*; first published in 1698, it inaugurated a series of defenses, counterattacks, and reprints which continued throughout Defoe's career. (According to one bibliography, almost eighty publications joined in the debate between 1698 and 1726.)[2] "The business of *Plays* is to recommend Virtue, and discountenance, Vice,"[3] begins Collier, and although he wants to show that the English stage fails in this design, he admits that the stage has some purpose. Collier's arguments suggest the reform rather than the abolition of the theater.

Defoe's position (at least as it is articulated in the pages of *The Review* in the first decade of the eighteenth century) is similar to Collier's.[4] Although one biographer claims that Defoe knew "Butler, Dryden, and the leading Restoration playwrights so intimately that he could quote their works from memory as long as he lived,"[5] Defoe endorses Collier in *The Review* and generally offers the stage reluctant praise and ready criticism. He expresses particular outrage at the collaboration of church and stage (June 20, 1706 and August 3, 1706)[6] and he tries to create a public scandal when plays are presented at Oxford in 1706 (August 8 and August 10, 1706). However, Defoe does call for reformation: "I will not deny, but publick Actings and Representations may be in themselves lawful, and in some Respects beneficial" (August 30, 1709). He asks for a theater which would be "a Discouragement to Vice, and an Illustration of Virtue . . . untainted with Indecency and Immoralities" (October 26, 1706).

Defoe's contribution to the debate about the theater may have consisted in his attempt to shift the blame from the actors and playwrights to the spectators. "In short," he writes in 1705, "the Errors of the Stage, lie in the Auditory; the Actors, and the Poets, are their Humble Servants" (May 3, 1705). (Defoe—whose own writing was accused of pandering to vulgar taste—signs himself both in *The Review* and elsewhere at this time as "the Age's Humble Servant.") He claims that a moral stage would have to be subsidized by the throne since no one would go to see it (October 26, 1706) but the proposal for subsidization he eventually presents is more like twentieth-century farm subsidies than public television: the plan calls for a national subscription that would allow the state to buy all the playhouses and pay all the actors in England not to act—in effect, suppressing the stage once again (September 1, 1706). If there is irony in the text of this proposal, it is neither plain nor explicit.

Indeed, it is consistent with the strict Puritan stance Defoe takes in his *Family Instructor* of 1715, where dialogues show a mother taking away her daughter's plays as well as her romances, and a father telling his son to "leave off the playhouses, and reading plays, as not only introductory to vice, and an extravagant mispender of time; but as . . . destructive to any sober character in the world."[7]

We know, of course, that Defoe could have a range of positions on any issue; and we shouldn't forget that the condemnations of theater in *The Family Instructor* appear in the form of dramatic dialogues that repeatedly make use of theatrical imagery.[8] I am suggesting, however, that although the moral climate of the early eighteenth century was more reformist than when Prynne and Gosson were in the limelight, the traditional Puritan attack on theater still carried weight for Defoe. Although Defoe often sounds like Collier, there is also something anachronistic about his position. (The preface to *Moll Flanders*—a book which claims to be written in 1683—refers to the controversy about theater "in all ages.") I want to argue that in writing *Moll Flanders* Defoe is closer to seventeenth-century condemnations of theater than to Collier. In saying this I don't mean to assign Defoe a strictly antitheatricalist point of view, although I have suggested that he felt more condemned for his play-acting than for his fiction; and his defense of his fiction in the preface implies that he has succeeded where stage plays have failed. My point is that the legacy of Puritan ideology about the theater offered Defoe a view of the world (in particular a vision of the ontological conditions of theater) which in some sense could be separated from the moral values that were supposed to invest that view. I will argue that even where Defoe rejects or simply does not attend to the moral judgments of the antitheatricalists, he still is influenced by the terms and categories they used to characterize play-acting. What is significant in *Moll Flanders* is not Defoe's anxiety about the morality of his enterprise—although with Defoe anxiety is never far removed—but rather his devalorization or even reversal of the values of the antitheatrical tradition. I suggested earlier that the Puritan attack on the stage informs and characterizes

Defoe's work; in particular, I mean that the antitheatricalist attempt to characterize the essence and world of actors serves to define Moll Flanders and the world she inhabits.

We saw that the band of "play-actors" that Defoe dramatizes in *A Journal of the Plague Year* fits the seventeenth-century characterization of actors as homeless vagrants who were suspected of spreading the plague. In the same manner, many of the other accusations that Puritan moralists directed against the actors and the theater sketch the characteristics of Moll Flanders. The playhouse was viewed as the scene of crime, theft, fraud, cheating, and deception; not only because criminals were said to frequent the public theater, but also because stage plays were seen as an idle waste of time: actors in effect stole their spectator's money since they didn't return anything of value in exchange. According to Prynne, "the very Profession of a Stage-Player being unlawfull (as Divines agree:) the mony they receive for acting . . . must certainly be theft."[9] Futhermore, playhouses "are the Schooles, Playes the Lectures which teach men how to Cheate, to Steale."[10] Antitheatrical tracts obsessively berated stage-players for dressing in the clothing of the opposite sex (violating *Deuteronomy* 12:5).[11] Acting itself was said to represent (in form and content) as well as inspire adultery and prostitution; the playhouse was analogous to the brothel and was a brothel itself since actors prostituted themselves figuratively and female play-actors were considered "notorious whores."[12] Prynne claimed that actresses had been prostitutes since classical times; and during the Restoration, when women were allowed on the English stage, many actresses (like Roxana) gained notoriety by becoming mistresses to noblemen and even royalty. All of these characteristics used by the antitheatricalists to describe the world, profession, and character of the actor also add up to a picture of Moll Flanders. A woman who is actually a female impersonation, a man dressed up in a woman's clothes, Moll is cast as a whore, a mistress, an adultress, a thief, a pickpocket, a cheat, a master of deception, fraud, and disguise. We have been satisfied to call her world of crime, corruption, deception, and sin a rogues' gallery, and clearly it fits into a popular Newgate genre; but in the context of the problematic status of the theater it also begins to sound like the world represented to the Puritans by the playhouse.

Moll Flanders—who repeatedly changes her name and appearance—also could be seen to embody perhaps the greatest threat that actors represented for the antitheatrical tradition: the theater's disruption and undermining of the concept of a stable identity. We saw how a dramatic method of personating, multiplying, and dividing the self, of distinguishing between an outward and an inward character, finally undermines Shaftesbury's search for a stable, true, authentic, and genuine self. Antitheatricalists would have considered Shaftesbury's enterprise doomed from the outset since they saw the actor's art as radically opposed to the concept of an absolute and knowable identity. Jonas Barish calls this threat to the self the "ontological subversiveness"[13] of the theater. In *The Antitheatrical Prejudice*, his authoritative account of the tradition, Barish refers to the literalness which marks Tertullian's concept of the self: "One's identity, for Tertullian, is absolutely given, as one's sex is given; any deviation from it constitutes a perversion akin to the attempt to change one's sex."[14] Barish discusses how later antitheatrical tracts, exemplified by Prynne, "make explicit the concept of an absolute identity that was only implied in Tertullian."[15] Prynne writes in *Histrio-mastix*:

> For God, who is truth itselfe, in whom there is no variablenesse, no shadow of change, no feining, no hypocrisie; as he hath given a uniforme distinct and proper being to every creature, the bounds of which may not be exceeded: so he requires that the actions of every creature should be honest and sincere, devoyde of all hypocrisie, as all his actions, and their natures are. Hence he enjoins all men at all times, to be such in shew, as they are in truth: to seeme that outwardly which they are inwardly; to act themselves, not others . . . . God requires truth in the inward parts; in the soule, the affections; yea, in the habit, speeches, gestures, in the whole intire man.[16]

Thus, actors were guilty because they sought to change their identities, as if competing with God in creating a self; and because they misrepresented themselves. Like the writer of fiction, the actor was a liar. What is hypocrisy, asks Prynne, "in the proper signification of the word, but the acting of anothers part or person on the Stage: or what else is an hypocrite, in his true etimologie, but a Stage-player, or one who acts anothers part."[17] In *Playes Confuted in Five Actions*, published in 1582, Stephen Gosson defines a lie as "an acte executed where it ought not. This acte is discerned by outward signes, every man must show himselfe outwardly to be such as in deed he is. Outward signes consist eyther in words or gestures, to declare our selves by wordes or by gestures to be otherwise than we are, is an act executed where it should not, therefore a lye."[18] These attacks on the theater represent more than objections to local corruption or specific plays: the essence of acting is at stake—and not only on the stage. Players were subversive not just for what they did on the stage but because their metamorphoses and counterfeiting threatened to destabilize the world of human relations. They opened the possibility that identities—social as well as personal— were not necessarily fixed, circumscribed, transparent, legible, and knowable, that appearances might not be trustworthy.[19]

In the antitheatrical tradition actresses doubled the sin of play-actors since as women they were considered to be deceptive, dissembling, protean, mere surface, and counterfeit to begin with. Women were attacked for embodying the hypocrisy and falseness of actors, for changing themselves from one moment to the next or for concealing their true selves beneath a disguise of insincerity or makeup. Katherine Eisaman Maus has argued persuasively that "both women and theater were subject to attack from the same rhetorical position. In the middle ages and the Renaissance anti-theatricalists and antifeminists strike exactly the same notes again and again, so that suspicion of the theater and suspicion of female sexuality can be considered two manifestations of the same anxiety."[20] The characterizations of the actress as a Proteus and a prostitute suggest an answer to the question of why Defoe should twice play, in the disguise of a fictive autobiography, the role of a woman who would be considered a "notorious whore." Such a character offers Defoe a figure for the play-actor; and the play-actor—especially the doubly deceptive female play-actor—offers him a figure

for himself. Defoe seems to adopt the Puritan antifeminist characterization of the woman but he does so to identify with the woman's
character, not to condemn it. We have seen that Defoe could be
more worried about the lie of theater—what Prynne calls "the acting of another's part or person"—than about the lie of fiction; and
that Charles Gildon claimed that the "Fabulous *Proteus* . . . was
but a very faint Type of [Defoe], whose Changes are much more
numerous, and he far more difficult to be constrain'd to his own
Shape."[21] In appearing in the person of Moll Flanders, Defoe accepts Puritan antitheatrical characterizations but not their value
judgments; and he creates a character who has all the characteristics
of an actor. These characteristics suggest the possibilities and advantages that the art of acting could present to a different point of
view—a perspective that would find theater appealing rather than
threatening. I will argue in the pages that follow that the characteristics of the actor also outline a portrait of Moll Flanders: she inhabits the theater, even if she never sets foot on a literal stage. In this
sense *Moll Flanders* (together with *Roxana*) might be seen as autobiographical fiction rather than a fictive autobiography.[22]

        To discuss Moll Flander's character as a play-actor we
must acknowledge her status as a disguise—not just a role played by
Defoe but a costume created by the assumption of a fictive first-
person narrative voice. The preface tells us that the book has been
"put into new Words . . . modester Words" which constitute "a
Dress fit to be seen" (3). This "new dressing up" of the story which
tries "to wrap it up so clean" (3) that it will be fit to be read resembles
the "dressing up" of Roxana's story "in worse Cloaths than the *Lady*
. . . prepar'd it for the World."[23] Robinson Crusoe (in his *Serious
Reflections*) calls lying "the sheep's clothing hung upon the wolf's
back . . . the thief's cloak" yet he also compares the "decency of
words" to the "decency of clothes."[24] It is not only lying that acts as
concealment and covering; truth itself, as we saw in *The Storm*, is a
"garb." Language itself is a costume for Defoe. Leo Braudy has

written that for Defoe "the plain style becomes a mask like any other
style. . . . The speakers in his novels manipulate the plain style to
disguise and dissemble."[25]

In *The Complete English Tradesman*—in which he discusses the "stage of trade"—Defoe includes a chapter on the
"Trading Stile" which advises the tradesman to speak "his own dia-
lect," the "language of trade"; he must always "suit his language to
his auditory."[26] *Street Robberies, Consider'd,* a short account of the
adventures of a reformed thief that is similar to *Moll Flanders,*
includes a glossary of "the Canting Language," a list from A to Z of
Newgate slang with English translations.[27] Throughout his career
Defoe was interested in the rhetoric that gave voice to an identity;
the recognition that social roles and ideologies carried with them
their own style and discourse helped make his satirical political
tracts so convincing. Indeed, information like this, catalogued to
advise tradesmen or help the public spot a thief, becomes most
useful to those who would counterfeit an identity—whether their
purpose is social mobility or fictive impersonation. *Moll Flanders,*
then, as a text, is as much a costume as "Moll Flanders" is a role;
and the text itself, dressed in clothes which conceal what shouldn't
be seen in the "original" (3) of the story, speaks the lines of a
character who spends her life concealing and disguising herself.
Once again, in looking for the self in a text we must read at several
removes.

That disguise is a fundamental aspect of Moll Flanders'
character is suggested in her account of her origins: her first recol-
lection is "that I had wandred among a Crew of those People they
call *Gypsies,* or *Egyptians*" (8). Gypsies in the sixteenth and seventeenth centuries were believed to combine the worst traits of thieves
and actors: nomadic dissemblers who dressed in unnatural clothes
and entertained and cheated the curious, gypsies had a reputation
for counterfeiting. Furthermore, English rogues often disguised
themselves as gypsies in order to take advantage of loopholes in
English law, thus becoming counterfeit Egyptians (which is to say
counterfeit counterfeiters). The vagrancy laws, aimed especially at

actors, included a special statute "for the punyshement of Vaga-
boundes, callyng them selues Egiptians" which was directed against
vagabonds guilty of "transformyng or disguysyng them selues in
theyr apparell, or in a certayne counterfait speache or be-
havuour."[28] Moll escapes from the gypsies before they discolor her
skin but her later traits and skills reflect the time she spent in her
formative years with people who, according to seventeenth-century
accounts, were "metamorphosers" "so skilled in assuming different
shapes" that one couldn't trust them "to look the same when one
sees them next."[29]

    Throughout the various stages of her life Moll Flanders
displays the need and ability to disguise herself and change identities. She passes from being a destitute orphan to a position in a
wealthy family where she learns "by Imitation and enquiry" (15)
how to be "as much a Gentlewoman as they were with whom I liv'd"
(16). An affair with one of the brothers necessitates dissembling and
for the first time Moll wears a "Hood" and "Mask" (23) to conceal
herself in public. She eventually becomes a gentlewoman by marrying the other brother in the family; but her metamorphoses take a
new turn when she must face the world after the disappearance of
her second husband. Unable to remarry and pursued by her credi-
tors, she decides "to go quite out of my Knowledge, and go by
another Name: This I did effectually, for I went into the *Mint* too,
took Lodgings in a very private Place, drest me up in the Habit of a
Widow, and call'd myself Mrs. *Flanders*" (51). Baptising herself with
a new name and contriving a costume which to the world represents
a new identity become Moll's characteristic responses to a need to
conceal herself and begin a "new Scene of Life" (83). They represent an almost ritualistic transformation by which she can "change
my Station, and make a new Appearance in some other Place where
I was not known, and even to pass by another Name if I found
Occasion" (61). Such transformations usually begin with an inventory of Moll's wealth and possessions: a literal taking "Stock"
(100) of the self which accounts for or "tells" oneself—as if she were
too literally taking Shaftesbury's advice that we can't know ourselves

"without first taking an inventory of the same kind of goods within ourselves, and surveying our domestic fund" (1:124).

I will not attempt to recount all of Moll's metamorphoses: in the first part of the book they usually are in service of "the Fraud of *passing for a Fortune without Money,* and cheating a Man into Marrying me on Pretence of a Fortune" (67). This ruse, which Moll says is "to Deceive the Deceiver" (61), backfires when she finds herself married to her Lancashire husband "upon the foot of a double Fraud" (116). In this scene both husband and wife are guilty of "putting the Face of great Things upon poor Circumstances" (118), and although this husband has represented himself in false colors, Moll forms a lasting affection for him. Long before they meet again in Newgate it is clear that they are a perfect match: both are actors, con artists skilled in the same game. Moll uses theatrical deception at other times as well, such as when she disguises herself as a servant to find out about her lover from Bath. It is when she begins her career as a thief, however, that Moll becomes a master of disguise, impersonation, and dramatic fiction. At first she performs these acts to get money but eventually she seems motivated by the pure pleasure of play. In short, she becomes "Moll Flanders": "the greatest Artist of my time" (167). In order to create new ruses and avoid the dangers of being known, Moll invents a repertoire of identities and costumes: "generally I took up new Figures, and contriv'd to appear in new Shapes every time I went abroad" (205). She becomes a Proteus who has "several Shapes to appear in" (185)—such as a "Disguise of a Widow's Dress" (188) or the "uneasie Disguise" (198) of a beggar woman; she plays gentlewoman or servant maid, depending on the scenario and fraud she is engaged in. Moll probably would have agreed with Defoe's arguments that apprentices and masters, servants and the upper classes, should be distinguishable by their dress; a society structured by classes that each have their proper costume offers a range of recognizable roles for an actor to counterfeit.

Moll's most impressive role is perhaps her impersonation of a man; the most concealing of her impostures to the other characters in the narrative, it is her most telling disguise for the reader since it is her most explicitly theatrical impersonation. She deceives her comrades—even the man she shares a bed with "never knew that I was not a Man" (168)—and when she is pursued by the police she is able to "throw off my Disguise, and dress me in my own Cloths" (168–169), thereby disappearing as the thief fleeing from a mob. Moll refers to this near capture as an event that "put an end to this Life" (168); the impersonation seems more an incarnation than a role. Yet we can see in this episode more than an illustration of Moll's uncanny artistry; her transformation of her sex and identity evokes the condition of the Renaissance stage that most infuriated Puritan moralists: actors impersonating the opposite sex. We noted that this practice was supposed to violate *Deuteronomy's* decree that "the woman shall not wear that which pertaineth unto a man, neither shall a man put on a woman's garment" (12–15)—as well as the bounds of one's true, God-given self. To the Puritans it represented the immorality of the stage and the sin of acting itself.

Of course, male actors appeared in female roles on the Renaissance stage; yet Moll Flanders uses precisely Puritan rhetoric when she refers to her costume as "a Dress so contrary to Nature" (167). Furthermore, we are reminded that as Moll is dressing up in a man's clothes to play the part of a man, Defoe is dressing as a woman to play the part of Moll Flanders. Once again we have a double imposture as Moll mirrors Defoe's activity, as if we were watching a production of *As You Like It* in which a boy plays the part of Rosalind playing the part of a boy playing the part of Rosalind. Moll's impersonation recalls the text's theatrical character and transports us to the vertigo and controversy of the Renaissance playhouse. Defoe goes to unusual lengths to underline this allusion: Moll uncharacteristically provides the information that while disguised as a man she went by the name of Gabriel Spencer. That this should be one of the few times that she unnecessarily reveals a name—even a pseudonym—makes sense if we recall that Gabriel Spencer was the name of a known English actor who was a member of the Earl of Pembroke's company and whose major claim to fame is that he was killed in a duel by Ben Jonson.[30] The name does more than point to a specific actor; it identifies the theater.

The play of names continues: shortly after the scene about "Gabriel Spencer," we read: "It was now a Merry time of the Year, and *Bartholomew Fair* was begun" (175). In this scene, Moll Flanders goes to the fair, encounters a rich gentleman, drinks with him, sleeps with him, and then robs him of "a gold Watch, with a silk Purse of Gold, his fine full bottom Perrewig, and silver fring'd Gloves, his Sword, and fine Snuff-box" (176). Moll needs no particular disguise for these acts but perhaps this is because she is already in the theater: to enter Bartholomew Fair is not simply to enter a colorful festival and market where rogues like Moll Flanders flourished; it is also to enter the play of that name by Ben Jonson. (Written in 1614, *Bartholomew Fair* was performed often on the Restoration stage for exactly the span of Defoe's lifetime: 1661 to 1731.)[31] In the space of two words we are transported to a literary world of spectacle, roguery, deception, drunkenness, and fraud where thieves, whores, and pickpockets reigned; this description fits not only the world of the play but also the world of the playhouse as it was characterized by antitheatrical tracts. Furthermore, in the play one character disguises himself and counterfeits another identity, another character is systematically stripped of most of his possessions by thieves, and all of the characters assemble at the climax of the comedy to themselves become an audience to a play. This spectacle, performed by puppets, stages a debate about the theater between a religious hypocrite and the "Puppet Dionysius." The argument, in which the puppet representing the theater defeats the person who takes the part of Puritanism, centers around the following exchange: Busy, the Puritan, calls actors an "abomination" because they "putteth on the apparel of the female, and the female of the male"—to which the Puppet Dionysius replies: "It is your old stale argument against the players, but it will not hold against the puppets; for we have neither male nor female amongst us."[32]

Thus, by entering Bartholomew Fair, Moll Flanders enters a realm famous for its tradition of spectacle and deception:

the world of Jonson's plays (Moll fits into *Volpone*, for example, almost as well as she fits into *Bartholomew Fair*); the realm of the playhouse; and the realm of theater itself—whose space both Jonson and Defoe inhabit and represent. Furthermore, one allusion (to the play Jonson authored) circles us back to another allusion (to the actor who died at Jonson's hand)—not only because of the connection of Jonson, but also because of the Puritan condemnation of the stage for allowing the sexes to exchange clothes. These associations also circle back to the preface which introduces Moll Flanders in the context of the debate about the theater. These associations occur at the height of Moll's play-acting; after her impersonation of Gabriel Spencer, Moll performs another theatrical sin condemned as counterfeiting by the Puritans: in her relations with the man she meets at the fair, Moll "for the first time us'd a little Art," which is to say she yields "to the baseness of Paint" (184). These allusions form a network of interrelated signs, texts, and events—all of which identify the narrative and its subject as theater.

Moll Flanders' play-acting continues after her life as a criminal is over, just as it predated that life. Even in Newgate, after her supposed repentance, she schemes to see her Lancashire husband by pretending she had been robbed by him: "I so disguis'd myself, and muffled my Face up so, that he cou'd see little of me, and consequently knew nothing of who I was." She appears before him with a "Hood over my Face" and "as I conceal'd my Face, so I Counterfeited my Voice, that he had not the least guess at who I was" (232). When she does reveal herself she still misrepresents herself by creating a fiction about how she came to be imprisoned in Newgate. In addition, when Moll returns to Virginia and from a distance spies her son, she again disguises her appearance although she has aged twenty years: "I had no Mask, but I ruffled my Hoods so about my Face, that . . . he would not be able to know any thing of me" (251). Each of these false appearances has a specific motivation but it is clear that disguise is a reflex response for Moll Flanders. Although Moll may present a consistent and recognizable voice for her reader throughout her retrospective monologue, throughout the scenes of her life Moll's identity seems to be defined by its resistance to definition. The identity she presents to the world is put on and off, donned and abandoned, as if it were a costume. Her self is made up of a series of roles and disguises—some lasting for a number of years, some appearing for the space of an episode, some passed over in a sentence. The counterfeiting gypsies who acted as her first family, the social mobility she exhibits in becoming a gentlewoman, her repeated misrepresentations of herself, her uncanny ability to appear as other persons, the shapes and figures with which she counterfeits the outward signs of a self—all add up to make Moll Flanders an embodiment of the ontological subversiveness of the actor.

As the Puritan antitheatricalists might have predicted, the self in *Moll Flanders* becomes a series of personations and impersonations whose outward characteristics can't be trusted to have reference to an inner reality. Rather than presenting a transparent and legible self in which any outer character would be uniform with an inner character, Moll depends upon others mistaking her identity—which is why the scene in which she is inadvertently a victim of mistaken identity has so many layers of irony. While imposing on the world in the disguise of a widow, Moll is taken as a thief before she has had a chance to steal anything; when she is vindicated—in this specific case she is innocent of an actual crime—she is enormously self-righteous in seeking damages. She starts out as a thief playing the part of a respectable widow in order to avoid being taken for a thief, yet she finishes the scene by playing a widow who a shopkeeper thought looked like a thief. Moll succeeds as a thief because people continually mistake her identity; only by mistake does someone read her correctly, but when this happens she is able to reverse the terms and escape with her mistaken identity (the widow) appearing genuine and her genuine identity (the thief) appearing mistaken. We are a long way from the case of mistaken identity by which a man speaking in the person of someone else converts an atheist on a staircase in order to justify the imposture of Daniel Defoe.

One often has the sense that Moll Flanders is less a person with numerous faces and guises than a succession of different people. When she takes inventory of herself to prepare "to make the World take me for something more than I was," she tells us: "With this Stock I had the World to begin again; but you are to consider that I was not now the same Woman" (100). She speaks specifically of her age here, but as with her incarnation as Gabriel Spenser she repeatedly acts as if she can become new people. When Moll returns to Virginia she hears a neighbor narrate the story of her own past misfortunes. The uncanny experience she describes retrospectively is created by hearing the story of herself told as if it were about someone else—or told as if *she* were someone else, which for all practical purposes she is as she appears in a new identity with her face concealed. The incident is a prefiguring of the autobiography in which Moll will double and divide herself to become witness to the story of her life.

Another figure for this retrospective multiplication and division of the self occurs when Moll describes her reception at Newgate. She offers a montage of her past incarnations: "what! Mrs. *Flanders* come to *Newgate* at last? what Mrs. *Mary*, Mrs. *Molly*, and after that plain *Moll Flanders*?" (215). These are only a few of the various identities she has passed as and passed through, the variations on the arbitrary name that mysteriously follows her from shape to shape; but the dizzying echo of Mrs. Flanders, Mrs. Mary, Mrs. Molly, and then Moll Flanders—resounding like the ringing of a bell and then blending together into one plain Moll Flanders—represents the coalescing of all the past versions of herself into one captured criminal. She says of her entry into confinement: "I was now fix'd indeed" (214) and this is the significance of her arrest: locked more firmly, it seems, than Proteus in the grip of Odysseus, she is held in a single shape—Moll Flanders—and no more quick changes or transformations seem possible. She can tell her Lancashire husband that she has been "taken in the Prison for one *Moll Flanders*, who was a famous successful Thief" (233) but that one name, written in the "Dead Warrant" (224), still identifies and condemns her.

The anticipation and dread of what happens to a criminal in Newgate can be seen as a manifestation of the obsessions that govern *Moll Flanders*, a figure that provides a literal rendering of what it means to be found out and identified. (It makes more sense at this point to ask why Defoe wrote so many books in the person of someone whose circumstances demanded that he or she avoid being discovered than to say that Moll is worried about being caught because she is a thief.) From the outset, Moll Flanders seeks to avoid being named or known. Even the preface tells the reader—who might expect Moll's life to be an open book—that the autobiography is a "private History" in which "the Names and other Circumstances of the Person are concealed" (3). Moll's first sentence declares that since her "True Name is so well known in the Records, or Registers at *Newgate*" she will write under the name of *"Moll Flanders"* until "I dare own who I have been, as well as who I am" (7). From the first pages on, Moll is obsessed with concealment, secrecy, privacy, anonymity, hiding from knowledge, withholding knowledge, refusing to acknowledge who she is; she lives in fear of being known, found out, uncovered, discovered, disclosed, undone, and revealed. In "Daniel Defoe and the Anxieties of Autobiography," Leo Braudy speaks of the "paradoxical mixture of reticence and revelation, self-protection and self-exposure" in Defoe's work.[33] In "The Displaced Self in the Novels of Daniel Defoe," Homer O. Brown also discusses the "double compulsion" of Defoe's characters "to expose and to conceal themselves."[34] Focusing mostly on *Robinson Crusoe*, he provides this formulation: "fear of the other, determining need for concealment; necessity, allurement of the world offering some form of completion to the self, determining the impulse to risk exposure."[35] Indeed, Moll's governess offers the first reading of this text of contradictory desires in Defoe: "A Fine Story!" she exclaims to Moll, "you would be Conceal'd and Discover'd both together" (137). I am suggesting that in *Moll Flanders* the need for concealment is primary and that discovery can be afforded only if it comes together with concealment; self-revelation is whenever possible not exposure, and if it is, it necessitates concealment. The need to conceal determines the character of any self-disclosure; and the interplay of concealment and exposure must be understood in the context of the theatrical character of Moll Flanders as well as Defoe's image of the self.

From her first experiences as a servant to a family, Moll finds herself in situations that call for concealment. Her affair with the brother makes her afraid that her secret will be made public—to the extent that she is even compelled to conceal from her lover her fear that their secret has been found out. She goes to the Mint in order to "be conceal'd" (53) and takes "Lodgings in a very private Place" (51) when there is no one "I durst Trust the Secret of my Circumstances to" (51). At this point she begins her series of disguises and ruses to delude prospective husbands; and she maintains that a woman has no power in looking for a husband because she is prevented from "enquiring into his Person or Character" (60) while the man can look into the woman's life without allowing himself to be seen.

Moll's disguises and frauds effectively screen her from the enquiring eyes of any suitor; when she is revealed as a counterfeit to her counterfeiting Lancashire husband, she rejoices that "I had not discovered myself or my Circumstances at all; no not so much as my Name" (117). Even when he "let me into the whole Story of his own Life" (124) Moll resolves "not to let him ever know my true Name, who I was, or where to be found" (125). The husband's position is to some degree analogous to that of the reader. Moll's reticence in this episode is not surprising since the one time when her identity was revealed proved to be a disaster. The revelation of one's true name—even to oneself—seems dangerous: Moll's mother-in-law tells a story that "requir'd telling her Name" (70) and this act of self-disclosure names Moll as the sister of her husband. Like Oedipus, she uncovers a secret (previously unknown to everyone) that names and identifies her—and dooms her present life; yet Moll's impulse at the discovery of incest is to blind others, not herself. She enters a period of great anxiety—"to reveal it . . . I cou'd not find wou'd be to any purpose, and yet to conceal it wou'd be next to impossible" (70)—and she fears that she will talk in her sleep. The words "reveal," "secret," "conceal," and "tell" punctuate every page until she allows the story to be drawn out of her so she can leave Virginia and start a new life in England. Moll and her husband agree "he should pretend to have an Account that I was Dead in *England*" (82). In or out of Newgate, being named and known seems to mean death for Moll Flanders; at the least it means abandoning one life and beginning another.

Twenty years later in the narrative, Virginia is the scene of the same dilemma for Moll. She is curious to see her husband-brother "if it was possible to do so without his seeing me" (251); fortunately for Moll, he is indeed blind but she seeks the same privileged point of view in seeing her son. She can mask herself temporarily but she can't decide "in what manner I should make myself known, or whether I should ever make myself known, or no" (253). Her fear of revealing herself to her son is related to the concealment of her past from her present husband—and from a wider audience as well: "It was not a Story, as I thought that would bear telling . . . and it was impossible to search into the bottom of the thing without making it Publick all over the Country, as well who I was, as what I now was also" (254).

Publishing the story of her past and present selves to her husband would lead to making herself public all over the country. It is no coincidence that Moll goes on to boast that although some say that women are not able "to keep a Secret, my Life is a plain Conviction to me of the contrary"; then to reflect upon people who are obliged to talk in their sleep and disclose their most secret crimes; and then to remark that it is not an "unnecessary Digression" to discuss "some People being oblig'd to disclose the greatest Secrets" since "publishing this Account of my Life" is supposed to warn and instruct "every Reader" (255). Recounting her fear of making her self public, allowing her story to be known, reminds Moll of her present act of publishing and disclosure. She feels called upon to remind her reader of the moral justification for making her adventures public; people don't publish themselves— appear before the eyes of the world—without a good reason, or compulsion, or disguise.

Besides the secrets which Moll occasionally allows to be coaxed out of her, there are two major scenes in which she truthfully tells her story to someone. How can we account for these

autobiographical disclosures, considering Moll's apparent agree-
ment with Roxana that "Secrets shou'd never be open'd, without
evident Utility"?[36] The first scene of autobiography takes place with
the governess, with whom Moll has lodged to give birth to one of
her several inconvenient yet forgettable children. Although Moll
claims "that I am not in any pain about being seen, or being publick
or conceal'd" (127), this is exactly the opposite of what is true; and
she is attracted by the governess' promise that "I do not desire to pry
into those things" (126). She offers Moll the privilege of seeing
without being seen: "tho' I do not enquire after you, you may
enquire after me" (127). Yet after Moll has had her child, which the
governess arranges to conceal, the governess begins to pressure Moll
to tell her story. At first Moll insists that it is impossible for her "to
commit the Secret to any Body" (134) but eventually, as the governess insists that she could be "trusted with the greatest Secrets of this
Nature, that it was her business to Conceal every thing," Moll
resolves to "unbosome myself to her" (134). She writes: "*In short,*
she had such a bewitching Eloquence, and so great a power of
Perswasion, that there was no concealing any thing from her" (134).[37]

The minister at Newgate, who shares Moll's second
scene of self-disclosure, has similarly irresistible rhetorical skills.
After he importunes Moll to discover her secrets, his inquiries finally "unlock'd all the Sluices of my Passions: He broke into my
very Soul by it; and I unravell'd all the Wickedness of my Life to
him: In a word, I gave him an Abridgement of this whole History; I
gave him the Picture of my Conduct for 50 Years in Miniature"
(226). Even if we didn't know about Moll's anticonfessional temperament, the language here would suggest the violence of a rape,
or at least a coercive seduction. The minister does not share
the female bond that eventually joins the governess with Moll, as
Roxana is joined with Amy. What sort of readers do the minister
and the governess represent?

What is remarkable about these scenes—indeed, what
allows them to take place—is that they don't really represent disclosure. Moll tells the governess that "I cou'd not speak of it to any

one alive" and the governess' response includes the claim that "to unfold my self to her was telling it to no Body; that she was silent as Death" (134). When revealing herself implies no revelation, when the other who demands knowledge becomes nobody at all, Moll can afford to tell her story. Accordingly, the minister convinces Moll to tell all by insisting "that whatever I said to him should remain with him, and be as much a Secret as if it was known only to God and myself; and that he desir'd to know nothing of me" (226). Moll's secret will remain a secret, as if she had told it to no one. (She is not called upon to confess to God, that unseen spectator whose presence is rarely alluded to in this supposedly religious book.) Confession is possible when it seems to speak to no one; exposure is neutralized by the pretense that there is no spectator to one's self-display.

We can see that theater and obsession with concealment make sense of each other in *Moll Flanders*. Moll lives in constant fear of being known, identified, recognized, found out; play-acting protects the self from being known. Disguise and impersonation offer a shield to sight; they provide identities that Moll can afford to expose, names she can afford to speak. Furthermore, besides offering a false appearance to the world, Moll's dramatic construction of the self undermines the notion that there really is a single, uniform self underneath the dizzying accumulation of false identities and changing appearances. Whenever Moll is named or revealed—or merely in danger of identification—the assumption of a new identity allows her to abandon her known self and to replace herself in new privacy and concealment, at a safe distance from sight and recognition. On this stage raising the curtain means lowering the veil. Acting allows one to declaim and disclaim oneself simultaneously, to appear before spectators without being seen. Thus Moll Flanders revels in the conditions of theater that so alarmed Prynne, Gosson, and other Puritan moralists; one might say they agreed on the meaning of theater but not on its value. While the Puritan antitheatricalists demanded that people be "such in show, as they are in truth," that "every man must show himselfe outwardly to be such as in deed he is," Moll's philosophy is expressed in her exclamation: "O! what a felicity is it to Mankind . . . that they cannot see into the Hearts of one another!" (142).

In an age when sceptics were insisting on the distance and difference that make other minds unknowable, Moll Flanders embraces the epistemological void that turns selves into texts that must be deciphered and interpreted. Yet such a void is not enough: lest the signs of the self should prove too legible, the self must present a counterfeit text, a fiction that stands as a mask to those who would read it. In fact, despite the difference in their moral views, Moll Flanders' position comes close to the stance that Shaftesbury took in the decade before Defoe's romances. We saw that the self as it is constructed in Shaftesbury's writings is a series of personations and impersonations set into play by the dramatic method of philosophy; yet in order to take a form that can bear publication, it must find the guise of an outward character that can withstand its theatrical position before the eyes of the world. As a mask or a fictive role, a manner of writing that will preserve a curtain or veil, it can speak and remain silent. Moll, too, divides herself into an outer character which protects the self by acting as a screen to spectators and an inner self which finally appears as a character to be personated—a series of parts and persons. The same dialectic of theater as exposure and theater as mask that we saw in Shaftesbury's work seems to operate in Defoe's text; although in *Moll Flanders* theater seems to serve the cause of concealment and protection more than it threatens to expose the self on the stage of the world. Unlike *Roxana*, *Moll Flanders* represents a stage in Defoe's work when theater responds to rather than creates anxiety.

Moll Flanders' control of the resources and conditions of theater help explain how she can write her autobiography. We saw that in her narrative Moll can bring herself to tell her story only when it feels like no one is listening. Her memoir is dressed in a costume which conceals her true name and identity; yet how can she avoid a sense of exposure in revealing herself to a reader whose presence is often evoked? We should recall that Moll's confession to the minister follows an experience of repentance and religious conversion. When Moll sees her former husband arrive at Newgate, she begins to reflect upon her past life until she is seized with abhorrence and: "in a word, I was perfectly chang'd, and become another Body" (220). We are not meant to read this as a simile; in the rhetoric of religious conversion, Moll has become another person. We should also recall now that before Moll tells her story to the governess, she describes herself as being as comforted with the woman's assurances of concealment that "I was quite another Body" (127). Autobiography becomes possible for Moll when she becomes another body, when she in effect is telling someone else's story. She narrates from the standpoint of a new identity about the life of a self (the lives of many selves) she has left behind. In the same manner Roxana announces at the beginning of her autobiography that she intends "to give my own Character . . . as if I was speaking of another-body."[38] This is a retrospective version of the *dédoublement* by which Shaftesbury multiplies and divides himself in his dramatic method.

At this point we can recognize the dramatic method inherent in the structure of autobiographical literature of conversion. Defoe has underlined both the problem and the possibilities of this form in the preface to *Moll Flanders*: "We cannot say indeed, that this History is carried on quite to the End of the Life of this famous *Moll Flanders*, as she calls her self, for no Body can write their own Life to the full End of it, unless they can write it after they are dead" (6). The structure of conversion allows one to tell the full story of one's life because one is, in a sense, already dead—although also reborn, with a new life and new body. Saul becomes Paul. Conversion (or its parody or imitation) allows one to put a period to one's life, a point of retrospection from which one can look back on a completed narrative.[39] This is a principle of autobiography: John Freccero has written of Dante: "The experience of conversion for Dante is at the same time the experience of writing the novel of the self, just as the novel of the self depends for its very existence on the conversion which is its subject matter."[40] Joyce paints his self-portrait "as a young man" who looks forward to an image of himself looking back. Flaubert, in posing Frédéric on a riverbank considering his own death, offers a figure for himself looking back to a former self: "il voyait son cadavre flottant sur l'eau."[41]

Moll Flanders can tell her story (in its novel form and in its abridgement) because she writes from beyond a type of death—a death which she dies many times in the course of the book.[42] Defoe recognized that the structure of autobiography and the literature of conversion is also acted out by the theater; and that theater could be turned into a repetitive narrative structure in which an actual religious conversion would represent only one change of identity in a series of impersonations, disguises, and transformations. Passing from role to role, changing identities as if they were costumes, Moll Flanders seems to enact a cycle of death and regeneration. She characterizes her reprieve as "coming back as it were into Life again" (228). Her joy at this rebirth brings her "a real transport" (229) which is followed by actually being "Transported" (230) to Virginia: a virgin state where "we should look back on all our past Disasters" and "live as new People in a new World" (238). In this Eden for the fallen, they have the world before them: a new world, at least to them, where they will become new people. Yet this new land, which sounds like it's located somewhere between autobiography and heaven, is just another stage for new identities and impersonations. Eventually Moll will find it necessary to conceal herself and to leave Virginia and return again "as from another Place, and in another Figure" (257). The transport of conversion and the transport of criminal exile are only manifestations of the metamorphoses enacted continually by the theatrical character of the narrative and its subject.

I would like to end this chapter by looking at one more figure that Defoe provides for the versions and conversions that constitute the self. This context can help us to understand what is otherwise one of the most bizarre and puzzling episodes in *Moll Flanders*. The story is simple: one day as Moll walks down the street with the hope of looting a burning house, a feather bed flies out of a window and lands on top of her, knocking her to the ground. Defoe is famous for his verisimilitude, so perhaps incidents like this often occurred in seventeenth-century London; but why does it happen in this book, for the space of a brief paragraph? The event, Moll tells us, "almost put a Period to my Life" (174), in other words, ended the story of her life; and in fact, lying unconscious and ignored, her limbs no doubt sticking out from beneath the feather bed like a character in a silent film comedy, Moll "lay like one Dead" (174). In another sentence, however, no simile appears: the weight of the bed "beat me down, and laid me dead for a while" (174). Dead? For a while?

It is no coincidence that this story follows Moll's account of her impersonation of Gabriel Spencer and the events that "put an end to this Life" (168), nor that it occurs immediately before Moll's entrance into the theatrical world of Bartholomew Fair. The passage stands as a figure for Moll's passages between incarnations throughout the book. Here she spells out what happens in the rest of her story: repeatedly, Moll dies and then gets up again, resurrects herself. Each new identity lasts as long as it is useful as a disguise, as long as Moll can't be held to one shape. If she is named—by her mother or in a list of criminals to be hanged—she dies for a while and then becomes another person. This passing from part to part occurs, of course, as that character we know as Defoe conceals himself behind the mask of Moll Flanders—one role in a long series of impersonations. For both Defoe and the character he poses as a figure for himself, theater makes possible the publication of the self before the eyes of the world. In the reading of *Roxana* which follows, we will see what happens when the self becomes pinned down and theatricality represents an unbearable sense of exposure.

CHAPTER 6

Roxana and the Theater
of Reading

IN 1724, two years after the appearance of *Moll Flanders*, Defoe published the narrative that is commonly known as his last novel: *The Fortunate Mistress: or, a History of the Life and Vast Variety of Fortunes of Mademoiselle de Beleau, afterwards called the Countess de Wintselsheim in Germany Being the Person known by the Name of the Lady Roxana in the time of Charles II.* As this list of titles and names suggests, *Roxana*—and I will want to consider what it means that this single name has emerged as the book's title—follows the pattern of *Moll Flanders:* through a succession of fortunes, misfortunes, husbands, and "scenes" of life, a heroine who considers herself a whore passes between names, identities, personations, and impersonations. Posing as an editor's version of the autobiography of a woman who writes from the other side of repentance ("as if I was speaking of another-body"),[1] *Roxana* rehearses both specific episodes and the general narrative structure of *Moll Flanders.*

Set among royalty and the rising mercantile class that Defoe saw could replace royalty, rather than among Newgate rogues who sought to live like gentlemen and gentlewomen, *Roxana* might be considered an upper-class sequel to *Moll Flanders.* What is most important from the perspective of this chapter is that the two narratives share a preoccupation with the terms and figure of theater. In the preface to *Roxana*, the "dressing up the Story in worse Cloaths than the Lady . . . prepar'd it for the World" is called a "Performance" (1).[2] We are told that when "Scenes of Crime" represent vice "painted in its Low-priz'd Colours, 'tis not to make People in love with it, but to expose it" (2)—a formulation that both pictures the text as spectacle and evokes the traditional defense of the theater. Roxana herself refers to the "History of my Actings upon the Stage of Life" (75) and "the vast Variety of Scenes that I had acted my Part in" (200). Indeed, references to scenes, acting, cues, and parts, as well as episodes in which looking, being seen, dissembling, costumes, and disguises figure prominently, recur throughout the text.[3]

I do not mean to suggest, however, that *Roxana* is merely *Moll Flanders* dressed up in new clothes. Indeed, I would argue that it is the manner in which the problem of theater is acted out in the two narratives that accounts for their fundamental difference. *Roxana* represents a shift in focus regarding the terms and conditions of theater. *Moll Flanders* is a celebration of theater's potential: Moll manipulates roles, masks, disguises, and impersonations not only to protect the self but also to constitute the self. Theater as concealment responds to and compensates for theater as exposure. In *Roxana* we become witnesses to the problem of theatricality itself: the threatening relation formed between spectator and spectacle. *Roxana* tells the story of the increasing theatricalization of a character's stance before the eyes of the world—and the perception of that condition as a problem which must be counteracted, avoided, or eliminated. In this chapter I will examine how theater for Defoe ceases to represent a screen which blocks the sight and will to knowledge of others, becoming instead a stage on which a curtain is thrown open and an actor is exposed to an audience who would see and know too much. I will argue that our place as readers of a veiled autobiography becomes a primary concern of *Roxana* as the theatrical aspect of the book's published and public status comes increasingly into play.

We have considered Moll Flander's desire for a privileged point of view in relation to the world: to see without the risk of being seen. This is Robinson Crusoe's desire, as he constructs enclosures for himself on his island; it also describes the position of H. F., whose relentless curiosity compels him to observe plague-stricken London. The difficulty of maintaining such a position, safe from the eyes of others, is repeatedly dramatized in *Roxana*. Early in the narrative, the sense of being watched is built into the structure of most scenes by the presence of Amy: Roxana's maid, confidante, and intimate companion. Amy stands as a witness to these scenes, even to Roxana's seduction. Roxana notes that her landlord-suitor is not at all affected by Amy's presence: "he made no Scruple to kiss me, and say all these things to me before her, nor had he car'd one Farthing if I would have let him Lay with me, to have had *Amy* there too all Night" (36). However, whether the landlord's class bias denies Amy standing as a person and consequently as a spectator, or whether the presence of a witness is a source of eroticism for him, it becomes clear that Roxana does not share her suitor's attitude. After she agrees to enter into a common-law marriage with him (which she regards as her fall) Roxana compels her new husband and Amy to go to bed together before her eyes. A detailed description shows Roxana stripping the maid of her clothing and pushing her into bed. This scene is usually read as a sign of Roxana's depravity⁴ but Roxana suggests another reading:

> Had I look'd upon myself as a Wife, you cannot suppose I would have been willing to have let my Husband lye with my Maid, much less, before my Face, for I stood-by all the while; but as I thought myself a Whore, I cannot say but that it was something design'd in my Thoughts, that my Maid should be a Whore too, and should not reproach me with it. (47)

Looking upon herself as a whore, Roxana fears the point of view of her witness, Amy; so she reverses the situation and becomes a bystander to Amy's identical act. As a beholder, she can look upon Amy as a whore, transforming her from an audience into another actress who plays the same part. This episode prefigures Amy's role as Roxana's alter-ego in the narrative; indeed, it explains the necessity of that role, from Roxana's point of view. As a reflection of Roxana—"*like* Mistress, *like* Maid" (83)—Amy becomes a version of the self rather than an other who watches the self.

However, even if Roxana does not have to worry about the regard of Amy, she still must contend with the eyes of the world.

During her stay in Paris, Roxana's affair with a prince necessitates that she stay "wholly within-Doors" and pretend that she has gone back to England. If not, "the World wou'd conclude I was maintain'd by somebody, and wou'd be indefatigable to find out the Person; so that he shou'd have Spies peeping at him, every time he went out or in" (66–67). These spies are not some particular foreign or political agents but rather "the People of *Paris*"—who, "especially the Women, are the most busie and impertinent Enquirers into the Conduct of their Neighbours . . . . When deep Intrigues are close and shy,/The GUILTY are the first that spy" (67). When Roxana enters into another "Confinement" (76) during a pregnancy, she has an old woman attendant dismissed because "she look'd so like a Spy"; she insists that besides some English nurses ("not one of [whom] should know who he was, or perhaps, ever see his Face" [77]) and the prince himself, no other "Witnesses" (77) are necessary. All of these situations require discretion and concealment for reasons of decorum, but Roxana's recurrent fear of being spied upon—as well as Defoe's proliferation of scenes in which Roxana must fear being known or seen—is motivated by more than a concern for public reputation.

It is well known, of course, that Defoe himself acted as a spy for Harley's government while the union with Scotland was being considered; he also advocated a secret police force for Britain. Defoe knew from experience how spies turn the world to theater not only by becoming actors, posing under false identities, but also by becoming spectators who would watch others without being seen themselves. Roxana imagines a "World" of spies; consequently, she conceals herself and, as she does with Amy, she tries to act as an unseen spectator rather than as an unseeing spectacle. This is her response when she discovers her first husband in Paris: keeping her fan before her face, "so that he cou'd not know me," she positions herself where she might "take a full View of his Dress, that I might farther inform myself" (85). Soon after, she positions herself in a window to watch her husband participate in the "most glorious show" of the king's guards; she emphasizes her ability to "take as

critical a View, and make as nice a Search among them, as I pleas'd"
(86).[5] Then, having become a spectator to her husband in a literal
sense, she sends Amy to spy upon him. At this point the text is
transformed into a dialogue to show us the theatrical exchange in
which Amy sees through the husband's misrepresentations but presents a story which is "all Hypocrisie, but acted so to the Life, as
perfectly deceiv'd him" (91). Roxana resolves that in order to avoid a
"fatal Discovery," "all that I had now to do, was to keep myself out
of his Sight" (94). However, it is not enough that her husband can't
see her or find her out. She decides to place him under constant
surveillance:

> I found out a Fellow, who was compleatly qualified for the Work of a
> Spy . . . and he was especially employ'd, and order'd to haunt him
> *as a Ghost*; that he should scarce let him be ever out of his Sight; he
> perform'd this to a Nicety, and fail'd not to give me a perfect Journal
> of all his Motions, from Day to Day. (94)

It is not clear how this retrospective account of her husband's daily
actions—which Roxana says she reads every week—helps her avoid
the man she would shun "as we wou'd shun a Spectre" (95); but by
appointing a proxy to haunt him like a ghost or a spy—an unseen
observer—she can act to avoid his sight: "never to see him, and,
above all, to keep him from seeing me" (96). In this way Roxana
becomes both a reader and a spectator of her husband's life; the
theatrical perspective of the spy allows her both to conceal herself
and to expose a potential spectator.

However, at the same time that Roxana is acting to
ensure her privileged point of view in relation to the world, to
counteract spies by spying on others, behind the closed doors of her
bedroom and parlor she enters a stage in which she becomes increasingly theatricalized. Her stage-manager, director, and primary
spectator is the prince, who begins his affair with her by turning her
to a spectacle:

> He stood up, and taking me by the Hand, led me to a large Looking-
> Glass, which made up the Peir in the Front of the Parlour; Look

there, Madam, *said he*; Is it fit that Face, pointing to my Figure in
the Glass, should go back to *Poictou?* . . . and with that, he took me
in his Arms, and kissing me twice, told me, he wou'd see me again,
but with less Ceremony. (59–60)

In a moment Roxana is shown to herself and framed: presumably
she sees a picture of both herself as spectacle and the prince, looking
at her within the mirror, directing her regard to the glass where her
face is turned to a figure. After this command performance, the
prince does indeed see Roxana again, although not with less ceremony. The scene before the looking-glass prefigures the scenes of
intimacy and exhibition which follow, in particular one in which
the prince requests Roxana to display the best of the many clothes
he has provided for her. Roxana willingly outfits herself, and after
offering her readers a description of her dress, she relates: "In this
Figure I came to him, out of my Dressing-Room, which open'd
with Folding-Doors into his Bed-chamber." With this brilliant detail Defoe creates a gesture which transports Roxana from her dressing room onto the stage: the doors which unfold to reveal her posing
in a stunning dress. At this dramatic entrance the prince sits "as one
astonish'd, a good-while, looking at me, without speaking a Word"
(71): a silent audience to a spectacular dumb-show. There is more
voyeurism and exhibitionism in this bedroom than there would be if
Amy or some other witness were present.

   This sense of being watched is compounded by Roxana's
reflections on the scene both at the time and in the retrospective
perspective of her narrative. Roxana is moved to tears by the prince's
response, and she explains that she cries tears of joy: "It is impossible for me to see myself snatch'd from the Misery I was fallen into,
and . . . to contain the Satisfaction of it" (72). As in the scene with
the mirror, as Roxana appears before an admirer she is lead to
contemplate an image of herself; and as she represents herself looking at herself, she reflects on how these scenes will appear to another audience: the reader. "It wou'd look a little too much like a
Romance here," she writes, "to repeat all the kind things he said to
me, on that Occasion; but I can't omit one Passage" (72). Defoe
ironically acknowledges the frame of his romance and the presence

of his audience as Roxana draws attention to both the self-drama-tization inherent in the scene itself and the self-consciousness which leads her to refer to an exchange between herself and the prince as a "Passage"—as if she sees it as a text before she actually writes it.

It is appropriate, then, that the passage dramatized in the text by Roxana underlines that the prince himself experiences Roxana's self-presentation as if it were theater. Moving to dry her tears but hesitating, "as if he was afraid to deface something" (72), the prince responds to Roxana's aspect as if he were facing a theatri-cal illusion. Ironically, Roxana reacts to the supposition that she is wearing makeup with some indignation: "Have you kiss'd me so often, and don't you know whether I am Painted, or not? Pray let your Highness satisfie yourself, that you have no Cheats put upon you; for once let me be vain enough to say, I have not deceiv'd you with false Colours" (72). When Moll Flanders speaks of deceiving others with false colors she speaks figuratively; Roxana speaks liter-ally. The situation feels so much like theater that the prince must be convinced that Roxana's beauty is real and not made up. However, this is accomplished by a "Demonstration" (72, 73), a show in which Roxana washes her face with hot water to prove that what the prince sees is not a false representation. Theater here has a totally different effect than it does in *Moll Flanders*: exposed rather than concealed, Roxana must follow her costumed display with a dem-onstration that she is uncovered. Theater (as false representation, impersonation, or disguise) has been replaced in these scenes with theatricality: display and exposure before the eyes of a beholder.

The climax of Roxana's exhibition occurs after the prince is convinced that he has not been imposed upon by the woman who poses for him. Roxana narrates that after "taking his View of me as I walk'd from one End of the Room to the other," the prince approaches her, clasps her neck, and "in half a Minute more, led me to a Peir-Glass, and behold, I saw my Neck clasp'd with a fine Necklace of Diamonds. . . . I was all on fire with the Sight" (73). The prince rehearses the theatrical gesture with which he first framed Roxana in a mirror, this time ornamenting and underlining

the figure he sets off as an object of sight. Roxana herself is en-
flamed with the sight, as if she were looking at someone else. The
episode is both a confirmation and a culmination of the ka-
leidoscopic images of theatricality that have been multiplying in the
text. What is perhaps most remarkable, however, is the "behold"
which leaves behind the preterite of the narrative and directly addresses the reader. This is no mere figure of speech, no merely
formulaic pause that punctuates the rhythm of Roxana's exclamation. Just as the prince told Roxana to "Look there" in the first scene
with the mirror, the narrative instructs us to "behold" as if the scene
were occurring before our eyes. Once again, the framing of Roxana
as a spectacle includes a gesture toward our presence as spectators of
the dramatic performance and representations of the book. As readers, we are like Amy watching in the bedroom or perhaps like the
attendant who looked like a spy; except Roxana can neither switch
places with us nor dismiss us.

        As Roxana's narrative proceeds, her increasing the-
atricalization seems to eclipse her fear of being seen. Returning to
England as a wealthy gentlewoman, she at first goes "Incognito"
(164) and leaves "the World to guess who or what I was, without
offering to put myself forward" (165). Soon, however, "dress'd to the
height of every Mode" and making "as gay a Show as I was able to
do . . . I understood that the Neighbours begun to be mighty inquisitive about me; as who I was?" (165–166). Such neighbors would
have made Moll Flanders rather anxious—and indeed, they troubled Roxana during her affair with the prince. Here, Roxana
responds by assuming a public "Posture" that "expos'd me to innu-
merable Visiters" (169) and by joining the "glorious Show" (172) of
the world of courtiers. "And now I began to act in a new Sphere"
(172), she writes, as she enters an arena of pure theatricality: a world
that looks like both a playhouse and a decadent court masque.
These scenes can be read as Defoe's Puritan exposé of aristocratic
corruption, meant to scandalize the reader and condemn Roxana

for embracing a world of immorality. I want to emphasize, however, the degree to which the scenes are described as theater; if there is an exposé here, it is primarily a story about Roxana's exposure and what it means to appear before the eyes of the public.[6]

No longer content to be a spectacle for one beholder, Roxana organizes a ball for her admirers. We are told that a gentleman has sent "a Sett of fine Musick from the Play-House" and that the male guests arrive "in Masquerade" (173). Roxana wonders with both excitement and embarrassment whether the king himself is present—but all of the gentlemen are concealed behind masks, seeing without being seen. These theatrical positions are further signaled to us by what we might call the "blocking" of the scene: as the guests arrive Roxana places herself in her drawing room "with the Folding-Doors wide open" (173). Then, when the company is assembled, she prepares to outdo the private spectacle that won her royal acclaim in Paris. First, she withdraws to dress herself "in the Habit of *a Turkish Princess*" (173); next she orders "the Folding-Doors to be shut for a Minute or two" in order to give the Ladies "a full View of my Dress" (174) but more importantly, to frame an especially spectacular entrance. As she is accompanied by a masked guest, "the Folding-Doors were flung open, and he led me into the Room: The Company were under the greatest Surprize imaginable; the very Musick stopp'd a-while to gaze" (175).

The moment of theater to which the prince was an astonished spectator is here repeated and magnified, as the same dramatic gesture introduces Roxana in another stunning dress. Here the folding doors reveal the costumed Roxana to a public audience—in a dazzling synecdoche even music is granted sight— and the conditions of the playhouse are reproduced, not merely evoked. After Roxana displays herself and gives directions that she will dance solo, "all the House rose up, and paid me a kind of a Compliment, by removing back every way to make me room" (175); in other words, rather than dancing with her, they remove themselves to create the psychological and physical distance that separates spectators from actors. At the conclusion of the dance (which is a counterfeit representation of a Turkish dance) the "Company clapp'd, and almost shouted" (176).

Roxana's role as a performer of a "Show" (176) staged in a public arena could not be more evident. The situation no longer merely seems like theater; it is theater. Furthermore, the effect of this theater is what we have come to see as pure theatricalization: Roxana's exotic costume, "unlac'd, and open-breasted, as if I had been in my Shift" (181), exposes rather than conceals or disguises. At the same time, Roxana's spectators (at least the men, the real audience of her performance) are masked and anonymous, hidden from sight and knowledge. Roxana dances with an admirer "who had no Name, *being all Mask'd*, nor would it have been allow'd to ask any Person's Name on such an Occasion" (174). By contrast, Roxana's face is as bare as it was in the scene with the prince: "I had no Mask, neither did I Paint" (180), she writes; and her dance is the occasion of her being named. As the crowd applauds, "one of the Gentlemen cry'd out, *Roxana! Roxana!* by ———, with an Oath; upon which foolish Accident I had the Name of *Roxana* presently fix'd upon me all over the Court End of Town, as effectually as if I had been Christen'd *Roxana*" (176). As if a parody of an oath sworn with God as a witness, this baptism in the presence of a theatricalizing audience *fixes* Roxana as Roxana, the name we still call her today. We know from *Moll Flanders* the threat of being named and fixed[7] and we will consider what it means for Roxana to be fixed with a name at this supremely dramatic moment. For now, however, it will be enough to see that this occasion names Roxana as an actress. Summarizing her public gatherings and performances, Roxana writes, "I was now in my Element" (181) and if there is any doubt what to call this element, Roxana herself characterizes it later in the book. Posing as someone else, she becomes an auditor to the story of her dance in the Turkish dress and she comments: "*I suppose*, your Lady was some *French* Comedian, *that is to say*, a Stage *Amazon*, that put on a counterfeit Dress to please the Company, such as they us'd in the Play of *Tamerlane*, at *Paris*" (289). Later, when she is accused of actually being Roxana, she protests: "Why,

wou'd you have me taken for an *Actress*, or a *French Stage-Player?*"
(294); and yet again, she objects "to be so liken'd to a publick
Mistress, or a Stage-Player" (303).[8] Roxana tells us how to read the
story of her masked ball, whether presented from the point of view
of the performer or the spectator or the reader. The circumstances
Roxana describes must be characterized as theatrical.

    I have suggested that such theatrical situations offer
none of the security provided by the dramatic roles, fictions, and
disguises of Moll Flanders. One might assume that the anxieties
about being seen displayed by Roxana are counteracted by the increasing pleasure she seems to take in appearing before admiring
beholders. This might be read in the context of the narrative's supposedly Puritan point of view as a sign of Roxana's depravity or at
least of the vanity that she dates as beginning with the prince's first
theatricalizing "Look there." However, we have been tracing an
emerging dialectic of exposure and concealment in *Roxana*. Even
in the episodes surrounding Roxana's acts of exhibition in Paris, we
saw her attempts to hide from witnesses and to regain the position of
an unseen spy or spectator in relation to others—as if she were
seeking to compensate for her exposure. Not surprisingly, then,
Roxana's performances in London lead directly to acts of concealment which indicate that either despite or as a result of her theatrical behavior, she still wants to avoid being seen.[9]
    The first act of concealment we witness in these scenes
is directed toward us: in the paragraph immediately following the
description of the second ball, we read, "There is a Scene which
came in here, which I must cover from humane Eyes or Ears; for
three Years and about a Month, *Roxana* liv'd retir'd . . . with a
Person, which Duty, and private Vows, obliges her not to reveal, at
least, not yet" (181). Writing about herself in the third person, regarding the role of "*Roxana*" as if she were a spectator "speaking of
another-body" (6), Roxana covers her story just as she and her lover
retired from the public. Of course Roxana's secrecy is meant to

convince us that she is speaking of the king, but this act of self-censorship is repeated when, in speaking of a subsequent affair, Roxana says that the vice of a particular lord "is not fit to write of" (199). Elsewhere, referring to some accounts that might justify her conduct "if I cou'd suffer myself to publish them," she writes: "that Part of the Story will not bear telling; so I must leave it, and proceed" (207). After committing herself to exposing to the world her past vice in a narrative that combines autobiographical self-revelation and social exposé, and after detailing scenes of both private and public self-exposure, Roxana develops a new shyness in relation to the reading public—before whom she must publish her accounts of her private and public acts. I will suggest that her reticence in this regard (a problem that we, as readers, will have to face again) is less a product of discretion or an attempt at titillation than a response to the position of being exposed before the eyes of the public.

Roxana's concern with the presence of witnesses and knowing beholders is revealed increasingly in the episodes that follow the ball scenes. At this point in the narrative, Roxana decides to search out the children she abandoned in her years of destitution; this requires secrecy since she resolves "not to discover myself to them, in the least" (188). She enacts these contradictory desires to act as a mother while not letting anyone know "that there was such a-body left in the World, as their Mother" (188) by sending Amy as her surrogate. Posing under a false name and various fictions in order to "blind [them], and provide against farther Enquiries" (193), Amy plays the benefactor to two of Roxana's children. This screen is designed to allow Roxana to see her children (if indirectly) without being seen, just as she managed to spy on her husband in Paris. By accident, however, it is discovered that a maid in Roxana's household is actually another of Roxana's daughters. Both Amy and Roxana react with the same anxiety that Moll Flanders exhibits upon seeing her grown son in Virginia; however, whereas Moll uses her ability to disguise herself and appear in new figures to resolve her conflicting desires for revelation and concealment, Roxana finds her situation more difficult to control. Worried that her decadent life has been witnessed by her daughter, just as she found it intolera-

ble to be seduced by the landlord before the eyes of her young maid
Amy, Roxana seems to fantasize the primal scene from the point of
view of a parent: "tho' I was much out of her Sight, yet she might
have had the Curiosity to have peep'd at me, and seen me enough to
know me again, if I had discover'd myself to her" (198). The girl tells
Amy that the only time she saw Roxana was on "that publick Night
when she danc'd in the fine *Turkish* Habit, and then she was so
disguis'd, that I knew nothing of her afterwards" (206). If Roxana's
appearance before the public had indeed disguised rather than exposed her—if, in other words, we were reading *Moll Flanders*—the
story might have ended there. In any case, thinking "that I was not
known to her" (206), Roxana has her daughter sent away, to be
provided for by a surrogate arranged by the surrogate Amy.

   In these same pages following the scenes of the performances, as Roxana worries about being seen by both the reader and
her daughter, she tells of her desire "to be a little less publick" (185).
Concerned that she is too well known "not by my Name only, but by
my Character too" (208) and thinking about "putting a new Face
upon" her "Manner of Living" (207), she resolves to transform herself—to reform herself in a literal sense. Roxana thinks of moving to
another part of the city where she might "be as entirely conceal'd as
if I had never been known" and Amy instructs: "you must put off all
your Equipages . . . change your Liveries, nay, your own Cloaths,
and if it was possible, your very Face" (208). Roxana and Amy
imagine the sort of metamorphosis that made Moll Flanders the
greatest artist of her time: they propose to "transform ourselves into
a new Shape, all in a Moment" (209), hoping to erase all trace of the
figure who appeared in public under the name of Roxana by effect-
ing, in Amy's words, "a perfect entire Change of your Figure and
Circumstances, in one Day, and [you] shall be as much unknown,
Madam, in twenty-four Hours, as you wou'd be in so many Years"
(209). To enact this scheme Roxana moves to the house of a Quaker
woman in another part of town where she feels safely "remote from
the Eyes of all that ever had seen me" (211). In addition, she tries
out the Quaker dress "to see whether it wou'd pass upon me for a
Disguise" (211); according to Amy, it is a "perfect Disguise" that

makes her look "quite another-body" (211). In this costume, and in the coach that she calls "a farther Disguise to me," Roxana boasts "there was not a Quaker in the Town look'd less like a Counterfeit than I did" (213). In a world in which people depend upon reading exterior signs to identify other people, where social and even religious roles are equipped with recognizable costumes, Roxana can feel "compleatly conceal'd" dressed as a Quaker and "depend upon being not known" (213). Like Moll Flanders, Roxana describes a world in which both counterfeiters and "authentic" people are reduced to using the same conventional signs to represent and personate their identities. At this point Roxana would appear to have mastered Moll Flanders' use of theater as a means of counteracting the exposure of her past theatricality.

The reappearance of the Dutch merchant suggests that Roxana's web of concealment might be unraveled. She reacts to an accidental near-encounter with him in the same manner she reacted to the discovery of her first husband in Paris: she hides her face behind a fan so "he should not know me" (219). The Dutch merchant nonetheless tracks Roxana down; Roxana's description of the scene reveals the potential risk involved in the discovery of a past identity. As she stands hesitantly in one room, reluctant to face her former lover, the Quaker acts to effect her entrance: "on a sudden she unlocks the Folding-Doors, which look'd into the next Parlour, and throwing them open, There, says she, (ushering him in) *is the Person who, I suppose thou enquirest for*" (223). By this point in the narrative the significance of this dramatic gesture is clear: to be inquired after, found out, discovered, and revealed is to be placed on a stage or theatricalized. The Folding-Doors (which themselves seem to be capable of sight) flung open by the Quaker as she plays usher to the Dutch merchant return Roxana to past scenes of exposure. Indeed, husbands, as we are later told, "are inquisitive creatures, and love to enquire after any-thing they think is kept from them" (246).

However, Roxana manages to control the situation; she ends up marrying the merchant "privately" (243), in exchange for which she receives two new titles: two new names. When her husband finds out about her Turkish dress she agrees to appear in it for him on the condition that he never ask her "to be seen in it before Company" (247). Roxana seems capable of containing this limited exposure as she incorporates her husband into her retired life. With the help of her new identity, Roxana can look back on her past and reflect that her "Life of Crime was over" (243). She can feel like "a Passenger coming back from the *Indies*" (243). Like Robinson Crusoe and Moll Flanders after their protean transformations and religious conversions, Roxana appears to be converted and re-formed—as if brought back from the dead, as if transformed into a new shape—and she and her husband transport themselves to Holland to take up a new "contemplative" (264) life.

Chronologically, Roxana has reached the end of her story and at this point the narrative almost ends. If we were reading *Moll Flanders*, the book *would* end here with a gesture toward repentance and a new life in a new world. However, although Roxana might be countess of a carefully bounded space, we learn that she has bad dreams. We are told that she dreams continually of "Nothing but Apparitions of Devils and Monsters; falling into Gulphs, and off from steep and high Precipices" (264). Then, after complaining that she had no "Confessor" to whom she might "unbosom" (265) the secrets causing this sublime terror, Roxana says to the reader: "But I have not gone thorow the Story of my two Daughters: I was so in danger of being known by one of them, that I durst not see her, so as to let her know who I was; and for the other, I cou'd not well know how to see her, and own her, and let her see me" (265).

Like the patient in the psychiatrist's office who says, five minutes before the end of the hour, 'by the way, there's something I haven't mentioned,' Roxana returns to a story she has left out of her autobiography. Indeed, more than Defoe's other narratives, *Roxana* at times appears to have the nonlinear structure of a psychoanalysis. The narrative continually omits facts and events, fragments itself, goes back to retrace episodes which occurred simultaneously with previously related episodes, fills in pictures we didn't know were incomplete—in general, the text surprisingly often proceeds non-chronologically. It is as if Faulkner and not Defoe had designed the story's unfolding and gradual revision before our eyes. The story Roxana goes back to tell is in fact never told completely. At crucial moments Roxana holds back disclosure, saying, "But this Tragedy requires a longer Story than I have room for here" (302), or referring to an act "of which I cannot enter into the Particulars here" (328). Finally, the same reticence in regard to the reader we saw displayed before seems to compel Roxana to write: "I can say no more now" (329); and after a brief hint of disaster the narrative cryptically breaks off, in what has been experienced as one of the most abrupt endings to a completed work in the history of English prose fiction. The reader can piece together a broken account, but one is left with a sense at the end of this story about the danger of being known and seen that he or she has been denied sight and knowledge.[10]

The story of Roxana's daughter has the suspense of a detective story and the anxiety of a nightmare. I would like to recall the basic outline of the story in order to emphasize the key terms in which Roxana casts the struggle between her daughter and herself. During the period when "the Masks and Balls were in Agitation" (198) and Roxana attempts to provide for her children through Amy and other surrogates, the daughter who by coincidence works in Roxana's house discovers that Amy is her benefactor. After concluding that Amy is her mother, she is led to reason back down the line of stand-ins all the way to Roxana: the woman she saw perform costumed in a Turkish dress on the night of the dance. Roxana, who has gone to great lengths to abandon and dispose of the identity of "Lady Roxana," "wou'd not have been seen, so as to be known by the Name of *Roxana*, no, not for ten Thousand Pounds" (271)—a figure which reveals the investment in remaining hidden on the part of one of Defoe's most canny financiers. However, the daughter's desire to inquire after Roxana and to find her out becomes relentless, and this "Search after me" (274) compels Roxana to advance her plans to leave the country. She decides to flee on a private ship "because I wou'd be sure not to go too publick" and "so as to take away all Possibility of being seen" (274). Her complaint about "the promiscuous Crowds" (275) on public vessels recalls the "promiscuous Crowd" (178) she described at her masked ball—thereby indicating the type of exposure she fears. In fact, by another coincidence, while visiting the ship she is introduced to a friend of the captain's wife who turns out to be the spectator from the ball who wants to name her as Roxana: her daughter. Calling her identity "the only valuable Secret in the World to me," Roxana writes, "if the Girl knew me, I was undone; and to discover any Surprize or Disorder, had been to make her know me, or guess it, and discover herself" (276). Roxana acts to counterfeit her voice and to prevent the girl from "having a full Sight of me" (278). She escapes without having been named and recognized, but she suspects that she has been suspected.

Roxana resolves that her daughter "should never see me again" (279) and henceforth a mad pursuit begins. The girl pays a call on Roxana and the Quaker and tells the story about the time "Lady Roxana" performed in the Turkish dress. Even more anxious than Moll Flanders was when she hears her past life narrated to her by the neighbor in Virginia—for Roxana is being confronted with her past theatricality—Roxana wonders "whether she knew me or no; or, *in short,* whether I was to be expos'd or not expos'd" (285). The scenes of past and present exposure come together when the Quaker reveals that Roxana (that is, the Quaker's boarder) also owns a Turkish dress. This reprise of the scene of Roxana's theatricality seems to confirm the daughter's suspicion that she had *"found it out"* (293). Exposed (perhaps) as the woman who was exposed before the eyes of the world, Roxana decides to flee her private quarters in London, despite her fear of going anywhere "where there were so many Eyes that had seen me before" (301). The girl, *"who was now my Plague"* (302), chases her from town to town and house to house in a game that requires detective work and the use of spies. Rehearsing the tactics she employed to avoid the sight of her former husband, Roxana has the Quaker act as her "faithful SPY" (309) and *"Trusty Agent"* (323). The girl hires a "SPY to watch" (318) the Quaker's house which causes Roxana to stay away since "I cou'd not think of being there under Spies, and afraid to look out-of-Doors" (323).

Finally, Amy acts again as a surrogate for the woman she repeatedly has doubled throughout the book; she decides to put an end to this diabolical game of "hide and seek" and (apparently) she murders the daughter. Roxana never acknowledges or admits any details concerning the daughter's fate. In fact, when Amy speaks of her desire to murder the girl, Roxana "bade her get out of my Sight . . . I wou'd never see her Face more. . . . I bade her get out of my Sight" (313)—as if she were playing King Lear but wanted to banish Cordelia and Kent and then blame the faithful servant for having disowned and condemned the daughter. In any case, the daughter disappears; but ironically, this does not stop Roxana's nightmare of being pursued by an unseen spectator. Just as the spy she hired in France was ordered "to haunt" her husband "*as a Ghost*" (94) and just as she shunned her husband "as we wou'd shun a Spectre" (95), Roxana imagines that her relentless spectator now pursues her as a specter: the ghost as spy rather than the spy as ghost. She writes: "she haunted my Imagination, if she did not haunt the House; my Fancy show'd her me in a hundred Shapes and Postures; sleeping or waking, she was with me" (325). Cast as both Macbeth and Lady Macbeth, Roxana abruptly closes the book.

Ostensibly, the nightmarish struggle at the end of the book occurs because Roxana can't bear the disgrace of being revealed (to her children, the Dutch merchant, and the world) as a notorious and scandalous mistress. I have been suggesting, however, another way in which to read both the inordinate anxiety of the text and the abrupt conclusion that not only ended *Roxana* but put a period to the prolific five-year stage that produced Defoe's most famous narrative fictions.[11] By now the threat posed by Roxana's daughter should be evident: the girl stands as one who would inquire after Roxana, to find her out, to discover her, to uncover her past identity, to name her, and to know her. Literally and figuratively, she threatens to see Roxana: to expose her. Yet she does not seek to reveal Roxana as the mother reduced to poverty in the early pages of the book, or even as a whore; she seeks the only Roxana she knows: the woman in the Turkish dress who performed one public night in a highly theatrical scene. She wants to name Roxana with the name that brands her as a stage actress, the name that was fixed upon her by her public audience at the zenith of her theatrical display. The daughter stands as a member of that audience. She embodies Roxana's audience and her presence—even the prospect of her presence—brings to light not Roxana's past decadence but the shame of theatricality: an exposure before the eyes of the world that has become intolerable.

Roxana has made every effort to act as Moll Flanders would and transform herself into a new person and shape, to avoid the eyes of all who saw her as "Roxana." But the daughter re-institutes the scene of Roxana's theatricality. She recalls it, rehearses it, and represents it by narrating the story of the performance— thereby creating a new audience for the dance, an audience that includes Roxana. By establishing that Roxana owns an "identical" Turkish dress, this story reveals and identifies Roxana as the actress the daughter witnessed. The dress that exposed Roxana on stage becomes a prop that literally and figuratively uncovers her; it is the symbol and telltale sign of her inescapable theatricality. However, the daughter's reenactment of the scene of Roxana's exposure is most threatening because it is present and continuing, not merely retro-spective or retroactive. The daughter's reappearance and pursuit, her relentless search to see and know her mother, thrust Roxana into a new and agonizing theatricality: a nightmare in which she is seen, revealed, exposed, and spied on, in which she can't close the folding doors that have been flung so widely open. The daughter is an audience that will not respect the boundaries of its place, that will not go home after the performance is over. She stands as an audience which pursues its position and role with (and like) a fury, refusing to let the players off the stage.

Roxana further characterizes the threat posed by the daughter by describing one of the meetings with her as an experi-ence that "put me upon the Rack" (281). I suggest that Roxana means more by this figure of speech than an image of torture. Earlier in her story, when she is unjustly accused of murder, the

Dutch merchant explains to her the danger of being put on the rack: "If they come to have you to the Rack, *said he*, they will make you confess you did it yourself, whether you did it or no . . . ." He continues: "the most innocent People in the World have been forc'd to confess themselves Guilty of what they never heard of, much less, had any Hand in" (118–119).

Being with the girl is like being put on the rack: that which would force one to confess. Roxana's situation is especially precarious because she does have a hidden history she doesn't want revealed. We saw that Moll Flanders can overcome her secrecy and confess only when she is assured she is telling her story to no one; and then she uses her conversion to leave her exposed self behind. Amy plays the role for Roxana that the Governess plays for Moll Flanders: an alter ego who does not really seem like an other. But unlike Moll, Roxana meets no minister capable of unlocking her soul. She declines to go to Catholic confession and she remarks that, unlike others, the fear of death does not prompt her to confess her sins. Her "Maxim" is *that Secrets shou'd never be open'd, without evident Utility*" (326). The girl would force Roxana to tell her story, name herself, confess her past—everything that Roxana is increasingly reluctant to do. Unable to manipulate disguise and protean transformation as well as Moll Flanders can, she seems unable to counteract the potentially theatrical aspect of autobiography. In the final stages of the book the act of autobiography (about which Defoe's first-person narrators are always ambivalent) becomes less and less possible for Roxana in relation to both her daughter and the reader.

In fact, what the daughter demands from Roxana is that Roxana *own* her. When she thinks that Amy is her mother, she asks: "What have I done that you won't own me, and that you will not be call'd my Mother?" She continues, "don't disown me now you have found me; don't hide yourself from me any longer" (267). This is the demand that Roxana feels she must deny. *To own* means more here than the opposite of disowning. It means more than simply recognizing the girl as a daughter, in the way that Charles Bon is imagined to want Sutpen to speak the words "My son" to him in *Absalom, Absalom! To own* is also *to confess*; according to the

Oxford English Dictionary, it means "to make a full admission or confession"; Dr. Johnson lists "to acknowledge" among its definitions. For Roxana to own the girl would be to reveal herself—but not just in the sense of exposure and disclosure. It would be to admit herself; for although Roxana refers to her daughter as "the Girl" throughout her narration (that is, when she doesn't call her "the Slut" or "the Creature") she lets drop as if by accident in one and only one place in the text that the daughter's name is Susan— and that this is *her* name as well. In Roxana's words: "she was my own Name" (205).

To own the girl, then, would be to own herself, to acknowledge her own name. Ironically, Roxana's refusal to come out of hiding and name herself (with a name which appears nowhere in the list of names and titles on the title page of her autobiography) has the effect of fixing her as Roxana, the name she is trying to escape. The same girl who threatens to name Roxana as "Roxana"—the actress who performed in the Turkish dress—is capable of naming her as "Susan." Roxana must choose between self-revelation and a costumed impersonation that exposes rather than conceals. By refusing to own, confess, and acknowledge, Roxana acts to avoid autobiography and protect herself; but by posing for her daughter, imposing upon the world, she locks herself into the theatrical position she finds so intolerable. By acknowledging her daughter (even if this would mean acknowledging herself) Roxana might be able to remove the girl from her position as audience. By granting her her name, by presenting her with herself, she might allow the daughter to be known: allow her an analogously revealed aspect from which she would no longer look as a spy, seeing though unseen. If Roxana could redefine the girl as a "counterpart" of herself—which is how she describes the other daughter (329) who is successfully blinded by the Quaker disguise—she might be able to "own" what she has abandoned, to incorporate the girl back into what is "proper" to her. Such acts as these might break down the theatricalizing distance between them. But Roxana holds the girl at a spectator's distance; she will not allow her daughter to identify herself. In return, the girl must play the part of the spy and spectator and place Roxana on a stage.[12]

To see that Roxana fears being exposed, however, we must also consider that she fears being "expos'd, and undone" (280). Roxana repeatedly tells us that her daughter is a threat because "if the girl knew me, I was undone" (276); indeed, the fear of being undone is expressed throughout both *Roxana* and *Moll Flanders* (appearing in the two texts some fifty times). To be *undone* means more than to be ruined; it means to be opened, unlocked, uncovered, unfastened—and thus revealed. Furthermore, the dictionary tells us that *undo* also means to explain or interpret. (The *OED* cites a sentence from 1654 which speaks of undoing a text.) Both Moll Flanders and Roxana fear that the fictions and representations they present to the world might be interpreted; they fear that the texts of the clothing they have woven or fabricated in order to conceal themselves might be unraveled.

Moll Flanders faces readers in the world who stop taking her fictions at face value, begin to figure out her theatrical illusions, and solve the riddles she presents to those who would detect her; but she can always spin a new disguise with which to confuse the world. Roxana, however, meets someone for whom her meaning is too clear; despite her attempts to cover her tracks and create a new figure for herself, she is found out, figured out, seen through. The daughter threatens to expose Roxana because she faces her as a spectator who has seen too much; but she threatens to undo Roxana because she stands before her as a reader. As a reader, the girl would inquire into and interpret the appearances that Roxana presents to the world, expose her former poses and present imposture. She would name and know the author of the fictions Roxana hides behind; she would retell the scene and story that she witnessed; she would unlock Roxana's soul and force her to confess, make public her life story. The girl represents a reader who would not take Roxana at face value; such a reader would see too much, go too far—and therefore must be stopped.

We saw that Roxana's reticence in regard to her readers is associated with her desire to avoid the sight of her daughter; that is, Roxana begins to avoid both the reader and her daughter at about the same time in the narrative *and* the most important story that

Roxana withholds from her reading public concerns her daughter. I am suggesting that the girl is not merely like *a* reader; she is like *the* reader. Roxana writes at the end of her book that the girl would "have trac'd me out at last, if *Amy* had not . . . put a Stop to her; of which I cannot enter into the Particulars here" (328). This passage recalls the beginning of the book where the "editor" explains that "it was necessary to conceal Names and Persons" in the text lest "the Facts [be] trac'd back too plainly" (1). The writer responsible for publishing the text must use concealment or disguise since the reader, like Roxana's daughter, might try to trace Roxana, to uncover and know her. He defends his blind by claiming that without such covers, "if we shou'd be always oblig'd to name the Persons . . . many a pleasant and delightful History wou'd be Buried in the Dark" (1). But this imagery recalls (or prefigures) Roxana's reflection that "the most secret Crimes are, by the most unforeseen Accidents, brought to light, and discover'd" (297), suggesting that such stories might not be so pleasant after all.

At the end of *Captain Singleton*, an "autobiography" that ends with the narrator adopting a permanent disguise, Singleton signs off by saying that he will "say no more for the present, lest some should be willing to inquire too nicely after Your Old Friend, CAPTAIN BOB."[13] The end of *Roxana*, more desperate than graceful, shares the same concern. Here the narrator is exposed rather than disguised before a reader who would inquire after the author too nicely (as Singleton says with delicate irony), a reader who would trace too far, see and know too much. So the book closes, the text breaks off, the curtain suddenly is brought down, the folding doors are slammed abruptly shut. The reader, like the daughter, must be murdered. In silencing itself, the text would dispose of the reader as reader; it would murder further reading. Ironically, the story that can't be told—the story of the elimination of Roxana's threatening reader and spectator—is acted out in the conclusion of the text. The reader must play the part of the daughter just as the daughter has played the part of the reader.

It must be acknowledged that my inquiry into *Roxana*, my attempt to trace back the persons and fictions of the narrative, has indeed sought to name and know at least the character of the book's author. If the name of "Defoe" has been largely absent from this chapter, it is because I have been speaking of Defoe all along, naming *Roxana* as *his* autobiography.[14] Throughout these pages, in interpreting Defoe's narrative fiction in the light of his theatrical positions and impositions, I have been suggesting that paradoxically these "novels" are indeed autobiographies—if not of the people whose names appear on the title page, if not literally the life story of the historical personage named Defoe. We have seen how many of Defoe's texts reflect (at times obsessively) upon Defoe's activities of impersonation and imposture: the representing and misrepresenting of the self in order to present an outer character as a screen to the eyes of the world. We saw through our reading of *Moll Flanders* how theatrical disguise can make possible the publication of the self. *Roxana* fails in this regard because it succeeds in being too autobiographical; ironically, for Defoe (who was condemned for claiming that his fictions were true) the story of a stage-player for whom exposure on the stage of the world is intolerable proves to be too revealing. *Roxana* represents—that is, it both displays and en-acts—the overshadowing of the protective role of *theater* by the conditions of *theatricality*. Roxana acts the part of Defoe just as Defoe plays the role of Roxana; as we read, we watch the drama Roxana enacts become the exposition of Defoe's anxiety about his own theatricality. With *Roxana*, after five years of publishing ro-mances and autobiographical fiction and a lifetime of fictions and impersonations, Defoe discovers the theatrical act of publishing himself (disguises notwithstanding) to be intolerable.

It is clear that something has gone wrong at the end of *Roxana*, the conclusion of which closes the folding doors, so to speak, on Defoe's career as a "novelist."[15] What has gone wrong is the situation of the book itself and the relation between authors and readers. On almost the last page of her narrative Roxana worries about "going away, and leaving this Work so unfinish'd" (328); al-though she ostensibly is referring to the support of her remaining children, she must also be worried about the abrupt ending of her book. Earlier, however, in speaking of her relation to her the-

atricalizing spectator, the prince—in particular, of the circumstances that "put an end to our conversing together"—Roxana notes
that "such things always meet with a Period, and generally break off
abruptly" (80). In the sentence immediately following these uncannily prophetic words, she "look[s] back" to an "Observation" which
"may be of Use to those who read my Story" (80). Those who read
Roxana's story must recognize their role in the circumstances which
end the conversation of the narrative and abruptly, with a blunt
period, break off their audience with the book's author. The circumstances are the conditions of theater: conditions which offer Defoe
the prospect of negotiating a safe relation to his reader, but in the
end demand his retirement from the scene and stage of writing.

Afterword

STILL, we read the book. Defoe's full stop does not stop us. As Defoe writes in the preface to *The Storm*, a book is not the "sound of words spoken to the ear" but rather a performance which "conveys its contents for ages to come, to the eternity of mortal time, when the author is forgotten in his grave."[1] The book remains to be reread, rehearsed, and examined. As readers, we try to call the text back from its silence and demand that it tell its story; we try to undo the character of the author, insisting on sight after the author has acted to blind us. Is this our relentless pursuit? Is there a way, short of silence, to escape the positions which define the theatricality Defoe eventually finds unbearable? I suggested that Roxana might have counteracted the spectator in her daughter by allowing her to present and identify herself. In her shame Roxana supposes the girl ashamed to own "Roxana" as her mother; she will not admit her daughter's admission. In the same way that Roxana will not redefine her relation with her daughter after the daughter has seen through Roxana's disguise and threatens to expose her, Defoe does not ask us to end the theatricality he sees in the situation of books and reading. From the outset, in publishing his books, Defoe has prefaced our reading by inscribing us before him as the public, as his audience. He faces us on the stage of the world; his stance is a pose. He neither asks nor allows us to stop being spectators, to leave the individual and collective positions that keep us removed, withheld, seeing though unseen. For ultimately, the world Defoe desires is a world of theater: a world in which social relations are theatrical.

Like Shaftesbury, Defoe seems to prefer a world in which communication and knowledge stop short, in which one's character is concealed from the eyes of mankind. Defoe sees the world as a stage—or, to mix metaphors, as an archipelago of stages—on which people perform acts of solitude. This is the vision Defoe presents while concealed behind the mask of Robinson Crusoe in the *Serious Reflections*. "I have frequently looked back," he writes in the essay "Of Solitude,"

> upon the notions of a long tedious life of solitude, which I have represented to the world, and of which you must have formed some ideas, from the life of a man in an island. Sometimes I have wondered how it could be supported, especially for the first years. . . . Sometimes I have as much wondered why it should be any grievance or affliction, seeing upon the whole view of the stage of life which we act upon in this world it seems to me that life in general is, or ought to be, but one universal act of solitude.[2]

This is the drama one performs and observes by oneself; and, Defoe interjects, in a clause that reads like a signature, so should it be. Solitary, people face each other as spectators and spectacles. As with Shaftesbury, the threat of theatricality necessitates the protection of theater, even if theater threatens to expose one before the eyes of the world. Readers have noted that Defoe's narratives depict characters obsessed with isolating themselves;[3] I want to emphasize that in Defoe's view this isolation characterizes us as well. His autobiographies stop short of confessing or confiding, frustrating those readers who expect the intimacy or sensibility of a Clarissa, leaving us to experience our separateness and lack of knowledge. I want to emphasize also that this separateness characterizes the conditions of theater for Defoe. I think that Defoe would have agreed with Rousseau's formulation: "L'on croit s'assembler au spectacle, et c'est là que chacun s'isole"; but he would have rejected the vision of a collective experience that ends the *Lettre à M. d'Alembert sur les spectacles*. For Defoe, the theater of isolation that closes up people "dans un antre obscur" and keeps them "craintifs et immobiles dans le silence et l'inaction"[4] is the necessary "stage of life that we act upon in this world."

This is the world of Robinson Crusoe, who "liv'd just like a Man cast away upon some desolate Island, that had no body there but himself"[5] while on his plantation in Brazil, long before

his actual shipwreck. Once on his literal island, Crusoe builds a
fortress in which he can watch over the island and "avoid being
seen";[6] obsessed with remaining concealed and undiscovered, he
reflects that he could be "more happy in this forsaken Solitary
Condition, than it was probable I should ever have been in any
other Particular State in the World."[7] Homer Brown describes how
Crusoe's "first act is to begin to build a wall around himself. He
further insulates himself; he creates an island within the island."[8]
Crusoe's most terrifying experience is the single footprint in the
sand, the sign of another person.

     This "constant Snare of *the Fear of Man*"[9] described by
Crusoe also characterizes the world described in A *Journal of the
Plague Year.* Here is a city in which communication is fatal, in
which people must insulate themselves behind shutters and doors
and wear masks when venturing outside. "It is dangerous so much
as to speak with anybody," says the narrator, whose obsessive curiosity compels him to stay in London to watch the "dismal spectacles
[that] represented themselves in my view out of my own windows."[10] In the street, where one can only witness from a distance
the lamentations of the dying, unable to do more than imagine and
shun their pain, the narrator meets a waterman who survives by
living in his boat; he serves people who are sequestered in ships that
are anchored off shore, exchanging food for a few shillings, and he
preserves his family by carrying provisions to a stone near his house
where they can hurry out and fetch them. The narrator is so moved
by the waterman's story of suffering that he risks contagion (ety-
mologically related to "touch") and crosses the distance that safely
separates them to give the man his charity. In a sense the man is a
modern-day Noah, a just man who survives in his boat while God's
scourge depopulates the earth.

     The narrator is clearly fascinated, however, with the
man's role as a go-between, a messenger, a mediator and medium of
exchange for individuals who are separated by distance and confinement. The waterman is himself like the stone that mediates the
transactions and communication between himself and his family.
One of the most joyful visions the narrator describes in A *Journal of
the Plague Year* is the sight the waterman brings him to witness from

the top of a hill in Greenwich. He tells of "the number of ships which lay in rows, two and two, and some places two or three such lines in the breadth of the river." Describing in detail "several hundreds of sail," the narrator writes of his reaction to this prospect: "I could not but applaud the contrivance: for ten thousand people and more who attended ship affairs were certainly sheltered here from the violence of the contagion, and lived very safe and very easy." When he returns to the safety of his own home the narrator "rejoiced to see that such little sanctuaries were provided for so many families in a time of such desolation."[11]

Although this prospect offers reassurance about people's ability to survive, perhaps few spectators would really applaud such a spectacle. Perhaps few besides Defoe would find joyful the sight of ten thousand people, confined and separated on islands of their own making, protected from each other and deadly communication; each ship isolated, apart, a world unto itself. But this is a vision of the world that is inhabited by most of Defoe's personae, whether by choice or fate: where individuals are retired, confined, isolated, withdrawn, concealed, disguised, lost, marooned, floating at sea, private. The aerial view of ten thousand Robinson Crusoes or the dangerous strangers and boarded up houses of plague-stricken London are merely literal versions of the world inhabited by Defoe's urban characters. "I enjoy much more solitude," writes Defoe as Crusoe in the *Serious Reflections*, "in the middle of the greatest collection of mankind in the world, I mean, at London, while I am writing this, than ever I could say I enjoyed in eight and twenty years' confinement to a desolate island."[12] Robinson Crusoe's enjoyment here is similar to the rejoicing of the narrator in *Plague Year*; for Defoe, confinement represents less imprisonment than a reassuring boundary.

Indeed, Robinson Crusoe's essay on solitude in the *Serious Reflections* is really a meditation on safety, protection, and mastery. "There is no need of a wilderness to wander among wild beasts," he writes, "no necessity of a cell on the top of a mountain, or a desolate island in the sea; if the mind be confined, if the soul be truly master of itself, all is safe."[13] Defoe's realistic portrayal of the

isolation and alienation of late-seventeenth- and early-eighteenth-
century London may act as an indictment of his society, but given
Defoe's fears about being known by other people and being exposed
before the eyes of the world, it makes sense that he would feel safer
living with anonymity, social distance, and lack of trust. The tres-
passes of other people seem threatening enough to drive one to
desolate islands or wild beasts. Whether moved by the fear of contagion and deadly communication, the fear of being devoured by
others, or the fear of being named, known, seen, and discovered,
Defoe's characters feel safer on their own islands, performing acts of
solitude.

    Yet outside of the conditions of desolate islands, ships
anchored at sea, plagues, and crowded cities, how is the mind
confined? Robinson Crusoe's suggestion that he enjoys the most
solitude in the middle of a city—"I mean, at London, while I am
writing this"—implies that the greatest act of solitude might be
writing. Indeed, in a relatively unknown book on the origins of
writing, Defoe praises writing not as a means of overcoming distance and absence, but as a medium which allows and ensures
distance and absence. Published two years after *Roxana*, in 1726,
*An Essay upon Literature: or An Enquiry into the Antiquity and
Original of Letters; proving that the two Tables, written by the
Finger of God in Mount Sinai, was the first Writing in the World*,
discusses both the miracle and the evolution of written texts. Defoe
imagines that before the invention of writing, people "were sensible
of the Defect, had a Notion of something wanting, that when they
had spoken to one another Face to Face, they cou'd know nothing
more."[14] According to Defoe, God, "the first *Writing Master* in the
World,"[15] passed on through the man he knew face to face the
means for an alternative to that kind of knowledge. Whereas before
writing, "the World was not able to form any Method fully to Express themselves to one another at a Distance," with the invention
of writing they could speak "a hundred or a thousand Miles"
apart.[16] From Defoe's point of view, this divine gift offers an ideal
form of communication. Like the waterman who acts as a medium
of exchange, transporting letters between isolated people who live

in mortal fear of getting too close to each other, writing allows communication through distance. Defoe's attraction to the figure of Duncan Campbell, the deaf and dumb clairvoyant who hired him as a ghost writer, must have been related to a fascination with someone who communicated with the world through written texts; he tells in great detail a story about how he conducted a long dialogue with the boy in writing, although they sat only inches apart.[17] Writing for Defoe can be like the speech that Shaftesbury characterizes as "the involution, the shadow, the veil, the curtain," the "soft irony"; it can allow us to see each other through a glass darkly rather than face to face.

Finally, however, the mind is confined because the self itself is removed from others. "All reflection is carried home, and our dear self is, in one respect, the end of living,"[18] writes Robinson Crusoe in an essay that recommends solitude of spirit rather than vows of silence or hermitage. Taking up the role of his most famous *solitaire*, Defoe asks:

> What are the sorrows of other men to us, and what their joy? Something we may be touched indeed with by the power of sympathy, and a secret turn of the affections; but all the solid reflection is directed to ourselves. Our meditations are all solitude in perfection; our passions are all exercised in retirement; we love, we hate, we covet, we enjoy, all in privacy and solitude. All that we communicate of those things to any other is but for their assistance in the pursuit of our desires; the end is at home; the enjoyment, the contemplation, is all solitude and retirement; it is for ourselves we enjoy, and for ourselves we suffer.[19]

In a passage uncannily reminiscent of the *Philosophical Regimen* that Shaftesbury secretly wrote until his death, only eight years before the publication of the *Serious Reflections*, Robinson Crusoe appears before his readers to insist on the utter privacy of the self; or, at least, the privacy that ought to be. Sometimes this privacy takes great efforts to maintain, as in *Roxana*, where the daughter not only threatens to expose Roxana's identity but makes demands upon her sympathy and secret affections as well. Roxana tries to use Amy and the Quaker as mediators; at one point the girl almost forces her way into the Quaker's house and with "earnest Entreaties, and at last,

Tears" brings the Quaker "to be greatly mov'd indeed."[20] The girl pleads with her to "stand my Friend, if you have any Charity, or if you have any Compassion for the Miserable . . . . She is my Mother! and will not own me; *and with that she stopp'd, with a Flood of Tears.*"[21] Roxana recounts that the "tender-hearted QUAKER told me, the Girl spoke this with such moving Eloquence, that it forc'd Tears from her."[22] Like the governess in *Moll Flanders* who "had such a bewitching Eloquence, and so great a power of Perswasion, that there was no concealing any thing from her,"[23] like the waterman whose tears and moving story compel the narrator of *Plague Year* to contribute "tears to this man's story" and "charity for his assistance,"[24] the daughter forces tears and compassion from the woman acting to screen Roxana. But the Quaker cannot risk the charity with which H. F. assists the waterman; not asking for money, the daughter demands something more expensive. Acting to conceal Roxana, the Quaker resumes her former reserve and the girl realizes "She cou'd not indeed expect that she (the QUAKER) shou'd be affected with the Story she had told her, however moving; or that she shou'd take any Pity on her."[25]

The Quaker must play Roxana's part and deny the girl, leaving her in solitude and isolation. This refusal to be touched (contaminated) spotlights the girl's separateness and turns her from an interlocutor into a performer declaiming a moving speech. It also reinforces and redefines the girl's position as an audience in relation to Roxana: it keeps her in the dark. However, even if the sorrows of the girl meant more to the Quaker, the Quaker would still stand as a mediator, preserving the distance between the girl and Roxana. Roxana cannot afford to be moved; she describes her daughter as "this impertinent Girl, *who was now my Plague.*"[26]

At one point, during the accidental meeting on the private ship that Roxana hires to flee her plague-like daughter, Roxana does come face to face with the girl. She describes with great intensity the power of sympathy and the secret turn of the affections that touch her as she is called upon to kiss the girl while hiding behind a false identity, as if she were greeting a stranger.

No Pen can describe, no Words can express, *I say,* the strange Impression which this thing made upon my Spirits; I felt something shoot thro' my Blood; my Heart flutter'd; my Head flashed, and was dizzy, and all within me, *as I thought*, turn'd about, and much ado I had, not to abandon myself to an Excess of Passion at the first Sight of her, much more when my Lips touch'd her Face. . . .[27]

Roxana tells us of the impossibility of expressing the emotions she felt in the sublime moment that her lips touched the daughter she would not admit and she faced the impossibility of expressing her emotions. Despite her desires at this moment to kiss "again a thousand times" the girl who bears her name—"my own Child; my own Flesh and Blood, born of my Body"—she must keep herself concealed, unacknowledged. She withdraws the lips that will not speak her daughter's name, steps back, "not conversible for some Minutes,"[28] and prevents discovery; and in representing this scene for us, she reflects on the impossibility of expressing herself to either her daughter or the reader. Such a moment might represent the failure of language. Indeed, the thousands of pages published by Defoe are punctuated with a remarkable number of asides to the reader that recall the inability of language to convey emotion or perception. For some, this condition would speak the necessity of faith; for Defoe, it seems a blessing. Writing speaks but it also withholds, holds back. Language, like the invention of writing, itself preserves the radical separateness that keeps us "in privacy and solitude."

Paradoxically, the conditions of theatricality risked by revealing oneself are also instituted by Defoe's insistence on concealing himself from the eyes of others. As readers, we must confront our position as spectators to his acts of solitude. When his figures seem to turn against him and threaten him with self-revelation on the stage of the world, when his acts of concealment recreate the theatrical distance that turns us into spectators, when the inherently theatrical status of the published book becomes too visible, Defoe must shut his book; perhaps, like Prospero, he must drown his book, just as Amy might have drowned Roxana's daughter. We are left to imagine what he cannot say, in so many words: we are left to speak into the void of speculation, but not to know.

PART III

The Theater of Sympathy

With thinking we may be beside ourselves in a sane sense. By a conscious effort of the mind we can stand aloof from actions and their consequences; and all things, good and bad, go by us like a torrent. We are not wholly involved in Nature. I may be either the driftwood in the stream, or Indra in the sky looking down on it. I *may* be affected by a theatrical exhibition; on the other hand, I *may not* be affected by an actual event which appears to concern me much more. I only know myself as a human entity; the scene, so to speak, of thoughts and affections; and am sensible of a certain doubleness by which I can stand as remote from myself as from another. However intense my experience, I am conscious of the presence and criticism of a part of me, which, as it were, is not a part of me, but a spectator, sharing no experience, but taking note of it; and that is no more I than it is you. When the play, it may be the tragedy, of life is over, the spectator goes his way. It was a kind of fiction, a work of the imagination only, so far as he was concerned. This doubleness may easily make us poor neighbors and friends sometimes.

Henry David Thoreau,
"Solitude," *Walden*

CHAPTER 7

Adam Smith and the Theatricality
of Moral Sentiments

"WHAT are the sorrows of other men to us, and what their joy?" The question Defoe asks as Robinson Crusoe, while reflecting on solitude, the power of sympathy, and secret turns of the affections, could have served as the epigraph for *The Theory of Moral Sentiments*. First published in 1759, signed on the title page by the printed characters "Adam Smith, Professor of Moral Philosophy in the University of Glasgow," *The Theory of Moral Sentiments* explores the role of sympathy in a world in which people face each other as spectators and spectacles. Much attention has been focused on Smith's concept of the *impartial spectator*, the hypothetical figure who is supposed to govern our actions by granting or withholding fellow-feeling.[1] Scholars have discussed how Smith developed this concept from assumptions about social and moral behavior implicit in the works of Hutcheson and Hume; and debate has often centered on identifying, as it were, this impartial spectator.[2] He (and *he* is clearly masculine) is alternatively characterized as an ideal observer, an ordinary innocent bystander, the voice of the people, an omniscient deity, the normative values of society, a relativistic social code, absolute standards, the personification of conscience, the internalization of social repression, the superego, and simply a hypothetical, abstract third person.

T. D. Campbell argues in *Adam Smith's Science of Morals* that the impartial spectator represents "the average, or normal or ordinary man," and he provides an array of citations to show that Smith speaks interchangeably of "the 'spectator', 'spectators', 'bystander', 'a third person', 'every attentive spectator', 'every impartial bystander', 'every impartial spectator', 'every indifferent person', 'another man', 'other men', 'society', and most frequently of all, 'mankind'." For Campbell, the impartial spectator is "by definition, someone who is not acting."[3] Yet D. D. Raphael, in an article that traces the development of Smith's concept through early lectures, drafts, and revisions, shows how Smith refined his characterization of the impartial spectator from a general notion of "'any impartial person'" to a specific depiction of a spectator.[4] Scholars focus almost exclusively on what it means that Smith's hypothetical spectator is supposed to be *impartial*; I want to ask what it means that the impartial spectator is a *spectator*. What is at stake is the inherently theatrical situation that Smith describes when he pictures us appearing before each other as spectators and spectacles.

Only Jonas Barish, in a brief discussion of *The Theory of Moral Sentiments* in *The Antitheatrical Prejudice*, recognizes Smith's system as an "essentially theatrical construction" that "puts the condition of spectatordom at the heart of the moral experience."[5] It may be that the familiarity of the *theatrum mundi* metaphor has blinded us to the significance of Smith's theatrical perspective. Clearly, there is a context to this perspective: Hutcheson, for example, remarks in his *Inquiry Concerning Beauty, Order, Harmony, Design* (1725) that the world is a "stupendous Theatre" adorned by God "in a manner agreeable to the Spectators." His *Essay on the Nature and Conduct of the Passions and Affections* (1728) moves easily, often without distinction, between considerations of "Spectacles of Pity" on stage and in the world, between situations where people are spectators to the "characters" of others and to the "characters" in plays.[6] Twenty-five years later, in the *Enquiry Concerning the Principles of Morals* (1751), Hume describes someone who enters into the sentiments of others as a "beholder" and refers to someone who elicits "natural sympathy" as a "spectacle." He illustrates his assertion that everything "presents us with the view of human happiness or misery, and excites in our breast a sympathetic movement of pleasure or uneasiness" with the example of a "man who enters the theatre."[7] "L'Homme est né spectateur," writes the Abbé Batteux in his *Principes de la littérature* (1764),[8] following the Abbé Du Bos, whose *Réflexions critiques sur la poésie et sur la peinture* (1719) portrayed sight as the most powerful of the senses and explored the experience of being a spectator to both works of art and other people. For Du Bos, as for others in the eighteenth century, to talk about how people responded to the sentiments of others was to talk about representation and theatrical distance, while to talk about how people reacted to the characters in a tragedy was to talk about the structure and experience of sympathy.

However, we should not let the absence of boundaries between moral philosophy, aesthetics, and psychology in the eighteenth century, or Enlightenment desires to discover universal principles, allow us to overlook the implications of a perspective that casts people as spectators to each other; nor should we dismiss this theatrical view of social relations as mere convention, tradition, or figure of speech. I suggest that, for Adam Smith, moral philosophy has entered the theater. In this chapter I will argue that Smith's examination of sympathy in *The Theory of Moral Sentiments* is designed to address the theatrical character of the way people face each other in the world—and that this theatrical situation, which is implicit in writers such as Hutcheson and Hume, becomes not only explicit but finally problematic for Smith. In this sense Smith can be seen to share Shaftesbury's and Defoe's concern with the inherent theatricality of presenting a character before the eyes of the world and acting as a beholder to people who perform acts of solitude.

For the Abbé Du Bos, sympathy is a natural emotion which provides the first foundation of society. He writes in the *Réflexions critiques:* "Les larmes d'un inconnu nous émeuvent même avant que nous sachions le sujet qui le fait pleurer. Les cris d'un homme qui ne tient à nous que par l'humanité, nous font voler à son secours par un mouvement machinal qui précède toute délibération."9 Smith's mentor Lord Kames, who devotes a section of his *Elements of Criticism* (1762) to an examination of "the effects produced upon a spectator by the external signs of passion," maintains that "distress painted on the countenance" of someone "instantaneously inspires the spectator with pity, and impels him to afford relief." "I cannot behold a man in distress without partaking of his

pain," writes Kames, "nor in joy, without partaking of his pleasure."[10] Adam Smith bases his entire system of moral philosophy on
the experience of sympathy, but he is in many ways closer to Defoe's
view of the radical separateness, isolation, and solitude of people
than to the theories of universal fellow-feeling expressed by writers
such as Kames and Du Bos. *The Theory of Moral Sentiments* begins
by supposing a sceptical epistemology that assumes sympathy but
insists that neither sight nor the other senses will suffice to commu-
nicate to us the feelings and experience of another person. Under
the chapter heading "OF SYMPATHY" Smith writes:

> As we have no immediate experience of what other men
> feel, we can form no idea of the manner in which they are affected,
> but by conceiving what we ourselves should feel in the like situation.
> Though our brother is upon the rack, as long as we ourselves are at
> our ease, our senses will never inform us of what he suffers. They
> never did, and never can, carry us beyond our own person, and it is
> by the imagination only that we can form any conception of what are
> his sensations. (9)

Writing in a first-person plural that identifies himself with his readers and asks us to imagine that we share his position, Smith imagines that we are faced with a brother, a *semblable*; but he represents
this image of suffering in order to acknowledge that the sight and
signs of a figure in pain will not immediately or automatically raise
similar feelings in us. First we are confronted by the limits of our
senses, our inability to go beyond our own persons and know or
experience the suffering of another person. It is only through imagination that sympathy can take place. However, Smith continues,
"neither can that faculty help us to this any other way, than by
representing to us what would be our own [sensations], if we were in
his case. It is the impressions of our own senses only, not those of
his which our imaginations copy" (9). Through a representation of
our own feelings, we can represent to ourselves the feelings of the
person we witness. "By the imagination," writes Smith, "we place
ourselves in his situation, we conceive ourselves enduring all the
same torments, we enter as it were into his body, and become in
some measure the same person with him, and thence form some

idea of his sensations, and even feel something which, though weaker in degree, is not altogether unlike them" (9).

Although the person suffering is really present, we can experience what our senses deny us only through what Kames in his *Elements of Criticism* calls "ideal presence." Kames uses this term to describe a "waking dream," a "fiction of the imagination," through which (for example) a reader of a powerful description forgets himself and is "transported as by magic into the very place and time of the important action, and [is] converted, as it were, into a spectator, beholding every thing that passes."[11] For Kames, this presence *in idea* can feel like real presence. Smith, however, as we have seen, has less faith in the effect of sight and presence. Rather than insisting that a fiction of the imagination can convey the conviction an eyewitness would feel, he maintains that even an eyewitness must depend upon an imagined representation, at least in order to feel sympathy. Smith's description of our emotions when "we read in history" is similar to the act of identification he describes as occurring when we face our brother on the rack: "In imagination we become the very person whose actions are represented to us: we transport ourselves in fancy to the scenes of those distant and forgotten adventures, and imagine ourselves acting the part of a Scipio" (75).

It is no coincidence that Smith illustrates a discussion of how we enter into the sentiments and actions of others with a description of reading; whether we are confronted with a person or a text, we must face a fiction. We must imagine that we are persons who can be only representations to us; through imagination we transport ourselves to a distant place, try to place ourselves in someone else's situation. We take their part by trying to play their part. The other person's "agonies, when they are thus brought home to ourselves, when we have thus adopted and made them our own, begin at last to affect us, and we then tremble and shudder at the thought of what he feels" (9).

It is perhaps a measure of Smith's ability to imagine the sentiments of another person that his *Theory of Moral Sentiments* attempts to understand the situation of sympathy not only by considering the part of the spectator but also by entering into the mind of the person suffering. Smith's attempt to sympathize with the object of sympathy is not an attempt to know the sufferer's pain; he tries instead to imagine the experience of feeling pain in front of a spectator. He begins his representation of the sufferer's point of view at the same point where he began to imagine the spectator's point of view: "As nature teaches the spectators to assume the circumstances of the person principally concerned, so she teaches this last in some measure to assume those of the spectators. As they are continually placing themselves in his situation, and thence conceiving emotions similar to what he feels; so he is as constantly placing himself in theirs" (22). The mirror of sympathy in which the spectator represents to himself the feelings of the other person and places himself in the position and person of the other is itself mirrored in the experience of the person who knows he is being viewed. As the sufferer tries to look at his spectators with sympathy (which Smith defines simply as "our fellow-feeling with any passion whatever" [10]), he finds himself in the same epistemological void. Unable to know what they feel as they face him, he must represent to himself in his imagination what they feel as *they* represent to themselves in *their* imaginations what *he* feels. Smith writes:

> As they are constantly considering what they themselves would feel, if they actually were the sufferers, so he is as constantly led to imagine in what manner he would be affected if he was only one of the spectators of his own situation. As their sympathy makes them look at it, in some measure, with his eyes, so his sympathy makes him look at it, in some measure, with theirs, especially when in their presence and acting under their observation. (22)

As the sufferer identifies with his spectator, he must realize that the distance established by the epistemological impossibility of sharing another person's sentiments means that he will never meet with complete sympathy. In Smith's view, even if the spectator can "adopt the whole case of his companion with all its minutest incidents; and strive to render as perfect as possible, that imaginary change of situation upon which his sympathy is founded . . . the emotions of the spectator will still be very apt to fall short of the violence of what is felt by the sufferer" (21). The sympathetic passion will never equal the original in degree or duration, and by entering into his spectators' feelings, the sufferer conceives "some degree of that coolness about his own fortune, with which he is sensible that they will view it" (22). According to Smith, the sufferer longs less for relief from pain than for the relief that is afforded only by sympathy. He "passionately desires a more complete sympathy. He longs for that relief which nothing can afford him but the entire concord of the affections of the spectators with his own." The sufferer is aware of being watched and he longs for the distance and difference between himself and his spectator to be surpassed. This can be done, in Smith's view, only if the sufferer lowers "his passion to that pitch, in which the spectators are capable of going along with him." Thus sympathy has a social function: it forces us to moderate our passions in order to create a "harmony and concord with the emotions" of those who are watching us (22). The need for this concord more than doubles the theatrical positions Smith sees enacted in sympathy by compelling us to become spectators to our spectators and thereby spectators to ourselves.[12] In this kaleidoscope of reflections and representations in which the imaginary change of positions that takes place in the spectator's mind is imagined, reflected, and repeated in the mind of the sufferer, both of the characters in the scene of sympathy play the roles of spectator and spectacle.

The Theory of Moral Sentiments extends this theater of sympathy beyond the scene of a person suffering. According to Smith, we view people with an eye toward whether or not we can enter into their feelings; in particular, our judgments of virtue and vice are based on our ability to sympathize with the person we are beholding. "We either approve or disapprove of the conduct of another man according as we feel that, when we bring his case home to ourselves, we either can or cannot entirely sympathize with the sentiments and motives which directed it" (109). (Such acts of sympathy are doubled because we also place ourselves in the position of the person who is affected by the conduct of the person we are judging; Smith calls this a "compounded sentiment" that is made up of "a direct sympathy with the sentiments of the agent, and an indirect sympathy" with the person who is acted upon [74].) If we are always spectators, however, comparing the points of view of others with our fellow-feelings, we are also always spectacles to all of those who view us. For Smith, the average, unsuffering person acts in the same manner as the person he describes suffering; he looks to his spectators for sympathy and in doing so imagines himself as a spectator to his own spectacle. Smith writes:

> We either approve or disapprove of our own conduct, according as we feel that, when we place ourselves in the situation of another man, and view it, as it were, with his eyes and from his station, we either can or cannot entirely enter into and sympathize with the sentiments and motives which influenced it. We can never survey our own sentiments and motives, we can never form any judgment concerning them; unless we remove ourselves, as it were, from our own natural station, and endeavour to view them as at a certain distance from us. But we can do this in no other way than by endeavouring to view them with the eyes of other people, or as other people are likely to view them. (109–110)

Imagining ourselves as a spectacle, we look at ourselves in exactly the same way that we look at others: we attempt to sympathize with ourselves, to enter into our own feelings and persons. Like the sufferer in the scene of the rack, we must represent in our imagination the position and point of view of a spectator who tries to represent to his imagination our position and point of view. In Smith's view, one does not simply imagine oneself seen by others; one imagines oneself imagined by others who either can or cannot enter into one's feelings (as they imagine them).

 This condition of constantly imagining ourselves appearing before the eyes of other people inevitably places us in a theatrical relation to others; but it also creates an internalized sense that determines how we see ourselves, even if we are not in the presence of an actual spectator. According to Smith, we view ourselves "with the eyes of other people, or as other people are likely to view" us (110). This potential spectator leads to Smith's well-known concept of the "impartial spectator," the hypothetical, uninvolved witness that we imagine observing our character and conduct. According to Smith's system, we govern our actions and judgments—indeed, we know ourselves—by internalizing the regard of a spectator. "We endeavour to examine our own conduct as we imagine any other fair and impartial spectator would examine it. If, upon placing ourselves in his situation, we thoroughly enter into all the passions and motives which influenced it, we approve of it, by sympathy with the approbation of this supposed equitable judge. If otherwise, we enter into his disapprobation, and condemn it" (110). One becomes a spectator to oneself in order to determine if one can enter into one's own feelings; one knows if one sympathizes with oneself because one sympathizes with the sentiments of the spectator-judge one has become. One enters into the feelings of oneself as other and accepts the judgment based on "his" ability to enter into one's own person and feelings.

In Smith's view, the *dédoublement* that structures any act of sympathy is internalized and doubled within the self. In endeavoring to "pass sentence" upon one's own conduct, Smith writes, "I divide myself, as it were, into two persons; and . . . I, the examiner and judge, represent a different character from that other I, the person whose conduct is examined into and judged of" (113). Earlier in his book, Smith claims that in imagining someone else's sentiments, we "imagine ourselves acting the part" of that person (75); here he pictures us trying to play ourselves by representing ourselves as two different characters. "The first," writes Smith, "is the spectator, whose sentiments with regard to my own conduct I endeavour to enter into, by placing myself in his situation." The second character, according to Smith, is "the agent, the person whom I properly call myself, and of whose conduct, under the character of a spectator, I was endeavouring to form some opinion" (113). In the version of this chapter that appeared in the first edition, Smith made these roles explicit by stating that "we must imagine ourselves not the actors, but the spectators of our own character and conduct" (111n2). In his final exposition, he makes it clear that we are both actors and spectators of our characters. We are actors not just because we appear before spectators played by ourselves, but also because we personate ourselves in different parts, persons, and characters. The self is theatricalized in its relation to others and in its self-conscious relation to itself; but it also enters the theater because "the person whom I properly call myself" must be an actor who can dramatize or represent to himself the spectacle of self-division in which the self personates two different persons who try to play each other's part, change positions, and identify with each other.

Ironically, after founding his *Theory of Moral Sentiments* on a supposedly universal principle of sympathy, and then structuring the act of sympathy around the epistemological void that prevents people from sharing each other's feelings, Smith seems to separate the self from the one self it could reasonably claim to know: itself. In order to sympathize with ourselves, we must imagine ourselves as an other who looks upon us as an other and tries to imagine us. Indeed, calling the spectator within the self the judge, and the agent within the self the person judged of, Smith writes, "but that the judge should, in every respect, be the same with the person judged of, is as impossible, as that the cause should, in every respect, be the same with the effect" (113). Thus the actor and spectator into which one divides oneself can never completely identify with each other or be made identical. Identity is itself undermined by the theatrical model which pictures the self as an actor who stands beside himself and represents the characters of both spectator and spectacle.

Smith's depictions of the impartial spectator and the relations it creates within the self suggest that he has been reading Shaftesbury. The characterization of the impartial spectator as the "man within the breast" (130) recalls Butler's discussions of "the witness of conscience"[13] and Hume's discussions, in his *Enquiry concerning the Principles of Morals,* of the moral value of considering how we appear in the eyes of those who regard us.[14] But it is Shaftesbury who expounds a "doctrine of two persons in one individual self" and calls for an "inspector or auditor [to be] established within us" as he presents his "dramatic method" in *Soliloquy, or Advice to an Author.*[15] We saw that Shaftesbury advises that one "play the critic on himself" and that he translates the "Delphic Inscription" as "divide yourself, or be two."[16] He compares his dialogic method, by which the mind divides itself into persons and characters, to a "looking-glass" in which we can "discover ourselves, and see our minutest features nicely delineated." This "double reflection" which allows us "to distinguish ourselves into two different parties"[17] surely anticipates Smith's system of dividing oneself into actor and spectator—which Smith calls "the only looking-glass by which we can, in some measure, with the eyes of other people, scrutinize the propriety of our own conduct" (112). Scholars note in passing the relevance for Smith of Shaftesbury's *Inquiry Concerning Virtue and Merit*, usually as they compare Shaftesbury's and Hutcheson's notions of a moral sense and stress the originality of Smith's concept of the impartial spectator. Strangely, *Soliloquy, or Advice to an Author* is practically ignored.[18] My purpose, however, in reviewing Shaftesbury's essay on dialogue, is not to debate originality or influence but rather to point to a context for Smith's discussion in which the problems of theater and theatricality are specifically addressed. The terms and figures of theater are inscribed within Smith's characterizations of sympathy and the impartial spectator, but they are also clearly informed by Shaftesbury's meditation on the dramatic character of the self and the problematic theatricality that threatens the self as it appears before the eyes of the world. Shaftesbury's model for the self and its relations to both itself and others underlines the theatrical perspective from which Smith designs *The Theory of Moral Sentiments*.

For Shaftesbury, *dédoublement* and a representation of parts and persons are enacted in order to reach a view of the self. Smith seems less concerned about the constitution of the self in itself. His theory of sympathy presupposes a certain instability of self; it depends upon an eclipsing of identity, a transfer of persons in which one leaves oneself behind and tries to take someone else's part. (Rousseau claimed that this ability to represent someone else's character and forget oneself meant that actors annihilated themselves.)[19] Smith is interested in the relations enacted in the confusion of characters we have seen—specifically, in the relations between people in the world which the division of the self into actor

and spectator merely duplicates. For Smith what is at stake in the
question of who takes whose part in the reflections, representations,
and projections of sympathy is not so much identity as identification. Smith is concerned with the difference between the two actors
in the scene of sympathy who attempt to change places, parts, and
persons—who are divided in order to mirror each other and each
other's division.

"The man of real constancy and firmness," writes
Smith, "does not merely affect the sentiments of the impartial spectator. He really adopts them. He almost identifies himself with, he
almost becomes himself that impartial spectator, and scarce even
feels but as that great arbiter of his conduct directs him to feel"
(146–47). Although this firm and constant man affects the sentiments of the character he represents, he makes them his own; like
an actor who can become his role, he makes his imitated feelings
genuine. But it is difficult to say which part of Smith's formulation
is more bizarre: the "almost" or the "identifies," the "almost" or the
"becomes." He almost takes on the identity of the other he has
become in order to identify with himself—but not quite. The other
whose sentiments he shares remains an other who directs his feelings while standing at a necessary distance from himself. Of course
the confusion of identification and difference is complicated here
because both the character of the actor and the character of the
spectator are represented by the same person; but this confusion is
also present in situations where there are actually two persons.

Arguing against theorists such as Hobbes and Mande-
ville who claim that sympathy is selfish rather than altruistic because it springs from self-love, Smith rejects the position that one
sympathizes with (for example) misery because one imagines it oc-
curing to oneself. Smith argues that the "imaginary change of situations" from which sympathy arises "is not supposed to happen to me
in my own person and character, but in that of the person with
whom I sympathize." He continues:

> When I condole with you for the loss of your only son, in order to
> enter into your grief I do not consider what I, a person of such a
> character and profession, should suffer, if I had a son, and if that son

was unfortunately to die: but I consider what I should suffer if I was really you, and I not only change circumstances with you, but I change persons and characters. My grief, therefore, is entirely upon your account, and not in the least upon my own. It is not, therefore, in the least selfish. (317)

In the substitution of sympathy, then, my assumption of your sentiments and person does not mean that you become me (in my eyes); it means, rather, that I become you—although you are presently becoming me as you try to imagine my position and point of view. Sympathy, according to Smith's formulation, involves a loss of self, a transfer and metamorphosis.

Hume tries to refute Hobbes' charge of "self-love" by claiming the opposite of Smith's position. Although he appears to agree in general with Smith's conclusions, Hume writes: "No force of imagination can convert us into another person, and make us fancy, that we, being that person, reap benefit from those valuable qualities, which belong to him. Or if it did, no celerity of imagination could immediately transport us back, into ourselves, and make us love and esteem the person, as different from us."[30] For Smith, the imagination seems to have all of these powers: it can convert us into another person and transport us back and forth, offering both identity and difference. Sympathy seems to blur the boundaries of the self while somehow maintaining the integrity of the self.

It is as if Smith were endorsing the two theories of acting that Diderot opposes in his *Paradoxe sur le comédien*: both the position that an actor should merge himself with his role and the position that the actor must be a cool observer who can stand at a distance from his own performance. At the same time, however, Smith agrees with Hume that this view of sympathy requires an impossible situation. Early in *The Theory of Moral Sentiments*, he admits that sympathy must stop short of total identification: if we really changed persons and characters with the people we sympathize with, we might not feel sympathy. We pity a madman, for example, while he is perfectly content; we even sympathize with the dead, who have no feelings at all. Smith writes: "The compassion of the spectator must arise altogether from the consideration of what he himself would feel if he was reduced to the same unhappy situation, and, what perhaps is impossible, was at the same time able to regard it with his present reason and judgment" (12).

What is perhaps impossible here is not the doubleness that allows spectators to take the part of other people and still maintain their own perspective; such a combination of identification and difference provided the standard eighteenth-century explanation for the pleasure audiences take in watching tragedies. For Smith, the impossibility of sympathy is founded in a system that insists on the distance between people, depends on that distance, and dreams of making that distance disappear. We saw that Smith takes as a presupposition the separateness of other minds, the limitations of our ability to share other people's feelings. We also saw that the situation of sympathy as Smith represents it posits people as actors and spectators, creating a theatrical distance that separates people not only from each other but also from themselves. We have seen that simultaneously, however, Smith imagines the possibility of sympathy enacting identification, transfer, transport, presence; *The Theory of Moral Sentiments* represents acts of the imagination that would deny the distance and difference that divide people from each other and themselves. Of course Smith acknowledges that he is speaking of fictions of the imagination when describing sympathy; sympathy, after all, takes place in the imagination. He describes what we "conceive" and imagine when we face our brother on the rack and through a representation of his feelings "we enter as it were into his body, and become in some measure the same person with him" (9). But I suggest that the "as it were" in Smith's formulation signals more than the imaginary status of the translation of one person to another; it signals more than a lack of proper words to describe the experience of sympathy. This "as it were" provides more than a simile that helps Smith describe what sympathy feels like; it allows him to speak literally at the same time he must speak figuratively. Smith wants to say that we could enter into the sentiments of other people, transgress the boundaries that keep us ourselves and prevent us from becoming others; but he can't believe with the ease of Kames or Du Bos that fellow-feeling is automatic or even natural. Furthermore, even the structure that he assigns to the situation of sympathy depends upon the distance it aims to transcend. *The Theory of Moral Sentiments*, then, must describe what it is like to want to believe in the fiction of sympathy, and what it is like to live in a world where sympathy is perhaps impossible.

        The Theory of Moral Sentiments presupposes a universal need for sympathy: we look to other people for approbation (which, according to Smith, is guaranteed when others can enter into our sentiments) and we fear their disapproval (that is, their inability or refusal to sympathize with us). Smith offers as an example of our concern with sympathy a portrait of a man who has committed a murder and has begun to reflect upon his act. The man is represented as overwhelmed with remorse and anxiety, but not because he feels guilty or because he fears punishment by society or God. As Smith imagines the scene, when "his passion is gratified, and he begins coolly to reflect," the man must begin to imagine the regard of other people (84). First, the man tries to enter into his own feelings and finds that he cannot sympathize with himself. This view anticipates the unsympathetic view he imagines that others will have of him. He even sympathizes with the victim of his crime, whose suffering now calls upon his pity. These acts of sympathy add up to the inescapable conclusion that he has lost the sympathy of his real and imagined spectators. It is this prospect and not merely guilt or repentance that makes the man regret his actions and fills him with dread.

        Smith pictures the murderer as he "dares no longer look society in the face, but imagines himself as it were rejected, and thrown out from the affections of all mankind. He cannot hope for the consolation of sympathy in this his greatest and most dreadful distress" (84). Smith writes that the man's "fellow-creatures" have "shut out all fellow-feeling with him" and "the very thing which he is most afraid of" is the "sentiments which they entertain with regard to him." Faced with spectators who must withhold their sympathy, the man dreads the prospect of entering into the feelings of those who regard him and discovering that they will not enter into his feelings. "Everything seems hostile, and he would be glad to fly to some inhospitable desert, where he might never more behold the face of a human creature, nor read in the countenance of mankind the condemnation of his crimes" (84).

Smith represents in great detail the inner sentiments of the isolated murderer. Of course he looks at him with stern judgment and disapproval, as one might expect from a professor of moral philosophy; but he also clearly sympathizes with the man. Smith can enter into his feelings and vividly imagine and represent his point of view. It is not that Smith feels any sympathy with the man's crime; it is the man's predicament after the murder that moves Smith's fellow-feeling. For although Smith is describing a particular instance of remorse—"of all the sentiments which can enter the human breast the most dreadful" (85)—the situation of the man in this character sketch is a somewhat extreme example of what (in Smith's view) everyone must fear, if not experience. The great anxiety displayed in *The Theory of Moral Sentiments* comes from the specter of spectators who would withhold sympathy. Smith describes the sufferer on the rack as longing "for that relief which nothing can afford him but the entire concord of the affections of the spectators with his own" (22). One would think that a man on a rack would be satisfied with a cessation of pain—but as Smith portrays him he is preoccupied with the spectators whose regard he is compelled to imagine. The greatest desire of man, according to Smith, is to "act so as that the impartial spectator may enter into the principles of his conduct" (83).

Whether murderers or sufferers or simply moral beings deciding how to act, we are always dependent on the sympathetic regard of those who watch us (or whom we imagine watching us). Even the murderer, writes Smith, who would flee to the desert rather than read the sentence that condemns him on the faces of his spectators, is finally compelled to return to society "in order to supplicate some little protection from the countenance of those very judges, who he knows have already all unanimously condemned him" (85). Smith suggests that the slightest sympathy (what else on the faces of the spectators could "protect" the man?) would be better than exposure before the imagined spectators the man must person-ate in his solitude. According to Smith, we constantly need sympa-thy and we cannot act without representing and reflecting on the point of view we imagine our spectators to have.

This internalization of the regard of others suggests the degree to which Smith believes that the need for sympathy will socialize people and regulate their behavior to make it conform to moral values. One should think twice about murdering someone— not just because it might be wrong but because it would cut one off from the sympathy of one's spectators. But the need and desire for the sympathy of one's spectators leads to a problem in the world that Smith represents; it is not so easy, in the course of life, to act in a manner that will secure the sympathy of others. I noted earlier that Smith describes the sufferer as knowing that complete sympathy is impossible. No matter how successful the spectator is in exchanging places and persons, his emotions "will still be very apt to fall short of the violence of what is felt by the sufferer" (21). This is not only because of the epistemological limitations of sharing someone else's feelings. Smith acknowledges that "it is painful to go along with grief, and we always enter into it with reluctance." Smith even comes close to saying that sympathy is unnatural: "Nature, it seems, when she loaded us with our own sorrows, thought that they were enough, and therefore did not command us to take any further share in those of others" (46,47). Our condition, then, as Smith represents it, is to depend on the sympathy of others (real or imag-ined; but even real sympathy is imagined) in a world in which we face spectators who either are not inclined to be moved or are not capable of being moved—or both. Joy may meet more readily with fellow-feeling, but suffering, whose only consolation lies in the sympathetic sentiments of others, will meet with "this dull sen-sibility to the afflictions of others" rather than the sympathy it looks and longs for (47). Smith's description of us resembles his portrait of the murderer: we cannot bear the thought of unsympathetic specta-tors yet this is precisely the prospect we must confront.

In this context we can understand Smith's approval of the general principles of Stoicism.[21] In a lengthy discussion of self-command, for example, he praises a man who has "lost his leg by a cannon shot" for controlling his passions and sympathizing less with himself than with his spectators—who, of course, cannot know his suffering and probably do not want to know it. Although he is in "paroxysms of distress," the man mutes his expression and display of suffering (147,148). Smith suggests that he controls himself not because it is more noble to accept one's condition but because he realizes that no one can adequately enter into his suffering. Earlier, Smith has remarked: "It is indecent to express any strong degree of those passions which arise from a certain situation or disposition of the body; because the company, not being in the same disposition, cannot be expected to sympathize with them" (27). Although suffering "in the agony of the paroxysm," writes Smith, the man who has lost his leg receives some "recompense" in "his own complete self-approbation, and the applause of every candid and impartial spectator"; both the man himself and his spectators approve "not only the manhood of his countenance, but the sedateness and sobriety of his judgment" (148). He also avoids, at least to some extent, exposing his emotions before spectators who cannot feel adequate sympathy.

In this sense Smith's endorsement of Stoic ideas can be seen as the result of an antitheatrical sensibility; Smith stands for the opposite of exhibitionism. The moral of *The Theory of Moral Sentiments* is that one should not display one's sentiments unless one is sure of eliciting sympathy; indeed, it would be best not to display oneself at all, given the small likelihood of attaining fellow-feeling. This ethic of self-command (one might say self-concealment) helps explain the almost total absence of women from the world of *The Theory of Moral Sentiments*. One might expect Smith to have more to say about women in a treatise on moral sentiments written in an age that closely associated both sympathy and sentiment with "feminine" sensibilities. However, it is precisely these qualities that appear to exclude women from the book. Although Smith differs from the Stoics in admiring the ability to enter into other people's feelings, he insists that a man should maintain "the most perfect command of his own original and selfish feelings"

(152)—in other words, one should avoid exposing oneself as a spectacle before unsympathetic eyes.

The fear of appearing before the eyes of unsympathetic spectators may produce a "masculine," antiexhibitionist ideal of self-mastery; but Smith suggests that such a fear, combined with a need and desire for sympathy, can lead to a theatrical, exhibitionist society as well. *The Theory of Moral Sentiments* represents a society where everyone and everything seems motivated by the gaze of spectators. These spectators are not the imaginary, impartial judges who personify our conscience. Smith portrays a society that is directed by a more pervasive and more powerful point of view: the eyes of the public. Unlike the Stoics, he suggests, most people are preoccupied with the character they present before the eyes of the world, and they know what they can and can not expect from these spectators. In a chapter called "Of the origin of Ambition, and of the distinction of Ranks," Smith writes:

> It is because mankind are disposed to sympathize more entirely with our joy than with our sorrow, that we make parade of our riches, and conceal our poverty. Nothing is so mortifying as to be obliged to expose our distress to the view of the public, and to feel, that though our situation is open to the eyes of all mankind, no mortal conceives for us the half of what we suffer. (50)

It is a pleasure to display ourselves before the view of the public, before the eyes of mankind, if we are rich. However, if we are poor, we find this theatrical exposure unbearable. According to Smith, the exposure we fear is not the uncovering of our distress or poverty; it is exposure before the eyes of those who can not or will not enter into our suffering, imagine our place and point of view—at the moment we are most in need of sympathy.

Smith maintains that people seek wealth simply because they cannot bear the thought of unsympathetic spectators: "It is chiefly from this regard to the sentiments of mankind, that we pursue riches and avoid poverty" (50). He examines all the reasons why one might want more prosperity than is enough to satisfy one's basic material needs and he rejects all of them except the regard that we have for the regard of others: "To be observed, to be attended to, to be taken notice of with sympathy, complacency, and approbation, are all the advantages which we can propose to derive from it" (50). Thus the need to secure sympathetic spectators is translated into economic terms as the economist is prefigured by the moral philosopher who explains the wealth of nations with a theory of moral sentiments.

This theatricalization of society is based not only on the need and desire to display oneself before the eyes of sympathetic spectators; it also grows, Smith's discussion suggests, from the *scoptophilia* of that modern representative of mankind: the public or the crowd. Although the crowd, according to Smith, shuns the sight of a poor man, "or if the extremity of his distress forces them to look at him, it is only to spurn so disagreeable an object," the man of rank and distinction "is observed by all the world. Every body is eager to look at him, and to conceive, at least by sympathy, that joy and exultation with which his circumstances naturally inspire him." The man of wealth and rank described by Smith will find himself like Roxana at her masked ball: facing a crowd of gazing, admiring spectators. According to Smith, he has no trouble "rendering himself the object of the observation and fellow-feeling of every body about him"; as if they have no feelings of their own, the spectators face him as a *tabula rasa*, waiting to mirror what they imagine to be his feelings: "In a great assembly he is the person upon whom all direct their eyes; it is upon him that their passions seem all to wait with expectation, in order to receive that movement and direction which he shall impress upon them" (51).

Indeed, Smith pictures a state in which spectators are so obsessed with such public spectacles that they go against their natural inclination not to sympathize with the suffering of others. The characters of kings impress them so much that they willingly enter into sorrow they would shun in ordinary circumstances. "Every calamity that befalls [kings]," Smith writes, "every injury that is done them, excites in the breast of the spectator ten times more compassion and resentment than he would have felt, had the same things happened to other men" (52). The paradox that spectators should enjoy watching spectacles that call upon them to sympathize with painful emotions is one that is familiar to readers of eighteenth-century treatises on aesthetics and theater.[22] It is not surprising, then, that Smith should continue to remark, "it is the misfortunes of Kings only which afford the proper subjects for tragedy" and to reflect upon situations that "interest us upon the theater" (52).

The terms and situation of theater have been present in Smith's discussion all along. It is not simply that the public's attitudes toward great men can explain what happens in the theater or are mirrored in audiences' reactions to tragedies; "[p]erils and misfortunes" themselves, Smith writes, "are the only proper theatre which can exhibit [heroism's] virtue to advantage, and draw upon it the full applause of the world" (58n). In Smith's view, our state *is* the theater; and an intense concern with theatricality governs both our acts and our reactions. According to Smith we either dread or desire this theatricality, depending upon the point of view of the spectators who represent the eyes of the world. We are not dealing here with an individual spectator who happens to behold our suffering; Smith pictures a society in which we feel surrounded by an audience. "Of such mighty importance does it appear to be," he writes, "in the imaginations of men, to stand in that situation which sets them most in the view of general sympathy and attention" (57).

Smith sees this theater in which the rich and powerful crave and receive the eyes of the public—whose attention the poor and weak fear and shun and yet also lack—as "necessary both to establish and to maintain the distinction of ranks and the order of society" and "at the same time, the great and most universal cause of the corruption of our moral sentiments" (61). One measure, or at least one result, of this social hierarchy and corruption is that the philosopher, although not an object of contempt like the poor, also seems to suffer from a want of spectators and sympathy. "Two different characters are presented to our emulation," writes Smith, the "rich and the great" and the "wise and the virtuous" (62). Of the "two different models, two different pictures" that seem to compete for our attention and approbation, one is "more gaudy and glittering in its colouring; the other more correct and more exquisitely beautiful in its outline."

While the picture of the rich and the great is seen "forcing itself upon the notice of every wandering eye," that of the philosopher is described as "attracting the attention of scarce any body but the most studious and careful observer." The philosopher, then, is not an exhibitionist; he does not enter into the theatricality of the public stage. But this means the picture that is represented to us so "we may fashion our own character and behaviour," the spectacle that entreats its spectators to enter into its sentiments and approve of its principles, will be ignored by the eyes of the world (62). This might explain the ease with which Smith can place his name on his title page—where he signs himself "Professor of Moral Philosophy"—and publish six editions of his book.

Shaftesbury worried that the ideal genre of philosophy was at an end and that philosophy itself "is no longer active in the world, nor can hardly, with any advantage, be brought upon the public stage."[23] He worried about how to present philosophy in public characters, before the eyes of readers whose presence by definition would turn his book to theater. For Smith, philosophy is not so much out of place on the stage of the world as it is off the stage. Smith must appeal to the sympathy of those few careful and studious readers who might be found reading a treatise on moral sentiments; but despite the success and renown of his book, his place is not before the public. (This, perhaps, is also what it means to sign one's book in the character of a "Professor of Moral Philosophy.") The philosopher, like the Stoic, refuses to force himself upon the notice of every wandering eye; he does not display the sentiments he asks others to share on the public stage. Yet this does not mean that he is exempt from a role in the theater of sympathy.

Smith's apparent lack of anxiety about appearing in public, printed characters before the eyes of mankind can also be attributed to the changing status of the book in the middle of the century and to the less personal and more academic character of Smith's book. Unlike Shaftesbury, Smith rarely uses the first-person singular: his almost constant use of the first-person plural both screens himself and practically assumes that the reader shares his sentiments and point of view. Smith's ability to focus on his careful and studious readers and to ignore the public audience that he elsewhere describes as governing people's actions and reactions—an audience that Smith represents as mercifully ignoring the wise and virtuous rather than beholding them without sympathy—can be understood in the context of Smith's discussion of the impartial spectator. It can also help us to understand the importance of this character in Smith's system. The presence of the fair and uninvolved spectator we are supposed to imagine examining and judging our conduct according to his ability to enter into our sentiments invariably leads to conflicts of interest and contradictory points of view. Smith acknowledges, for instance, that "the mysterious veil of self-delusion" might distort or misrepresent our view of ourselves and allow us to act improperly. The counter to this self-interested point of view would be the view of others: "If we saw ourselves in the light in which others see us, or in which they would see us if they knew all, a reformation would generally be unavoidable" (158–159). But the phrase with which Smith qualifies his view of the view of others is significant; others can't know all, and what is more, Smith makes it clear that the spectators who surround us are not to be trusted to view us in a disinterested light or to sympathize with the most moral sentiments.

In this sense the impartial spectator can be seen as a more reliable witness than the public; and I would argue that one of its primary roles is to counteract the presence of the public view. The impartial spectator is guaranteed to enter into our feelings if we act properly, thereby both compensating for and substituting for those spectators who withhold their sympathy. According to Smith, if we can be satisfied with the view of our imagined impartial spectator, "we can be more indifferent about the applause, and, in some measure, despise the censure of the world; secure that, however misunderstood or misrepresented, we are the natural and proper objects of approbation" (112). The view of spectators who might regard us without sympathy can be disregarded as we enter into a private relation with an ideal spectator who allows us to bypass, so to speak, the eyes of the world. Once again, we see an unbearable theatricality—yet not theater—avoided. Smith tries to respond to these conflicts of interest and point of view by resorting to the authority of an all-seeing spectator: "In such cases, the only effectual consolation of humbled and afflicted man lies in an appeal to a still higher tribunal, to that of the all-seeing Judge of the world, whose eye can never be deceived, and whose judgments can never be perverted" (131). The introduction of this literal *deus ex machina*— like the image of the Sun King at the end of *Tartuffe*—would release us from dependence on particular spectators, if not from the condition of being beheld. It is not so clear, however, from Smith's representation of society, that we could really disregard the regard of the spectators who face us.

The Theory of Moral Sentiments represents a world that is structured and governed by theatrical relations; it posits a necessary theatricality that is to be both sought after and avoided. For Smith, sympathy depends upon a theatrical relation between a spectator and a spectacle, a relation that is reversed and mirrored as both persons try to represent the other's feelings. We need this sympathy, we thrive upon it, and even when we are alone we double and divide ourselves in order to play the part of our own spectators. Thus the theatrical structure of sympathy is both acted out between people and internalized; the self as Smith represents it has a dramatic character, as it does for Shaftesbury. However, the same theatrical situation that is entered into in order to measure and attain sympathy becomes undesirable and even intolerable when it exists *apart* from an act of sympathy. This presents a problem in Smith's system because it turns out that sympathy is in many cases—in cases where it is needed the most—unlikely; indeed, perhaps unnatural, perhaps impossible. Faced with the prospect that people can't know each other's feelings and are reticent to enter into each other's pain, sufferers deny their pain in an effort to reach a concord with the sentiments of their spectators; or they refuse to exhibit feelings that can not be shared. Many people seek wealth and distinction in order to win the sympathy of the public, that crowd of spectators who love to enter into the sentiments of great men and who shun or regard with contempt those in distress. Those without wealth and power are grateful to be ignored rather than exposed before the eyes of spectators who will not sympathize with them; or they imagine an impartial spectator whose sympathy can help one disregard the unsympathetic regard of the world.

Thus the need for sympathy motivates both the moderation and the performance of emotions, both Stoicism and exhibitionism, both conformation to moral codes and the corruption of society. What each of these situations has in common is a desire to be seen with sympathy and, above all, a dread of being seen without sympathy. The theater of sympathy in *The Theory of Moral Sentiments* is based on the simultaneous necessity of spectators and fear of spectators; the ultimate threat in the world that Smith represents is the prospect of spectators who would deny sympathy. When spectators withhold sympathy they transform the situation of theater that structures and allows a representation and exchange of feelings into a situation of theatricality: the exposure before the eyes of the world that both Shaftesbury and Defoe found so threatening. Shaftesbury and Defoe looked for ways to conceal the self, to protect it behind an outward character. They used theater to avoid or negate the regard of an audience. Smith's epistemology pictures a self that is already partly concealed; but even if we repress or hide our sentiments, the need for sympathy compels us to imagine ourselves before the eyes of spectators, real or ideal. Smith's theory of sympathy poses us on the stage, where we must act our parts and appear before spectators who threaten to theatricalize us.

Smith provides a figure for this situation when he explains why it is better to be executed than humiliated. "A brave man is not rendered contemptible by being brought to the scaffold," writes Smith, "he is, by being set in the pillory." He continues:

> The sympathy of the spectators supports him in the one case, and saves him from that shame, that consciousness that his misery is felt by himself only, which is of all sentiments the most unsupportable. There is no sympathy in the other; or, if there is any, it is not with his pain, which is a trifle, but with his consciousness of the want of

sympathy with which this pain is attended. It is with his shame, not
with his sorrow. (60–61)

Smith pictures a man on a scaffold, on a stage. Although facing
death, he is spared being exposed to the most insupportable of
sentiments, the awareness of facing spectators who watch without
sympathy. The man in the pillory knows that there is no sympathy
in his situation; for him, there is no sympathy in the other who must
face him as a spectator. Ironically, if Smith were in the audience the
man would receive sympathy after all. In Smith's view he deserves
sympathy because he suffers the worst of all miseries: theatrical
exposure. But the sympathy of his spectators would only reinforce
the view that the man's condition is abhorrent. He stands like the
murderer represented by Smith, unable to face the regard of the
spectators who stand before him unmoved. His public stage has
become theatrical.

What is the difference between these two situations?
Both men face the eyes of the world from a stage. However, according to Smith's theory of moral sentiments, if the spectators withhold
sympathy, they remain spectators. If they grant sympathy—if they
enter into the sentiments of the person they are beholding, if they
become in some measure the same person as him, identify themselves with him through a transfer of persons and characters—then
they stop being spectators. The spectacle here is only a prelude if a
precondition for the situation of sympathy which in Smith's view
would deny the difference and distance between spectacle and spectator. The dream of sympathy, the fiction of sympathy, is that an
interplay and interchange of places, positions, persons, sentiments,
and points of view could cancel out the theatricality of the most
theatrical of situations. According to Smith, we desire and depend
on spectators but we can tolerate them only if we can believe in the
fiction that they can transport themselves from their distant position
and become us. Our greatest fear is that they will remain spectators.
The situation of theater determines our views and relations, for
better or for worse. In *The Theory of Moral Sentiments*, sympathy
comes to mean both theater and the only means of defeating theater. It is only through theater that we can escape the intolerable
situation that theatricality itself creates.

CHAPTER 8

Daniel Deronda
and the Wisest Beholder

"NO retrospect will take us to the true beginning," writes George Eliot in the epigraph to the first chapter of *Daniel Deronda*, insisting that we must always begin *"in medias res."*[1] Eliot allows, however, that "Men can do nothing without the make-believe of a beginning" (35), and in prefacing her novel with these reflections, she prefigures the importance of beginnings in the story of a young man who discovers his identity by discovering his Jewish genealogy and eventually sets out to find his origins in the Orient. This announcement of the novel's concern with the fictions of beginnings also serves to allude to the beginnings of Eliot's fiction: as a novel about origins, long-lost relatives, and the formation of identity, *Daniel Deronda* has its origins in the eighteenth century—a century known for its treatises about origins and its novels about characters' forgotten, unforgettable, avoided, or rediscovered origins. In this context Eliot's reference to beginning *in medias res* not only alludes to Horace's praise of Homer for beginning the *Iliad in medias res* rather than *ab ovo*; it also evokes Tristram Shandy's impossible attempt to begin his life story from his conception as well as in "the middle of things."[2]

Eliot's allusion to Horace includes Sterne's allusion and thus marks both her origins and her place in the middle of the history of the novel. Furthermore, the epigraph alludes to the novel's origins in the theater. As Barbara Hardy has noted, when Eliot writes in the epigraph, "whether our prologue be in heaven or on earth" (35), she evokes the double beginning of Goethe's *Faust* (885n). The first prologue of this play, called the "Vorspiel auf dem Theater," prefaces Goethe's *Schauspiel* by staging a dialogue between the theater manager, the playwright, and a jester which dis-

cusses the audience and the experience of watching a play. As it
considers beginnings, then, *Daniel Deronda* might be seen to declare its origins in both the eighteenth century and the theater as it
evokes the novel of origins, the origins of the novel, and the prologue of a play which discusses the theater (and promises a play that
will act like "ein Roman") by an eighteenth-century novelist whose
novels are concerned with actors, plays, spectators, and spectacles.[3]

   I have chosen to end this book with an interpretation of
Eliot's last novel because I take *Daniel Deronda* to be a continuation
of the investigations of theatrical relations that we have seen dramatized in texts by Shaftesbury, Defoe, and Smith. If I am interested
in the ways in which *Daniel Deronda* looks back to eighteenth-
century fiction and philosophy, however, I am less concerned with
Eliot's "true beginning" than I am with her elaboration of and reflections on the set of issues and concerns we have been examining.
Although *Daniel Deronda* was published in 1876, at a time when
authors had mastered the eighteenth-century anxiety about publishing a novel or any book before the eyes of the world, I will suggest
that this novel about someone who turns out to be living under a
pseudonym, written by a woman named Mary Ann Evans disguised
as a man named George Eliot, is concerned with its place before an
audience of readers who look on as spectators. *Daniel Deronda*
considers its own theatrical status as it dramatizes characters who
play-act on stage and in life; and it rehearses the problematic ways
in which people become spectators to the spectacles of others. In
this sense *Daniel Deronda* is about the interplay of theater and
sympathy; and I will suggest that as it explores the theatrical conditions of its own characters and world, the novel acts as a dramatization of Smith's *Theory of Moral Sentiments*.[4]

   Critics have discussed the importance of sympathy in
Eliot's novels, usually in the context of Eliot's concern with egoism
or egotism and her advocacy of what Felicia Bonaparte calls "man's
capacity . . . to make an imaginative leap in which he substitutes
self for others." In addition to analyzing characters according to
their proximity to the poles of sympathetic imagination and narcissism, critics have written of Eliot's belief in sympathy as a necessary

characteristic of the artist and of her desire to evoke the reader's sympathy, in Bonaparte's words, to force "the reader to enter into the consciousness of another self."5

However, although Eliot is seen as basing much of her moral system on the principle of sympathy, *Daniel Deronda* is often read as a warning about taking sympathy too far. While Gwendolen is viewed as a typical example of Eliot's "morally stupid" egoists, Deronda is seen as having an oversympathetic nature; Gwendolen's blindness to others is contrasted with his "aimless neutrality," his "too sympathetic, too passive" character, his "disease of sympathy."6 I will argue that Eliot's last novel is a more complicated examination of both the dynamics and the possibility of sympathy. Sympathy, for Eliot, is an epistemological and aesthetic as well as a moral problem. Gwendolen and Deronda can be seen to act out a theory of moral sentiments that amounts to a serious investigation of the epistemological conditions of sympathy as much as a romantic lesson in the failings of solipsism and the virtues of identifying with others. Although I am not concerned primarily with the question of influence, I will suggest that the sympathetic relations enacted between Deronda and Gwendolen, as well as between other characters in the novel, indicate that Eliot's depictions of sympathy are to a significant degree informed by *The Theory of Moral Sentiments.* Eliot shares with Smith not only particular descriptions and characterizations of sympathy, but also an understanding of sympathy based on its specifically *theatrical* dynamics. Eliot, like Smith, is concerned with the theater of sympathy.

In Book Two of *Daniel Deronda*, while rowing on the Thames Deronda sees a young woman who reminds him of "the girl-tragedies that are going on in the world" (228) and a few moments later he prevents the woman from drowning herself. She has heard him singing the gondolier's song from Rossini's *Otello* as he rowed and in their first words of conversation she speaks some lines from the song back to Deronda, as if they were in a scene from an opera; so it is not illogical that she asks him: "Do you belong to the theatre?" Deronda replies in what the narrator describes as "a decided tone," "No; I have nothing to do with the theatre" (232). For the reader of *Daniel Deronda*, this denial is rich in irony—and not only because of Deronda's melodramatic rescue of the woman Mirah (who turns out to be both an actress and a singer and his future wife), or because of his relations with Gwendolen (a theatrical would-be actress) and his mother (who also turns out to be an actress). The deepest irony comes from our sense that Daniel Deronda has everything to do with the theater. Indeed, one could read this brief dialogue, which occurs at a point in the narrative when Deronda knows nothing about his identity, as a Sophoclean joke and a signal from Eliot. I will argue that *Daniel Deronda*, a book which seems to have been planned in its first stages as both "a novel and play,"[7] in many senses belongs to the theater and has everything to do with the theater.

Ever since the publication of *Daniel Deronda* many readers have been troubled by the vast scope of the narrative and by the apparent incongruity between what has been considered the "Jewish" part of the novel and what might be thought of as the Henry James novel contained within Eliot's narrative—what F. R. Leavis, following James' own cue, insisted on calling *Gwendolen Harleth*.[8] My interpretation is not designed to change anyone's personal response to Eliot's story about a young Englishman who discovers that he is Jewish and agrees to carry on the mission of a nineteenth-century prophet, or her story about a young woman who gains wealth, status, misery, and consciousness at the hands of a brutal aristocrat, or the story that stages the interplay between these two plots. Implicit in my reading, however, is the argument that Eliot's concern with the figure of theater, and more specifically with the theatrical dynamics of sympathy, acts as a major organizing principle in *Daniel Deronda*. The figure of theater allows us to make sense both of Eliot's preoccupations in writing her last major work of fiction and of the ways in which *Daniel Deronda* offers not only retrospective but also prospective views in the history of the novel.

From the outset, the scene of *Daniel Deronda* belongs to the theater. "Was she beautiful or not beautiful? and what was the secret of form or expression which gave the dynamic quality to her glance?"(35). The first sentence establishes the point of view of a spectator as the narrator brings into focus Deronda's view of Gwendolen's eyes. As Gwendolen gambles—an activity once closely associated with the sins of the playhouse—we observe "player[s]" (37) "absorbed in play" before "spectators" (36). The "jeu" is described as a "drama" that "takes no long while to play out" (39) while a child stands nearby "as a masquerading advertisement on the platform of an itinerant show" (36). Accused by one of her companions of taking on "a new *rôle*" (42), Gwendolen is a player even when she is not gambling; described as a "very good furniture picture" (41), she is very much an object of sight. Deronda feels "the moment become dramatic" as his attention is "arrested" (37) by Gwendolen. Although she plays "unaffected by beholders" she becomes aware of "Deronda's gaze" (38): "Many were now watching her, but the sole observation she was conscious of was Deronda's" (39). Eliot's framing of this scene as theatrical could not be more explicit if it were set in the playhouse. The occasion of gambling allows her to use the vocabulary and characters of the theater; and the relationship of Gwendolen and Deronda is described in terms of the interaction between a player and a spectator. This literal and figurative presentation of the setting, activity, and relations of the theater sets the stage for concerns that Eliot will dramatize in the course of her novel.

Gwendolen's theatrical character is not just the result of the drama of the casino. We learn that she has been educated at "a showy school, where on all occasions of display she had been put foremost" (52) and that her life seems composed of "dramas in which she imagined herself a heroine" (68). This self-dramatizing tendency is displayed in the second chapter, where Gwendolen poses before a mirror "in an attitude that might have been chosen for her portrait" (46–47) and is moved to kiss "the cold glass which had looked so warm" (47). This almost childlike narcissism recalls the autoeroticism with which Roxana is "all on fire with the Sight"[9] of herself in a mirror. Gwendolen is attracted not just to the image of herself but also to the frame that sets her off as if she were a painting. She imagines her new home as "a good background" (54)

against which she might be painted as St. Cecilia or act "in charades
or theatrical pieces" (84). Like Roxana, Gwendolen improvises with
domestic architecture to replicate the conditions of the playhouse:
"The antechamber with folding-doors lent itself admirably to the
purposes of a stage" (90). Gwendolen, too, organizes a private performance before an invited audience. Mr. Gascoigne prohibits "the
acting of scenes from plays" but Gwendolen produces *tableaux vivants* that are "an imitation of acting" (89, 90) and perhaps even
more theatrical.

    The *tableau vivant* scenes in *Daniel Deronda* may re-
call the private theatricals of *Mansfield Park*, but more importantly,
I think, they cast Gwendolen in the role of Luciane from Goethe's
Die Wahlverwandtschaften.[10] Gwendolen, like Eliot, is "a student
of Goethe" (75) and she often resembles Luciane, the theatrical
young woman who performs "pantomimes and dances, in which
she was very good at expressing different characters" as well as
tableaux vivants. This affinity is underlined later in the novel,
when Deronda observes Gwendolen "standing with her back to
everyone." In this passage, the narrator advises: "If you have any
reason for not indulging a wish to speak to a fair woman, it is a bad
plan to look long at her back: the wish to see what it screens becomes the stronger" (463). Both the position depicted here and the
narrator's comment evoke the representation of the Ter Borch
tableau in *Elective Affinities* in which Luciane poses with her back
to the audience and (in Goethe's words) "the entirely natural wish to
see the face of the beautiful girl, after having seen her back for so
long" prompts a spectator to shout, "Tournez, s'il vous plaît."[11]
These allusions to *Elective Affinities* not only identify Gwendolen's
theatricality; they draw attention to the theatrical, pictorial, and
textual aspects of all the characters in Eliot's novels. *Elective Affinities* considers what it means to behold people as if they were
theatrical representations, paintings, or texts, and Eliot's *tableau
vivant* scenes can be viewed both as a signal of Eliot's relation to
Goethe and as a continuation of his inquiry.

    Daniel Deronda carries Goethe's consideration of the-
atrical relations further by posing Gwendolen in a *tableau vivant*
that represents "Hermione as the statue in the Winter's Tale" (90).
Here we see a dramatic representation of a scene that is already a

dramatic representation. Furthermore, not only is Gwendolen imitating a scene from Shakespeare's play; according to Hugh Witemeyer, Gwendolen is imitating popular pictures that represented "the attitude in which Mrs. Siddons and other eighteenth-century actresses regularly played the statue scene in *The Winter's Tale.*"¹² Gwendolen poses in a *tableau vivant* modeled after pictures of actresses performing a scene from Shakespeare's play in which a character poses as a statue, a painted representation. The *tableau vivant* stages the *tableau vivant* that is supposed to be staged by Hermione; Gwendolen turns herself into an unmoving representation of a woman who acts like a statue that looks like a person and appears to pass from art to life. This proliferation of frames is further compounded by Gwendolen's reaction to the unexpected panel showing the face of a dead man; after screaming yet standing "without change of attitude" she is said to look "like a statue into which a soul of Fear had entered" (91). Her eyes are "fixed" and when she falls, she is "mute" (92). Although she finally breaks frame, so to speak, she doesn't quite break character; at the moment that she plays a woman who is playing a statue that comes to life—in a *tableau* that poses all of its actors like statues or characters in a painting—Gwendolen really looks and acts like a statue, as if she were reversing the Pygmalion myth rather than following it as Shakespeare's characters appear to do. The irony and confusion continues as Klesmer responds to reversals of art and life in *tableaux* within *tableaux* by pretending to take the event as a "magnificent bit of *plastik*" (92). Eliot carries the joke further by having an unnamed spectator reject the theory that it was all part of the show since "Miss Harleth was too much affected" to have been acting (92). This is one moment when the often affected Gwendolen stops acting and almost becomes her part. Klesmer later disillusions Gwendolen when she asks his advice about her plan "to be an actress—to go on the stage" (295); but if her performance does not convince anyone of her talent, it displays for the reader the complex theatricality of Gwendolen's character, as well as the multiple levels of illusion and representation that structure the world of the novel.

I have dwelled upon the *tableau vivant* scene and its many illusions and allusions because it stands as an emblem for the relations enacted by characters throughout *Daniel Deronda*. The *tableau vivant* is not so much a figure as a literal demonstration of the way characters either pose for each other or are viewed as if they were paintings or statues. I am not speaking only of the theatrical characters such as Gwendolen or of the way that artistically inclined characters such as the Meyricks imagine turning people they see into paintings. The narrator, too, often turns characters into *tableaux vivants* by comparing them to paintings, describing them as if they were paintings, or describing the way they might appear to a painter. Deronda's hands, for example, are "such as Titian has painted in a picture" (226); Mirah's image in Deronda's mind is described as being "clear to him as an onyx cameo" (228). At another point the image of Deronda next to Grandcourt is described as a juxtaposition that "might have been a subject for those old painters who liked contrasts of temperament" (200).

Clearly, these passages and the many others like them are informed by the tradition of *ut pictura poesis:* the dream that texts could present images and *tableaux* to the reader's imagination. At times this illusion seems so strong that Eliot seems to feel that she can gesture toward an actual scene, commanding the reader to look. For example, she instructs the reader to "Imagine [Deronda] in such a scene" (202), to "look at his hands" (226). The reader is told to "see the perfect cameo [Mirah's] profile makes" (422). At other times the text reads not only as if it is to be visualized but also as if it is a script—almost a screenplay—that is to be enacted. Rather than simply describing Gwendolen's posture as she speaks to Rex, for instance, an authorial aside instructs: "Here should any young lady incline to imitate Gwendolen, let her consider the set of her head and neck: if the angle there had been different, the chin protrusive and the cervical vertebrae a trifle more curved in their position . . . " (100). This description is somewhere between stage directions and an analysis of Gwendolen as if she were a statue or *tableau vivant.*

Even characters who are neither painters nor actors seem to share a perspective that transforms people into living *tableaux.* The scene that describes Mordecai in the National Gallery (where "he look[s] at pictures as well as men") appeals to "some observant persons" who may actually have seen him; it speaks of a hat "which no painter would have asked him to take off" and describes the impression he would have made on hypothetical "spectators" (529), an impression that Mordecai is said to be aware of. We imagine Mordecai moving through the gallery, comparing pictures and people, as he himself is pictured as a portrait that would strike the eye of painters and beholders alike. Eliot's description is more than a conventional literary portrait; it is a *tableau* of a gallery that, like the novel itself, juxtaposes and interchanges painted and living *tableaux*. When, in her *tableau vivant*, Gwendolen acts like a painting of a woman acting the part of a woman who acts like a statue—as the audience wonders whether her mute, statuelike pose is representation or reality—she is dramatizing in explicit terms the way characters in *Daniel Deronda* appear both to each other and to the reader as *tableaux* come to life or life transformed to *tableaux*.

The transformation of Gwendolen's world to theater intensifies after she meets Grandcourt. From "the narrow theatre which life offers to a girl of twenty" (94) Gwendolen is thrust into a public arena which offers new roles as well as the props and characteristics of the stage. Grandcourt first tries to propose to Gwendolen in a landscape "where a bit of hanging wood made a sheltering amphitheatre" (183). Appropriately, the guests at Green Arbor agree that they are "playing an extemporised 'As you like it'" with Gwendolen in "the part of Rosalind" (188). Within this landscape Gwendolen's life seems "busy with a small social drama almost as little penetrated by a feeling of wider relations as if it had been a puppet show" (186); but the entry into this life of Grandcourt, who is earlier described as having a complexion "resembling that of an actress" (145), means only that Gwendolen will move into a more elaborately staged play. We should not be surprised to learn that Grandcourt's residence at Ryelands was "built by Inigo Jones" (354), Jonson's collaborator and rival in creating extravagantly theatrical court masques: Gwendolen's life with Grandcourt will take place in this grand court, as if on a stage set complete with façades, illusions, costumes, and an audience. The months leading up to Gwendolen's marriage are described as a "show, in which her consciousness was a wondering spectator" (405). As Mrs. Grandcourt, she feels herself "standing at the game of life with many eyes upon her" (402), as if she acts "the heroine of an admired play without the pains of art" (404).

Gwendolen is the most theatrical character in *Daniel Deronda*. We should realize, however, that our sense of her theatricality comes from at least two different levels of the narrative: the details of plot and character that show Gwendolen performing, posturing, role-playing, and imagining her life as a play; and the theatrical imagery and vocabulary that frame the presentation of the text. Between these two levels we find the tendency of the characters to turn each other to theater. In one "scene" between Gwendolen and Grandcourt, for example, it is hard to say exactly whose perspective theatricalizes Gwendolen. The narrator says: "A cruder lover would have lost the view of her pretty ways and attitudes, and spoiled all by stupid attempts at caresses, utterly destructive of drama. Grandcourt preferred the drama" (361). Gwendolen is striking attitudes, and we are told that she "played at reigning"; but the narrator suggests that if "Klesmer had seen more of her in this unconscious kind of acting, instead of when she was trying to be theatrical, he might have rated her chance higher" (361). Gwendolen seems to be unconscious of theater in this particular passage; Grandcourt, an imagined Klesmer, the narrator, and the reader all appear to provide the theatrical perspective. This suggests that Gwendolen is not always in control of the theatrical scenes and roles in which we see her, and that both author and reader participate in placing her on the stage.

In contrast to Gwendolen, both Deronda and Mirah are portrayed with antitheatrical sensibilities. K. M. Newton notes that Deronda and Mirah share "an intense dislike of acting."[13] I would suggest further that they seek to avoid not only the sort of posing and performing that Gwendolen seems to thrive on, but also the conditions of theatricality created when one appears as a spectacle before beholders. We have seen that both characters are repeatedly figured by the narrator as paintings or as subjects for paintings. Yet unlike the descriptions of Gwendolen posing as St. Cecelia, Hermione, or merely a woman in a painting, in the passages that picture them as paintings, neither Deronda nor Mirah are aware of the gaze of their real or hypothetical beholders. The scene we are asked to imagine, for example, when Deronda is introduced as a child in chapter 16, represents "a boy of thirteen, stretched prone on the grass where it was in shadow, his curly head propped on his arms over a book, while his tutor, also reading, sat on a campstool under shelter" (202).

To imagine this scene as a painting is to imagine the sort of *tableau* that Michael Fried calls a depiction of absorption: a painting in which the figures represented are so engrossed in an activity or meditative state that they appear to be oblivious of all beholders, especially the beholders who actually view the painting.[14] The *tableau* Eliot asks her readers to see fits squarely into the tradition of painting that, Fried has shown, seeks to deny or negate the presence of its beholders. Indeed, we are told that Deronda "objected very strongly to the notion, which others had not allowed him to escape, that his appearance was of a kind to draw attention" (226). At another point Hans Meyrick says to Deronda: "I forgot; you don't like sitting for your portrait" (513). If Deronda is pictured as a *tableau* in the course of the novel, it is never because he is posing for beholders. He resists the very idea of appearing before spectators; when, as a child, he is asked by Sir Hugo if he wants to be a singer who is "adored by the world" he responds with anger, "No; I should hate it!" (208). We have seen that he has a similar reaction when asked by Mirah if he belonged to the theater.

Deronda's avoidance of theatricality extends to his attitude toward Mirah. In a long argument with Hans Meyrick over the idea of painting Mirah as Berenice, what Deronda objects to is the public character of Hans' proposed *tableaux*. Deronda assumes that Mirah "would strongly object to being exhibited in this way" (516). Hans insists that his "pictures are likely to remain as private as the utmost hypersensitiveness could desire" and Deronda is said to recognize his "mistake as to publicity" (517); but he still insists that Hans "ought not to publish Mirah's face as a model for Berenice" (517). Like Shaftesbury, Deronda is concerned with a public and published exhibition that would place its subject on the stage of the world. He shows the same concern for Mirah's exposure before the public eye when she appears in a private performance sponsored by Lady Mallinger. (Earlier, Hans is said to act like Deronda when he remarks that a dress that Mirah calls "a very good stage-dress" for the occasion is "a little too theatrical" [545].) When Lady Pentreath suggests that Mirah learned to look demure "on the stage" Deronda is indignant that Mirah should be "remarked on in a free and easy way, as if she were an imported commodity disdainfully paid for by the fashionable public" (619). This analogy recalls Rousseau's condemnation in the *Lettre à d'Alembert sur les spectacles* of the roles the theater offers to women, both the actresses whose job is to "se montrer au public, et qui pis est, de se montrer pour de l'argent" and the female spectators who are "mises en étalage dans les loges comme sur le devant d'une boutique, en attendant les acheteurs."¹⁵ Deronda's imaginative and personal investment in this scene is revealed when he is reminded of the incident in his childhood when "Sir Hugo asked him if he would like to be a great singer" (619).

Of course, despite Deronda's hypersensitiveness about Mirah's public display, her performance is private, unpaid, and relatively untheatrical. It is not surprising that it is *Gwendolen* who strikes *Mirah* as "a new kind of stage-experience," as if she came out of "some unknown drama" (621). Indeed, in contrast to Gwendolen, who lacks the talent to be an actress or singer but seems innately theatrical, Mirah is a professional performer who appears to be singularly unsuited for the theater. Although she is raised by a show-business father "to sing for show at any minute, as if I had been a musical box," Mirah is said to have "no notion of being anybody but herself" (253). As for a career in the theater, it is judged that her voice "will never do for the public" (256) or "for the stage" (541); as for her manner off the stage, we learn that "her theatrical training had left no recognisable trace" (266). Thus, paradoxically, although she is raised in the theater and has a beautiful singing voice, both her characteristics and her disposition disqualify Mirah as an actress. She shares Deronda's antitheatrical sensibilities, rejecting not only a career on the stage but also theatricality as such. As I suggested before, however, this does not mean that either Mirah or Deronda have nothing to do with the theater. We can see again the complex mirroring and reversals that take place between the world of the stage and the stage of the world, as Eliot appears to define her characters in terms of their relation to the theater.

       Our recognition of Gwendolen as *Daniel Deronda's* most theatrical character would be incomplete if we overlooked the change that Gwendolen undergoes in relation to theater. I suggested earlier that she is not always in control of what makes her theatrical; this is especially evident after she assumes her most dramatic role: Mrs. Grandcourt. One indication of her changing relation to theater is the change in her attitude toward mirrors, which previously reflected her narcissistic and self-dramatizing disposition. It is perhaps no coincidence that Gwendolen Harleth, whose last name recalls not only Clarissa Harlowe but also harlot and harlequin, should have her life changed by a woman named Mirah and a woman named Glasher. Each woman serves as a kind of mirror or glass through which Gwendolen alters her image of herself. After receiving on her wedding day the letter and diamonds from Mrs. Glasher, Gwendolen sits before "glass panels" (405) but we are told that she "could not see the reflections of herself then" (407). Clearly she is upset and distracted in this scene after being accused of usurping the role of Mrs. Grandcourt from someone else, but afterwards she does not look at herself in the same way. Felicia Bonaparte writes that "the egoists of [Eliot's] novels are habitually attracted to mirrors" and remarks that "Gwendolen often kisses 'her fortunate image in the glass'"[16] but Gwendolen does not, in fact, do this often; she kisses her image in the glass only one time that we see, in chapter 2. As early as chapter 21 we learn that the "self-delight with which she had kissed her image in the glass had faded" (270) and the passage that Bonaparte cites specifies that Gwendolen "no longer felt inclined to kiss her fortunate image in the glass; she looked at it with wonder that she could be so miserable" (477).

When we see her "looking at herself in a mirror" it is "not in admiration, but in a sad kind of companionship" (485). Gwendolen as Mrs. Grandcourt sometimes seems deprived of her reflection: we see her "not recognising herself in the glass panels" (651) and covering her hair with "manifest contempt of appearance" (671) after standing before two mirrors. If mirrors remain an important index of Gwendolen's character, they do not always reflect the posing that characterizes her most theatrical moments.

Ironically, this change in Gwendolen's attitude occurs at the moment she is placed as never before on the stage of the world. The "grand dance" that Sir Hugo gives on New Year's Eve marks Gwendolen's public debut as Mrs. Grandcourt. Held in the "picture-gallery" where even the rows of portraits are described as "a piquant line of spectators" (495), this ball is as theatrical as the ball that features Roxana's most theatrical performance. Like Roxana, Gwendolen is described as "the cynosure of all eyes" (496); yet she reacts to the sort of exhibition that she would have desired previously with the sentiments that Roxana displays in her antitheatrical stage. "Are you persuading Mrs. Grandcourt to play to us" (495) asks Sir Hugo on the night before the ball when he finds Gwendolen and Deronda at the piano. Gwendolen, who is introduced to the reader and Deronda as someone who plays, replies: "I cannot persuade myself" (495).

Eliot compounds the irony in these reversals when she has Grandcourt accuse Gwendolen of "showing whims like a mad woman in a play" (502) after he has noticed her secret display of her necklace to Deronda. He insists that she "not make a spectacle of [her]self" (503) but what has angered him, aside from any jealousy about Deronda, is that she has stopped acting her part on their public stage. He objects that she has neglected her appearance before the eyes of the world and insists, "you will either fill your place properly—to the world and to me—or you will go to the devil" (503). Grandcourt, we are told, desires "a world of admiring or envying spectators" (646), like the rich and corrupt men Adam Smith condemns in *The Theory of Moral Sentiments*. Grandcourt demands that Gwendolen "be on the scene as Mrs. Grandcourt" and she feels herself "watched in that part by the exacting eyes of a husband" who would punish any "failure in her representation" (608). Gwendolen's life has never been so theatrical yet she finds herself imprisoned in a role, forced to act out a scenario controlled by a theatrical master of appearances who seems "to gratify himself with looking at her" (504) and gain "an intense satisfaction in leading his wife captive" in a manner that gives their life "a royal representation and publicity" (736). Gwendolen is in a double bind: she resists the once pleasurable role of appearing in costumes before admiring beholders, yet in Grandcourt's view when she neglects her part before the eyes of the world she acts like a character in a play and makes a spectacle of herself. Furthermore, Gwendolen is forced to continue in a role she despises because she dreads "any act, word, or look that would be a confession to the world" (608). She burns the letter from Mrs. Glasher "lest accusation and proof at once should meet all eyes" (407), but like Roxana, she must live in fear that "an involuntary confession" (608) will expose her before the eyes of the world and reveal her shame.

I am suggesting that Gwendolen, like Roxana, moves from exhibitionism to an abhorrence of being the cynosure of all eyes—particularly of being the object of Grandcourt's observation and display. This does not mean, however, that she seeks to escape from all theatrical relations. Indeed, the comparatively antitheatrical attitude she adopts in regard to both herself and her beholders develops at the same time that Gwendolen renews her investment in the private theater that Eliot represents in the first pages of the novel: the theater in which Gwendolen is a player and Deronda is her most significant spectator. As she rebels against Grandcourt's world of representation and publicity, Gwendolen increasingly places Deronda in the role of her beholder. I will argue that what is at stake in this private theater, what accounts for Gwendolen's risky investment, is sympathy.

In considering *Daniel Deronda* as a sympathetic spectator, we should note the frequency with which Eliot asks us to imagine her central character as a beholder of drownings. Two of the novel's most important turns of plot include the prospect of a drowning: when Deronda rescues Mirah on the banks of the Thames as she prepares her "drowning-shroud" (230) and when he stumbles upon the scene of Grandcourt's drowning, as bystanders rescue Gwendolen from the water. Such scenes of drowning, rescues, and prospects of ships and shores appear as figures throughout the narrative. Gwendolen is pictured like Mirah (in an image that might evoke Dido as well): "Deronda felt [Gwendolen's] look as if she had been stretching her arms toward him from a forsaken shore" (838). He comes to realize that "she too needed a rescue, and one much more difficult than that of the wanderer by the river—a rescue for which he felt himself helpless" (620). The helplessness Deronda feels when faced with Gwendolen is figured as his inability to save her from drowning: "It was as if he saw her drowning while his limbs were bound" (509). Eliot repeatedly portrays Gwendolen as a kind of shipwreck that is witnessed by Deronda from a distant shore: "Words seemed to have no more rescue in them than if he had been beholding a vessel in peril of wreck—the poor ship with its many-lived anguish beaten by the inescapable storm" (672–673).

I suggest that the image of Deronda as a spectator to the distress of a ship in a storm, and in general, Eliot's descriptions of beholding someone in danger of drowning, are meant to evoke the famous passage that begins Book II of *De Rerum Natura* where Lucretius writes of the pleasure of beholding a ship in peril at sea from the safety of shore.[17] I suggest further that in alluding to this passage Eliot is alluding to a complex figure which by the eighteenth century had become a trope for the experience of beholding a spectacle of suffering—and more specifically, a trope for the experience of watching a tragedy in the theater. Eliot's use of this trope evokes a history of other authors' revisions of Lucretius. The passage in *De Rerum Natura* illustrates the pleasure (literally, the sweetness) of watching suffering or danger from a safe distance. In *The Tempest*, in what might be considered Shakespeare's version of this scene, Miranda describes her response to beholding a shipwreck from the shore in different terms. Recounting the sentiments she felt as she witnessed what Prospero calls "the direful spectacle of the wrack," Miranda says, "I have sufferèd/ With those that I saw suffer." The spectacle, brought about by Prospero's "art," touches "the very virtue of compassion" in her.[18]

In the eighteenth century, in his influential *Réflexions critiques sur la poésie et sur la peinture*, the Abbé Du Bos quotes Lucretius in a chapter about the attraction of spectacles: "Il est touchant, dit Lucrèce, de voir du rivage un vaisseau luter contre les vagues qui le veulent engloutir."[19] That Du Bos would translate the Latin "Suave" ("It is sweet") with the French "Il est touchant" ("It is touching") (immediately before citing the Latin text) suggests that he is more interested in the sort of sympathetic response Miranda displays while watching a shipwreck than in the pleasing detachment and self-concern described by Lucretius. But it is precisely the ambiguity of this figure, or the desire to read it in opposite ways, that charges it with meaning in eighteenth-century discussions of sympathy and theater. Both aesthetics and moral philosophy in the eighteenth century are concerned with the combination of distance and emotional identification experienced by spectators of scenes of suffering or danger. For some, such as Du Bos and Kames, sympathy seems to act as a moral guarantee for the theater; for others, such as Smith and Rousseau, the failure of sympathy in the theater and consequently on the stage of the world is partially responsible for the corruption of morals in society.[20] Both the difference and distance described by Lucretius and the sympathetic identification exemplified by Miranda are crucial experiences in the history of aesthetics as spectators try to account for the experience of beholding tragedy in a theater.

In her descriptions of Deronda as beholder to shipwrecks or scenes of suffering, Eliot appears to identify Deronda with Miranda's interpretation of the role of sympathetic spectator. My point, however, is that in evoking the trope of someone watching the spectacle of a shipwreck or drowning, Eliot is raising the question of how one beholds the sight of someone suffering; and furthermore, in doing so, she is evoking a theoretical and historical context that has framed this question in specifically *theatrical* terms. It is no coincidence that when Grandcourt and Gwendolen set off on the boating expedition that will result in a drowning and a near-drowning, the narrator says: "the scene was as good as a theatrical representation for all beholders" (745). Deronda witnesses the last scene in this act, as he discovers a crowd of spectators standing on the shore, some with telescopes, watching the drowning and the rescue. Nor is it a coincidence that Mirah asks Deronda if he belongs to the theater immediately after he rescues her from her attempt to drown herself. As I have suggested, these episodes belong to the theater; and to imagine Deronda as the sympathetic spectator to Gwendolen (and others) is to ask the question posed by Smith and other eighteenth-century theoreticians of sympathy: what sort of sympathy is possible between people who face each other as spectators and spectacles?

From the first scene of the novel, Deronda seems to personify for Gwendolen Smith's role of the impartial spectator; he is a relatively disinterested observer whose opinion and regard seem to matter more than those of any other beholder. Later in the novel, we learn that Deronda has viewed the world with "impartial sympathy" (814); as the novel begins, Gwendolen feels that his "gaze seemed to have acted as an evil eye" (38). To Gwendolen, Deronda represents an unknown and distant spectator who will form some judgment of her actions. As he watches her with "a growing expression of scrutiny" (38) in his eyes, his regard becomes "the sole observation she was conscious of" (39). Gwendolen does not really seem to think that Deronda causes her bad luck; rather, she is disconcerted because from her first moments as a spectacle for Deronda she is preoccupied with imagining his sentiments and point of view. When she finally meets Deronda at Sir Hugo's and again sees "his eyes fixed on her with a look so gravely penetrating," she thinks: "I wonder what he thinks of me really" (376). Later she complains, "I object to any eyes that are critical" (462) but she asks Deronda why he "thought it wrong for me to gamble" (382).

Throughout the novel, Gwendolen increasingly thinks of Deronda not just as a spectator but as that projection of conscience and judgment that is represented by the figure of Smith's impartial spectator. Deronda becomes for Gwendolen what Smith calls "reason, principle, conscience, the inhabitant of the breast, the man within, the great judge and arbiter of our conduct."[21] Gwendolen imagines him as "being not her admirer but her superior: in some mysterious way he was becoming a part of her conscience" (468). Like Smith's impartial spectator, Deronda becomes a "monitor" in relation to Gwendolen, "the strongest of all monitors" (503). According to Smith, we "endeavour to examine our own conduct as we imagine any other fair and impartial spectator would examine it. If, upon placing ourselves in his situation, we thoroughly enter into all the passions and motives which influenced it, we approve of it, by sympathy with the approbation of this supposedly equitable judge. If otherwise, we enter into his disapprobation, and condemn it."[22] Gwendolen, too, begins to view herself by trying to enter into the sentiments that Deronda feels in trying to imagine her feelings. She learns "to see all her acts through the impression they would make on Deronda: whatever relief might come to her, she could not sever it from the judgment of her that would be created in his mind" (737).

Like Theophrastus Such (whose character Eliot sketched after completing *Daniel Deronda*) Gwendolen finds within herself "a permanent longing for approbation, sympathy, and love";[23] as in *The Theory of Moral Sentiments*, however, approbation and sympathy—which for Smith are practically synonyms—seem much more important than love. From the moment she imagines Deronda's disapproval in the casino, through her sense of guilt about wronging the illegitimate children with whom she assumes Deronda would identify himself, to the remorse with which she faces him after Grandcourt's death, Gwendolen longs for Deronda's approbation and dreads the prospect of his disapprobation. In her confession following Grandcourt's death, she asks Deronda, "you will not want to punish me now?" (757). She acts like the man Smith pictures on the scaffold, whose worst punishment would be the prospect of being watched and judged by unsympathetic spectators; indeed, she is like the murderer described by Smith, who is compelled both to imagine the spectators who will withhold their sympathy and to beg that they judge him for his crime. The possibility of divine retribution seems to be eclipsed by the judgment of the imagined spectator

Smith calls the "demigod within the breast."[24] Gwendolen thinks of Deronda as an "angel from whom she could not think of concealing any deed so as to win an ignorant regard from him" (737). As a demigod and internalized spectator, Deronda's regard seems omniscient; Gwendolen gives voice to "inarticulate prayers" and imagines salvation in "the form of Deronda's presence and words, of the sympathy he might have for her" (738). It is this "compassion" that seems to be "regarding her from a halo of superiority" (759) that Gwendolen longs for.

Gwendolen's obsession with viewing her life through Deronda's eyes in order to see if she can imagine his sympathy may help explain the shift in her attitude toward mirrors. She uses Deronda's perspective to become a spectator to herself just as she used a mirror—except the theater here takes the form of a court of judgment rather than a court of admiration. Deronda becomes for Gwendolen what Smith calls "the only looking-glass by which we can, in some measure, with the eyes of other people, scrutinize the propriety of our own conduct."[25] Deronda is the impartial spectator who causes her to disregard the image in her mirror, as well as the image of her reflected in the eyes of the world. Their conversations sometimes occur in proximity to mirrors; at one point Gwendolen turns "from the glass and look[ed] at him. He looked full at her in return" (501), as if he has taken the place of her mirror. At another point, after standing before two mirrors, Gwendolen meets Deronda and sees "in his embarrassment some reflection of her own" (671). Most of all, she desires that reflection of her own sentiments that would guarantee the approbation that comes in the looking-glass of sympathy. Gwendolen tries to see herself as Deronda sees her in order to see if he can find in her a reflection of his sentiments.

As much as she fears his judgment, Gwendolen does in fact imagine that Deronda will be able to imagine what goes on in her mind; in this sense, she believes that Deronda regards her with sympathy. Deronda is described as combining the judgment, compassion, and ability to enter into the thoughts of another that Smith includes in his characterization of sympathy. Deronda is "inclined to judge her tenderly, to excuse, to pity. He thought he had found a key now by which to interpret her more clearly" (488). Gwendolen feels "confidence in his interpretation of her" (500); as if he could read her mind and share her feelings, she imagines him "free from all misunderstanding . . . or rather, that he should misunderstand her had never entered into her mind" (504). She may feel that she could never avoid his regard, but she is "unvisited by any dream of his being a man who could misinterpret her" (625).

Deronda's position as a sympathetic spectator is in part defined by his opposition to Grandcourt, whose solipsism prevents him from having "the least conception of what was going on in the breast of this wife" (734). In a passage that appears shortly after an instruction to the reader to "enter into the soul" of Gwendolen, the narrator describes Grandcourt's total lack of sympathy: "Some men bring themselves to believe, and not merely maintain, the non-existence of an external world. . . . How, then, could Grandcourt divine what was going on in Gwendolen's breast?" (734–735). Like Deronda, he stands as a constant spectator to Gwendolen—"he would not leave her out of his sight"—but unlike Deronda he is said to "interpret" the "signs" of Gwendolen's sentiments "with the narrow correctness which leaves a world of unknown feeling behind" (742). Not only does Grandcourt hold Gwendolen captive on a public stage before the eyes of mankind, he himself represents the theatricalizing spectator whose specter haunts *The Theory of Moral Sentiments*. "You don't in the least imagine what is in my mind" (744), says Gwendolen to Grandcourt just before they compose the "scene" which is "as good as a theatrical representation for all beholders" (745). Unable and unwilling to regard her with sympathy, Grandcourt must face Gwendolen as a spectator who will turn her into theater.

By contrast, Deronda appears to be the ideal sympathetic spectator. As she turns to him for sympathy, Gwendolen seems to have good grounds for her belief in his ability to enter into the thoughts and feelings of other people. Although he watches others with critical scrutiny, Deronda embodies "the most exquisite sensibility both to the original and sympathetic feelings of others" that

Smith pairs with self-command to represent the "man of the most perfect virtue."[26] The well-known passage in which Eliot poses Deronda as both Wordsworth and Rousseau[27]—floating in a boat on the water, forgetting himself in a "half-involuntary identification of himself with the objects he was looking at, thinking how far it might be possible habitually to shift his centre till his own personality would be no less outside him than the landscape" (229)—is only a Romantic application to nature of the imaginative transport that Smith less romantically described in relation to other people.

Throughout the novel we find examples of Deronda's "keenly perceptive sympathetic emotiveness" (553), his "habit of thinking himself imaginatively into the experience of others" (570). He offers Mordecai, for example, "words of sympathy" such as "I feel with you—I feel strongly with you" (557); for Gwendolen, he not only acts out Smith's theory of moral sentiments, he actually preaches a sort of gospel of sympathy. "I suppose our keen feeling for ourselves might end in giving us a keen feeling for others" (507), says Deronda as he tries to teach Gwendolen to take "an interest in the world beyond the small drama of personal desires" (507). Deronda undoubtably appears as the representative of sympathy in the novel, which helps to explain Gwendolen's investment in him as both a real and imagined beholder. He represents a sympathetic spectator who will act as a guardian angel to teach her to leave the world of Grandcourt's solipsism and imagine a world of others; he stands as an all-seeing judge onto whom Gwendolen can project her conscience; and his apparent ability to exchange parts and persons with the object of his compassion, to transport himself so he can imagine what passes in her mind, seems to neutralize the theatrical conditions that first place them in a spectator-spectacle relationship—perhaps even neutralize the threatricality of her position on a public stage. With his "many-sided sympathy" (412) Deronda seems to carry sympathy to its limits. However, it is at the limits of sympathy that Eliot's inquiry into moral sentiments really begins.

I have noted that many readers of *Daniel Deronda* have emphasized Deronda's need to become less sympathetic. In an often-cited passage, the narrator explains: "His imagination had so wrought itself to the habit of seeing things as they probably appeared to others, that a strong partisanship . . . had become an insincerity for him. His plenteous, flexible sympathy had ended by falling into one current with that reflective analysis which tends to neutralise sympathy" (412). It is as if Deronda has become so much a spectator that he risks losing his ability to be an actor in the world: "A too reflective and diffusive sympathy was in danger of paralysing in him . . . the conditions of moral force" (413). Deronda seems to be in danger of losing himself, as when he forgets himself while floating aimlessly in the river, until the discovery of his identity allows him "the noble partiality . . . that makes sympathy practical" (814). No longer suffering from the *oubli de l'homme* that Rousseau claimed afflicted the actor who gave up his own feelings for those of the part he adopted, Deronda seems to move away from the suppression of one's "own original and selfish feelings" that, according to Smith, characterizes the man of virtue and sympathy.[28] "His judgment no longer wandering in the mazes of impartial sympathy" (814), Deronda seems to abandon his role as the purely impartial spectator to the spectacle of other people.

What, however, does Deronda learn that alters the dispositions of his sympathetic imagination? What accounts for the shift in his position of sympathetic spectator to the thoughts and sentiments of others? If the answer to these questions is that Deronda discovers his Jewish identity—his vocation, his calling, his past and future—then we should recognize that this discovery is practically simultaneous with Deronda's largest act of sympathy: his vow to his mother to "identify myself, as far as possible, with my hereditary people" (724). From this moment on, Deronda will adopt the identity of an entire people once considered different from himself; in particular, he will accept the role of Mordecai's "executive self" (530). However, it is during these highly charged and pivotal conversations with his mother that Deronda learns about the limits as well as the risks of sympathy. It is no coincidence that Eliot places the conversations between Deronda and his mother in close juxtaposition to the description (from which I have quoted) of Grandcourt's solipsism and his inability to imagine the sentiments of another person. Book Seven of *Daniel Deronda* is not so much about the inadvisability of extreme sympathy as it is an examination of the very possibility of sympathy. In this sense Deronda and Grandcourt represent not so much opposites of each other as somewhat distant points on a continuum. Deronda and Grandcourt may represent different extremes of the ability to sympathize, but the dialogues between Deronda and his mother suggest that they are closer than he or we had thought.

Upon meeting his mother, Deronda discovers that the woman whose face he had often imagined "as one which had a likeness to his own" reveals "likeness . . . amidst more striking differences" (687). Faced with difference where he might have expected likeness, he says, "I used to think that you might be suffering" and the Princess replies, "I *am* suffering. But with a suffering that you can't comfort" (688). Once again, Deronda finds himself a witness to someone who is suffering but the Princess suggests that he will not be able to enter into her sentiments—either her suffering or the past sentiments she is trying to justify. She is proud and self-assured but, like Gwendolen, she wonders about how Deronda will view her: "Shall you comprehend your mother—or only blame her?" (692). Deronda fully expects to regard his mother with sympathy, to act as he always has by transporting himself to someone else's place and person. He insists, "What I have been most trying to do for fifteen years is to have some understanding of those who differ from myself" (692). Expecting that he can enter into his mother's pain, imagine her thoughts and feelings, he asks her to recount her motives: "Though my own experience has been quite different, I enter into the painfulness of your struggle. I can imagine the hardship of an enforced renunciation" (694). The Princess, however, responds to Deronda's declaration of sympathy with a denial of his fellow-feeling: "No. . . . You are not a woman. You may try—but you can never imagine what it is to have a man's force of genius in you, and yet to suffer the slavery of being a girl" (694). Clearly, these lines constitute a deeply personal as well as polemical statement for Eliot; one source for the intensity of the confrontation between Deronda and the Princess must be the utterly divided sympathies that Eliot experienced as she portrayed the protagonist of her novel and a woman who knew what it meant to be an artist in nineteenth-century Europe. However, for the purposes of this reading, I want to suggest that the issue of sexual difference here is a specific manifestation of the more general question of difference that Eliot is insisting on in this chapter.

The Princess insists that Deronda cannot transport himself across the difference and distance that separates them. Deronda, as usual, is standing within the Romantic tradition of sympathy that expects finely tuned sensibilities to enable one to imagine the feelings of another person. The Princess acts as if she has adopted the more sceptical and even Stoical aspects of Smith's *Theory of Moral Sentiments*. She denies that Deronda can enter into her feelings, imagine her pain; she acts coldly, as if afraid to reveal her emotions. As Deronda is leaving she reflects, "How do I know that I can see you again? I cannot bear to be seen when I am in pain" (703)—as if she has read Smith's stoical explanation of why it is improper to display pain, especially physical pain: "passions which take their origin from the body . . . excite either no sympathy at all, or such a degree of it, as is altogether disproportioned to the violence of what is felt by the sufferer."[29] She fears being seen by a spectator who might not be able to sympathize with her; as she cries she seems to wish "that they should not look at each other" (702). She has not exactly blushed to acknowledge her son, but she must continue to avoid his sight. Like Gwendolen, the Princess tries to see herself through Deronda's eyes; however, the point of view she represents to herself as she imagines Deronda imagining her feelings is one that leaves her exposed. She cannot believe in his sympathy. She teaches him his difference as well as his identity.

After his audience with the Princess, Deronda's relations with Gwendolen are not the same. The possibilities before them have been redefined (Deronda could now marry either Gwendolen or Mirah) but I think the difference in their relations can be described in terms of sympathy. After his second conversation with his mother, and after the narrator's discussion about Grandcourt's inability to enter into the sentiments of others, Deronda feels he should find Gwendolen and "manifest the continuance of his sympathy" (748). Instead, he discovers from the strand the shipwreck that began as if a "theatrical representation." From this point on, Deronda is closer to the distant beholder of a shipwreck described by Lucretius than to Miranda; he neither stops sympathizing with Gwendolen nor takes pleasure in her pain, but he no longer plays the role of the ideal sympathetic spectator. Although the "sight" of Gwendolen after the accident "pierced him with pity" (753), Deronda is described as keeping "his more passionate sympathy . . . in abeyance" (752). Before he accepted the role of demigod or angel; now he resents the part of a "priest. He dreaded the weight of this woman's soul flung upon his own" (754). "You cannot bear to look at me" (764), says Gwendolen to the observer she regards as her judge and conscience. As usual, she looks to his sympathy; but although his "heart was pierced" his sympathy appears to be qualified: we are told that Deronda's appearance made "his ready sympathy seem more personal and special than it really was" (765). There are, of course, complicated and intense feelings at stake in this chapter, as Deronda faces Gwendolen in her guilt and grief; for the first time, however, their conversations end with Gwendolen's realization that "the distance between them was too great" (767).

Although, at the end of the novel, Deronda is assumed by Sir Hugo to be "the man who knew most about what Mrs. Grandcourt felt or did not feel" (784), Deronda no longer stands as the privileged beholder and interpreter of Gwendolen's sentiments. Difference and distance are the topics of conversation as Deronda and Gwendolen meet again for the last time in the novel. To his declaration that he is a Jew, she asks: "What difference need that have made?" and he replies: "It has made a great difference to me" (873). However, the lines that follow make it clear that the difference in question is not merely one of religion or vocation; Deronda feels that "the distance between her ideas and his acted like a difference of native language, making him uncertain what force his words would carry" (873). When Deronda first meets his mother he can "not even conjecture in what language she would speak to him," although her facial expressions during their first moments together are described as a "tacit language" (687). She speaks English, but with a foreign accent, to say what she has to say about what bonds and separates them. Gwendolen and Deronda have always assumed that they shared a common language, indeed that words between them were not entirely necessary. Now, their dialogue encounters "misunderstanding" and Gwendolen imagines "mountainous travel for her mind before it could reach Deronda's" (874). Eliot's Wittgensteinian metaphor of an unshared language stands for the distance between two minds. Although Deronda is still disposed to sympathize with Gwendolen, just as he always has tried to represent to himself the experience of others, he finds he "could not quite divine what was going on within her" (874). No longer is misunderstanding or misinterpretation not a question; Deronda must divine her sentiments and he recognizes that he may not be able to decipher their language. More happens in this scene than Gwendolen's sense that she has been "dislodged from her supremacy in her own world" (876). Both Gwendolen and Deronda are forced to confront the limits of sympathy. "If we had been much together before, we should have felt our differences more, and seemed to get farther apart," explains Deronda; "But our minds may get nearer" (878). Neither Deronda nor Gwendolen sees the world of others as Grandcourt did; in fact, Gwendolen is learning to be less like Grandcourt than ever before. Yet the promise that their minds may get nearer must follow a new acknowledgment that they are apart.

If Deronda in some sense becomes disillusioned about sympathy in his conversations with the Princess and Gwendolen, this, of course, does not mean that sympathy ceases to influence his actions or view of the world. I would like to return to the suggestion I made earlier that Deronda's decision to identify himself with his Jewish heritage could itself be construed as a far-reaching act of sympathy. Deirdre David writes that when Deronda "is finally released from social paralysis into action by the discovery of his racial heritage, he abandons one meditative passive role, sympathetic confessor to women, for another, Jewish epic hero with a destiny to

be fulfilled rather than a career to be chosen."³⁰ Although I think
that Deronda's paralysis and passivity have been overemphasized—
indeed, it is not so clear that sympathy is passive in the novel—I
think it is important to recognize the similarity between Deronda's
roles both before and after his "conversion" (or perhaps we should
say his "unconversion"). In many ways the practical, partial sympathy that Deronda is supposed to display after his meeting with his
mother—what is supposed to rescue him from the loss of self
brought about by what one critic calls the "fatal intensity of absolute
sympathy"³¹—is strikingly similar to the sympathy that Deronda
enacted earlier in the novel, particularly in relation to Gwendolen.
Indeed, Deronda's relation to Gwendolen is often evoked by the
terms in which Deronda's conversations with Mordecai are described. Just as Gwendolen has complete confidence in Deronda's
understanding of her sentiments, Mordecai is "conscious of no bar-
rier to a complete understanding between him and Deronda" (551).
Deronda responds to Mordecai's faith in him with a sense of ap-
prehensiveness but with "keenly perceptive sympathetic emotiveness" (553). His hand is "sympathetic" (558) as he speaks "words of
sympathy" (557). The two are said to share a consciousness as intense "as if they had been two undeclared lovers" (552), and when
Deronda accepts the "transference of self" (553) that Mordecai has
dreamed of, it is characterized by Mordecai as "the marriage of our
souls" (820). Such a sympathetic communion goes beyond any understanding that may have been shared by Deronda and Gwendolen. Deronda, in fact, marries himself both to Mordecai's mission
and to Mordecai's sister—his female counterpart, so to speak. In
some sense Mordecai is as much a "rival" for Gwendolen as Mirah
is, and Deronda's decision to marry Mirah is in part a decision to
join himself to Mordecai.

When Deronda vows to identify himself with his hereditary people he tells his mother, "I shall be all the more the grand-
son whom also you willed to annihilate" (727). However, how
much or what part of Deronda's identity remains after the marriage
of true minds that takes place in his sympathetic exchange with
Mordecai? Mordecai has searched for "a man who differed from

himself . . . who would have all the elements necessary for sympathy with him, but in an embodiment unlike his own" (529). This "marriage," based on sympathy and difference, seems analogous to the doctrine of Jewish identity Deronda inherits from his grandfather—the doctrine described as a "balance of separateness and communication" that would preserve identity and difference, rather than "the many sorts of grain going back from their variety into sameness" (791).

I am inclined to agree with David Carroll's suggestion that the "discussions on the Jewish state and its religion are a definition on a national level of the meaning of the personal relations in the other half of the novel."[32] Yet Mordecai thinks of Deronda as "my new self" (551) and vows to him, "I shall live in you" (603). It is not so clear that the doctrine of separateness and communication is really carried out in the transference, conversion, and substitution of selves that turns Deronda into Mordecai's translation as well as his translator. In what sense does Deronda's extended act of sympathy actually annihilate his self, in the way that Rousseau fears the actor annihilates himself in taking someone else's part? In my attempts to trace the narrative of sympathy that unfolds in the course of *Daniel Deronda*, I have suggested that Eliot is engaged in an exploration of the risks and possibilities of sympathy: the conditions of its existence and the consequences of its presence and absence. I have implied that this exploration leaves Eliot ambivalent about sympathy; nowhere is this ambivalence more apparent than in the novel's implication that sympathy means subjection or loss of self.

The defense the Princess offers to Deronda for why she refused to identify herself with her hereditary people is based on a view of human relations as a struggle between selves. She describes her rebellion against "the slavery of being a girl" and against men who "turn their wives and daughters into slaves" (694); and as she strives for some "mastery" (694) in her conversation with her son, she explains, "I obey something tyrannic . . . I have been forced to obey my dead father" (693). She describes Deronda's father as a man "I knew I could rule" (695).[33] At issue here is not only the struggle of a woman against patriarchy in its individual and institutional forms;

for the Princess, it is love itself that leads to subjection: "I know very well what love makes of men and women—it is subjection. It takes another for a larger self, enclosing this one. . . . I was never willingly subject to any man. Men have been subject to me" (730). Threatened with slavery by a tyrant, the Princess (we can now recognize the appropriateness of the title that names her) finds instead a man she can rule. What is at stake is not just power but the self itself—whether the subject will be subject to another self. We can see now that regardless of how much the Princess believed in the power of sympathy, she clearly would find such a power threatening. Eliot displays the dangers of subjection in the marriage of Grandcourt and Gwendolen, a union based from the outset on a struggle for power that is almost devoid of sympathy. We are told in the chapter immediately following the Princess' characterization of love as subjection that Gwendolen "meant to rule and have her own way" when she married, but her "disposition to dominate" (732) loses out to Grandcourt's demand for total control. With "the courage and confidence that belong to domination" (744), Grandcourt takes "an intense satisfaction in leading his wife captive" (736), in keeping her "under his power" (734). Gwendolen's only means of resistance is a determination that "if he must tyrannise over her, he should not do it precisely in the way he would choose" (743). Gwendolen's fate is to some degree an example of what the Princess sought to avoid; perhaps the Princess merely had more luck in finding a man she could rule.

    One might expect that the novel would offer—particularly through Deronda—an alternative to a marriage based on a struggle for domination. The Princess, however, casts Deronda's marriage in the same terms in which she casts her own. She asks if the woman Deronda loves "must have a path of her own"; he says that Mirah is not ambitious and is "not given to make great claims" (728). This compels the Princess to reassert her "claim to be something more than a mere daughter and mother" and insist that her son "acknowledge that I had a right to be an artist" (728). When it turns out that Mirah is a singer who has rejected the stage but not the religion of her father, the Princess remarks to Deronda, "I can see that you would never have let yourself be merged in a wife, as your father was" (729). She identifies her son with his grandfather rather than his father: he will not be subject to a woman. In this sense, however, Deronda represents the triumph of his grandfather over his mother—retroactively, as he fulfills the grandfather's will and at least in part thwarts his mother's rebellion, and by proxy, as he marries a Jewish woman who will forgo the right to be an artist. It is as if new actors will enact the same scenario while reversing their roles.

But are these the only roles imaginable in the novel, or is the Princess merely projecting her own experience onto her son's future? Deronda seems to acquiesce to the suggestion that Mirah would let herself be merged in her husband. Late in the novel, Mirah herself provides a clue to her understanding of the struggle of the self in love; the occasion is a *Midrash* parable that Mordecai recounts as an example of "the love which feels possession in renouncing," a love, he says, for which women are "specially framed" (803).[34] The story is about a Jewish maiden in love with a Gentile king who is in love with a woman in prison; the Jewish maiden "entered into prison and changed clothes with the woman who was beloved by the king, that she might deliver that woman from death by dying in her stead, and leave the king to be happy in his love which was not for her." For Mordecai, the parable is about "the surpassing love, that loses self in the object of love." However, in a rare expression of disagreement, Mirah, a representative of self-sacrifice and self-effacement in the novel, offers another interpretation: she argues that the maiden "wanted somehow to have the first place in the king's mind" and concludes that it "was her strong self, wanting to conquer, that made her die" (803). This is a reading one might have expected from Gwendolen; indeed, Mirah's sense that the story is about the Jewish maiden's "jealousy" (803) may be related to her feelings about Gwendolen and Deronda (whose Jewish identity is still unknown to her). What is remarkable, however, is Mirah's reinterpretation of Mordecai's story about the surrendering of self as a story about the will to conquer. She imagines that one could subject oneself to someone else, give up one's self for the sake of another, and still maintain one's strength and domination. Mirah does not reject the terms with which the Princess and Gwendolen define love; she insists that there is more than one way to rule.

Mordecai rejects Mirah's revision of his parable and complains that she has "read too many plays" (803). In fact, the parable could be read as having something to do with the theater: like an audience, the maiden lets someone else play the role she desires; like an actress, she disguises herself in a costume to take the part of someone else. In this sense, the parable is also about sympathy since the maiden substitutes herself for someone else, stands in the stead of another in an exchange of parts and persons.[35] But if the story is to be understood as alluding to the substitution and exchange of roles enacted in sympathy, this is also because it must be read as a parable about Mordecai and Deronda. Mordecai tells the story after speaking of the sacrifice in which he will "lay down this poor life upon its altar and say: 'Burn, burn indiscernibly into that which shall be, which is my love and not me'" (802).

Surely Mordecai is anticipating that transference of self through which Deronda will take his part when he says, as if Moses, "I hold the joy of another's future within me: a future which these eyes will not see" (802). Yet the parable and its different interpretations, as well as its associations with other discussions of the struggle of selves in the novel, raise the question: which self will be lost, which self will conquer, in the sympathetic exchange through which Mordecai will live in Deronda and Deronda will serve as a new self for Mordecai? Literally, Mordecai will lose his self as he accepts his own death; but Deronda, who already is "speaking from Mordecai's mind as much as from his own" (816) when the two meet again and Deronda reveals his hidden identity, also seems ready to take another for a larger self, enclosing his self in another. Deronda is about to be merged in a marriage of souls with Mordecai. As Deronda stands in Mordecai's stead and, so to speak, puts on his mantle, will he not be subject to Mordecai's strong self?

In one sense, in claiming his identity as a Jew and embracing the missions of his grandfather and Mordecai, Deronda undergoes a traditional conversion experience which establishes a new self and leaves him as if another person. Yet this is complicated by the sense that the conversion is really a reversion to a former self that was almost annihilated—and especially by the sense in which Deronda seems to be converted into Mordecai through the transmission and transference of selves that turns Deronda into Mordecai's new self. Thus we see that the partial, practical sympathy that is supposed to guarantee Deronda from loss of self feels similar to the flexible, plenteous sympathy in which identification seemed to shift his center of consciousness outside of himself. We see, also, that the self-forgetting Rousseau condemns in the actor is considered a risk in any union between two people in which it appears one must take the other for a larger self, merge in another, lose self in the object of love—while the self to whom one is subject rules, dominates, and conquers. It appears possible, however, to sacrifice oneself and still conquer, to rule when one seems to have given up one's place. Sympathy, too, seems to involve a play of power in which the balance between separateness and communication is precarious.

Two visions of theater emerge in *Daniel Deronda:* theater as separateness and theater as communication. The theater of communication is the theater of sympathy, in which difference gives way to sameness as one loses oneself in an act of identification with someone else. Here we see the enactment of communion, interchange, opening up and entering into, conversation, contagion, diffusion, sharing, affinity, the passage from one place to another, the transmission of knowledge by speech, writing, or signs. This is what I have called the dream of sympathy, the desire to transcend the difference and distance that separate people. For Adam Smith, this dream represents the only prospect of defeating or negating theatricality, although it is not a dream he really can believe in. For Defoe, such communication feels like the contagion of the plague. For him, as for Shaftesbury, the exposure of being known and seen by someone who could enter into one's inner character and identify one's thoughts and feelings feels as theatrical as appearing on the stage of the world before the eyes of the public—unless that stage allowed one a mask or outward character to hide behind. Eliot seems to share in the dream of sympathy, although she fears the loss of self it might involve. But the alternative to losing the self might be to lose the other; the alternative to the theater of sympathy or communication is the theater of separateness in which one accepts one's position as a distant beholder to other people.

This is the view of the world that motivates but finally defeats Smith's desire to found his theory of moral sentiments upon sympathy. It is the perspective that paradoxically comforts Shaftesbury as he pictures the self as a secret fiction that can be construed and believed by others but never really known. The theater of separateness is what the narrator of A *Journal of the Plague Year* applauds as he views from a hill a community of isolated ships at sea, each an island unto itself. Speaking as Robinson Crusoe, Defoe questions the hardship of life on an island, "seeing upon the whole view of the stage of life which we act upon in this world it seems to me that life in general is, or ought to be, but one universal act of solitude."[36] Eliot writes in a letter: "When I spoke of myself as an island, I did not mean that I was so exceptionally. We are all islands—'Each in his hidden sphere of joy or woe,/ Our hermit spirits dwell and roam apart'"; she explains that when we are young we think "that the world is spread out expressly as a stage for the particular drama of our lives."[37] In *Daniel Deronda*, Eliot reflects on what it means that we face each other across the epistemological void that prevents us from knowing other people's minds. As much as it explores the possibility of entering into someone else's sentiments, the novel considers our position *outside* of other people.[38]

In this context we can see it is significant that Deronda is first confronted with the limits of sympathy in conversation with an actress—not the theatricalized Gwendolen who imagines an ideal spectator who could enter into her thoughts and feelings, but rather a professional actress who understands that everyone is separated by theatrical distance. K. M. Newton views the way in which the Princess acts in her conversations with Deronda as an indication of her self-negation, claiming that "there is no depth to the Princess's feeling. . . . Role-playing is thus ultimately deadening, creating a 'double consciousness' in which part of her stands aside and observes her role-playing self. Instead of facing the real world, she lives in a world of make-believe."[39] I agree that a double consciousness with which one becomes spectator to oneself is important here but I think that Newton ignores what Eliot means by "sincere acting":

> The speech was in fact a piece of what may be called sincere acting: this woman's nature was one in which all feeling—and all the more when it was tragic as well as real—immediately became matter of conscious representation: experience immediately passed into drama, and she acted her own emotions. In a minor degree this is nothing uncommon, but in the Princess the acting had a rare perfection of physiognomy, voice, and gesture. It would not be true to say that she felt less because of this double consciousness. (691)[40]

If the Princess' sensibility "at once exalts and deadens" (692), this does not make her feelings any less deep or real. If she is acting, this does not mean that she is false. Like Smith, the Princess is aware that we can know other people's feelings only though a representation of them in our imaginations; to convey our own feelings to other people we must, like the actor Diderot praises in his *Paradoxe sur le comédien*, represent the exterior signs and symptoms of our feelings. Like Diderot's actor, the Princess is a self-conscious observer of human life who has perfected the expression of physiognomy, voice, and gesture. She may be too cold or stoical to gain the sympathy of some readers; but after all, she doesn't want sympathy. She carries to an extreme what the narrator says is not at all uncommon; indeed, as an actress she stands as a literal example of what is common among characters throughout the novel. The Princess realizes that her emotions must be acted, her sentiments must be represented. She must face Deronda as an actress and he must face her as a spectator—a spectator to the representation of herself that she enacts. The Princess stands for the view that the relations of sympathy (by which I mean the imaginative acts by which we feel we know other people) are inherently theatrical relations.

Throughout *Daniel Deronda*, characters are posed as actors, performers, *tableaux*, statues, paintings, and spectacles to each other; and conversely, they face each other as beholders who must interpret the representations that other people present. J. Hillis Miller and Neil Hertz each have written about Eliot's portrayal of the characters in *Middlemarch* as clusters of signs or texts that are interpreted and misinterpreted by other characters.[41] Gwendolen, like Dorothea, has problems with her interpretation of others; she suffers because she has no sense that men like Lush and Grandcourt, in particular, "were dark enigmas to her" (159). In *Daniel Deronda*, Eliot emphasizes the multiplicity of possible interpretations: writing that "all meanings, we know, depend on the key of interpretation" (88), she allows that "often the grand meanings of faces as well as of written words may lie chiefly in the impressions of those who look on them" (226). Deronda, especially, with his highly developed abilities to imagine the thoughts of other people, is posed as an interpreter. He senses that he has a "key now by which to interpret" Gwendolen (488), and after he receives the key to his grandfather's trunk, the key that unlocks his past and future identity, he is like one who has discovered "a new key to language telling a new story of races" (771); after this he feels able "to interpret [Mirah's] looks and words from a new starting-point" (814).

However, *Daniel Deronda* suggests that in recognizing that people are enigmas to us, we must acknowledge that we "recognise the alphabet" but "are not sure of the language" (145–146). We may need a key to interpret the key; the stories of other people and ourselves are not so easily unlocked. Our interpretations, even of ourselves, must be revised continually to correct misreadings or to account for new keys. Furthermore, Eliot is concerned with more than our need to decipher the signs of others or even with our responsibility for such interpretations; she is concerned also with what this means about our knowledge of others, what it means that we are faced with representations that we suppose refer to something inside or behind them.

In *Daniel Deronda*—about which Eliot could have claimed what Diderot claimed about *La Religieuse*: "C'est un ouvrage à feuilleter sans cesse par les peintres"[42]—Eliot is increasingly interested in our need to interpret other people as we would behold a painting: without access to the interior of characters. After completing *Daniel Deronda*, Eliot would take on the persona of someone named Theophrastus, thereby placing herself in the tradition of character books that reduced people to identifiable roles and measured the characteristics that allow us to read others. As Theophrastus, she reflects on the way in which one is known by others and writes, "Surely I ought to know myself better than these indifferent outsiders can know me; nay, better even than my intimate friends, to whom I have never breathed those items of my inward experience which have chiefly shaped my life."[43] Eliot had a longstanding interest in physiognomy and phrenology; she even visited a phrenologist in 1844 to have a cast of her head made.[44] In the late nineteenth century Eliot was writing in a context in which the eighteenth-century theories of physiognomy that had been developed by painters, actors, and philosophers had been appropriated by new and flourishing schools of physiology, psychology, and sociology; they surpassed Lavater in their dream of being scientific and they promised rational and absolutely reliable keys to the analysis of human character. Like the theoreticians of sympathy, the physiognomists traditionally believed in the possibility of penetrating the inner thoughts and feelings of others; they sought to deny the distance between people by turning their outer characteristics into transparent and legible representations of inner characters. However, despite Eliot's investment in these theories and in the necessity of reading other people, in *Daniel Deronda* she is increasingly preoccupied, as is Theophrastus Such, with the distance that separates "indifferent outsiders" and "inward experience." Even as partial spectators inclined to sympathize, the novel suggests, we must still face others as distant beholders: we are outside of the minds that others must represent if we are to know them.

I suggested earlier that the situation of beholding people as if they were paintings is both explored in Eliot's variations of *tableau vivant* scenes and figured in the frequent tropes that picture characters as if they were portraits. This situation is also figured in

Eliot's repeated attempts to imagine the scenes she describes from
the point of view of a spectator who knows no more than that which
a mere spectator could know. Take, for example, the description of
the scene between Gwendolen and Deronda after the drowning:
"Their attitude, his averted face with its expression of a suffering
which he was solemnly resolved to undergo, might have told half
the truth of the situation to a beholder who had suddenly entered"
(755). Who is this beholder that we are to imagine suddenly entering the room and interpreting the scene from the attitude and physiognomy of the characters—as if he or she had stumbled into a
theater for a single moment in the middle of a play? This is not the
point of view of either of the characters, nor is it the perspective of
either the narrator or the author, both of whom presumably know
more than half the truth of the situation. At another point a description of Grandcourt and Gwendolen is followed by the authorial
aside: "anyone seeing them as a picture would have concluded that
they were in some stage of love-making suspense" (344). What is at
stake here is more than a doctrine of *ut pictura poesis* (or its slightly
less ambitious and more self-referential form of describing characters as if they were paintings, rather than presenting images that the
reader is actually supposed to see). Who, after all, is seeing the
scene as a picture and drawing conclusions?

　　Characters in *Daniel Deronda* often imagine the eyes of
real or imagined spectators: Deronda, for example, worries about
"the impression his dialogue with Gwendolen had made on a distant beholder" (626). Gwendolen at one point is said to be unaware
of "considerations such as would have filled the minds of indifferent
spectators" (841); but this is an example of the many moments in the
novel when the eyes of the world are imagined by the narrator, not
by characters concerned with their appearance. The narrator reflects on what "anyone looking at [Gwendolen] for the first time
might have supposed" (73), on what "spectators would be likely to
think of" Mordecai (529), on what "any one overhearing might have
supposed" (690), on the hypothetical point of view of "a lover of
dogs" (161), "eloquent interpreters" (169), "a painter" (183), "a close
observer" (800), "all witnesses" (833), and even "the angels once
supposed to watch the toilet of women" (799).

None of these perspectives belongs to anyone actually present on the scene or the narrator or the reader—except for the moment we are asked to represent in our imaginations what would have been seen by a distant beholder, an indifferent spectator, or a beholder who suddenly entered the room. What these perspectives have in common is the point of view of an "outsider" who, having no knowledge of context or the "inward experience" of the characters in the scene, has to take what is seen at face value. No sympathy seems to give these beholders privileged access into the thoughts and feelings of the characters; if they are physiognomists, they know only what they can interpret from the exterior signs the characters display. Despite the voluminous details and information about place, society, character, psychology, and appearance provided for us by the realist nineteenth-century novel, we are continually reminded of what it is like to see other people as *tableaux vivants* about which we must make up stories. In other words, we are reminded of the theatrical distance that separates us.

In the scene between Gwendolen and Deronda in which the narrator reflects on the point of view of "indifferent spectators," we are told that Gwendolen "looked like a melancholy statue" of her former self (841). This image, along with Eliot's various descriptions of what scenes would look like to beholders, recalls the *tableau vivant* from *The Winter's Tale* in which Gwendolen literally imitated a statue—or rather, imitated a picture of a stage play in which an actress played a woman imitating a statue that comes to life. If we look at the last act of Shakespeare's play, at the scene which precedes Hermione's *tableau vivant*, we find this description of the king and Camillo: "There was speech in their dumbness, language in their very gesture. . . . But the wisest beholder, that knew no more but seeing, could not say if the importance were joy or sorrow" (V, ii, 13–18). Shakespeare in this scene is concerned, like Eliot, with the possibility of description and representation, as characters discuss scenes Shakespeare chose not to place on the stage such as "a sight which was to be seen, cannot be spoken of" (V, ii, 41–42) and an encounter "which lames report to follow it and undoes description to do it" (V, ii, 55–56). As both a playwright and an actor, he is concerned with the position of beholders who must

read and interpret the exterior signs of people representing characters, acting feelings, converting sentiments into drama.

Of course the beholders of a play, like the readers of a
novel, presumably know more than even the wisest beholder who
knows no more than seeing—more than the mere sight of a painting, a *tableau vivant*, or a still from a film that we may or may not
have seen.[45] But Shakespeare appears to be meditating on the most
basic conditions of theater: that people become spectators to the
spectacles of other people, whether or not they openly take them for
statues, painted representations, or actors. I believe that Eliot's multiple allusions in her last novel to the end of one of Shakespeare's
last plays declare her continuation of Shakespeare's meditation on
the ways of knowing that theater figures. Eliot must acknowledge in
Daniel Deronda the separateness that communication cannot bridge;
she must acknowledge that despite speech, stories, descriptions, and
explanations we stand outside of others' inward experience.

I argued earlier that Gwendolen's *tableau vivant* of Hermione in *The Winter's Tale* also alluded to Goethe's *Die Wahlver-
vandtschaften*. One could view *Die Wahlverwandtschaften* as a
"Vorspiel auf dem Theater" which prefaces *Daniel Deronda* and its
staging of the theatrical conditions separating "indifferent outsiders"
or "indifferent spectators" from the "inward experience" of others.
Goethe's novel is preoccupied with analogies between knowing people, reading texts, and beholding paintings, *tableaux vivants*,
dramatic spectacles, and monuments; it reflects on how we know
other people in the world—what it means, for example, to "speak to
a person who is in our presence as though we would speak to a
picture [als mit einem Bilde]." *Elective Affinities* explores mysterious and uncanny sympathies between characters, strange acts of
identification and substitution by which they take each other's parts
and places. It is not surprising to find Goethe beginning a chapter
with this remark: "When they all met again at breakfast, an attentive
observer [ein aufmerksamer Beobachter] would have been able to
discern the innermost thoughts and emotions of each one of them

from his or her behavior."[46] Goethe's concern with a spectrum of points of view which includes observing other people as if with access to their inner feelings and observing other people from the outside, as if they were paintings or *tableaux vivants*, prefigures Eliot's concern in *Daniel Deronda* with the theater of sympathy. Published in 1809 and divided between the third-person narrative of an anonymous narrator and the first-person autobiographical narrative of a diary, *Elective Affinities* is a particularly suggestive subtext for Eliot's novel because it seems posed on the threshold between the eighteenth- and the nineteenth-century novel. *Daniel Deronda* follows *Elective Affinities* in illustrating a particular transition and a particular tradition within the history of the novel. In raising epistemological questions which are central to the form and character of the novel—what the reader can know, what one's position is in reading a novel—it helps us to situate the novel within a continuing series of investigations into our ways of knowing characters: the characters in novels *and* the characters of other people.

The eighteenth-century novel might be said to begin inside the head of Robinson Crusoe. If writers of narrative fiction in the eighteenth century sacrificed the presence, sight, and voice of theater for the problematic theatricality of published books, they at least gained the possibility of presenting the inner thoughts of a man or woman. At a time when philosophers worried about the distance between minds, the novel offered legible characters and something that felt like interiority. Yet Defoe's characters seem to respond to the privileged point of view of readers by using autobiography to disguise rather than reveal themselves. "O! what a felicity is it to Mankind," exclaims Moll Flanders, "that they cannot see into the Hearts of one another!"[47] At the same time they recount inner experience, borrowing confessional forms from Puritan spiritual autobiography, Defoe's characters remind us of our place in an audience of outside observers, facing what Shaftesbury thought of as outward characters. Hugh Kenner has remarked on the significance that Lemuel Gulliver is cast by Swift as an "empiric physician" (a doctor who has learned his art by observation and apprenticeship rather than by education); Swift, according to Kenner, "has Gulliver apply the empiric method to the whole conduct of his intellectual life, in a way we should find deliciously absurd." Throughout the entire narrative, "we are told only the things an observer would have experienced, and told them in the order in which he would have experienced them," explains Kenner, who sees this method as ultimately linked to "that of the stage, where we see what we can see and nothing more." We may be inside Gulliver's mind but the scrupulousness of his empirical observation, filtered through "the discrete reports of the senses," ends by limiting our knowledge to that of mere beholders who happen to stumble onto a scene.[48]

If, however, the presentation of characters' inward experience is undermined by Defoe and turned into satire by Swift, it is taken entirely seriously by Richardson, who uses the first-person singular of *Pamela* to provide letters that were meant to be written "to those who had a right to know the fair writer's most secret thoughts."[49] Richardson might be said to be obsessed with Pamela's interiority: at the same time that Pamela is concerned with protecting her body and her self from Mr. B.'s invasion of her privacy, the reader is invited into the privacy of her closet to hear her most intimate and seemingly spontaneous thoughts. We see other characters but the novel takes place, so to speak, inside Pamela's mind. In Richardson's terms, to read Pamela's letters is to know her; and ironically, Mr. B. himself gains access to Pamela by becoming her reader. Richardson wrote to Sarah Fielding to praise her "knowledge of the human heart," suggesting that her brother had not shared such a knowledge. "His was but as the knowledge of the outside of a clock-work machine," wrote Richardson of Henry Fielding, "while yours was that of all the finer springs and movements of the inside."[50] Twelve years later Samuel Johnson used the same metaphor in making his now well-known distinction between "characters of manners," which he associated with Fielding, and "characters of nature," which he associated with Richardson: "Characters of manners are very entertaining; but they are to be understood, by a more superficial observer, than characters of nature, where a man must dive into the recesses of the human heart."

According to Johnson, "there was as great a difference between" Richardson and Fielding "as between a man who knew how a watch was made, and a man who could tell the hour by looking on the dial-plate."⁵¹ Fielding, of course, had no intention of revealing the inner recesses of the human heart, the finer springs and movements of the inside of his characters; as if he were still writing plays, he insisted that we face his characters from the outside. "Fielding avowedly and even ostentatiously refused to go too deep into the minds of his characters," writes Ian Watt, who cites the passage in *Tom Jones* in which the narrator remarks of Blifil that "it would be an ill office in us to pay a visit to the inmost recesses of his mind, as some scandalous people search into the most secret affairs of their friends, and often pry into their closets and cupboards."⁵²

Fielding presented his readers with "the knowledge of the outside" because he insisted that this was all that they really could know. In *An Essay Concerning Human Understanding*, Locke asserted that the thoughts of man "are all within his own breast, invisible and hidden from others," but he believed that through the signs of language "the thoughts of men's minds [might] be conveyed from one to another." "Propriety of speech," he writes, "is that which gives our thoughts entrance into other men's minds with the greatest ease and advantage."⁵³ Fielding, however, seems to think that the abuse of words is beyond remedies, and in "An Essay on the Knowledge of the Characters of Men," he denounces the imposition by which "the whole World becomes a vast Masquerade, where the greatest Part appear disguised under false Vizors and Habits; a very few only shewing their own Faces." Describing a world in which the outsides of people bear almost no resemblance to their inner characters, a world in which characters such as Moll Flanders and Roxana do not want to convey their inner thoughts to others, where physiognomy is unreliable because people are not accurate observers, Fielding insists that we judge others by their actions—"the justest Interpreters of their Thoughts."⁵⁴ What we read on the countenance or in the actions of others is indispensable because it provides the only knowledge that we can have of their characters. Patricia Meyer Spacks has argued persuasively that

Fielding rebelled against the theatricality of autobiography, as exemplified for him by both *Pamela* and the *Apology* of Colley Cibber.[55] However, at the same time that he condemns "exposing" virtue "to the publick View" and the assumption of "false characters, in order to purchase applause,"[56] Fielding is willing to turn his readers into the audience of a public performance—precisely because he wants to teach them about their positions as spectators. If Fielding never really leaves the theater when he turns to novels from plays, this is because he insists that *we* never leave the theater. Arguing against Richardson's fictions of immediacy and transparency, responding to the world of disguise that gave Defoe comfort and refuge, Fielding maintains that the only knowledge we can have of characters in novels and characters in the world is the knowledge we can construe from the outside.

    Sterne has Tristram Shandy explain his decision to "draw my uncle *Toby's* character from his HOBBY-HORSE" by evoking the famous lament of Momus (as recounted by Lucian) that Vulcan did not design man with a window in his breast to reveal his inner feelings: "had the said glass been there set up," writes Tristram, "nothing more would have been wanting, in order to have taken a man's character, but to have taken a chair and gone softly, as you would to a dioptrical bee-hive, and look'd in,—view'd the soul stark naked;—observ'd all her motions,—her machinations."[57] Sterne himself, as Ian Watt has observed, is "an extreme exponent of the internal and subjective approach to character";[58] indeed, he presents Tristram's inner life with a vengeance. At the same time, however, the Shandy household is an illustration of the consequences of the fact that people are not transparent, that their ideas and feelings are hidden or invisible. Specific chapters of the novel, especially those containing dialogues between Walter and Toby, might have been titled "Of the Imperfection of Words" or "Of the Abuse of Words," and the entire book might have been called *An Essay Concerning Human Misunderstanding*. We may gain some access to the inner workings of Tristram's mind, but we are continually reminded of the epistemological void which separates spectators and observers from the inward experience of others.

In the same manner Austen, as Dorrit Cohn has suggested, may set the pattern for the nineteenth century's reintroduction of "the subjectivity of private experience into the novel";[59] yet a
novel such as *Mansfield Park* (which is clearly a precursor of *Daniel
Deronda*) stages a crisis of meaning in which characters are faced
with the impossibility of knowing whether others say what they
mean or mean what they say. It is no coincidence that this novel
turns upon the problem of "playing" and the question, "what sig-
nifies a theater?"[60] Austen may anticipate James but she also follows
Sterne, presenting a less comic and a more anxious depiction of a
world in which stability is threatened by the opacity of the people in
one's own household.

In the nineteenth century, novelists such as Eliot tried
to pick up where Richardson had left off. In Fielding's hands, the
novel had become a sophisticated puppet show in which the author
manipulated characters who no longer told their own stories (except
in interpolated narratives); in this sense it prefigured the nineteenth-century novel. Yet the expanded epistolary novel offered the
possibility of entering into the minds of several characters by multiplying the autobiographical acts that take place within the covers of
one book. Readers were offered access to a composite picture of the
world that promised to release them from the single-minded empiri-
cism that previously had been multiplied only by the doubling
retrospection of autobiography and conversion. The abandonment
of Fielding's pervasive and intrusive third-person narrator and the
incorporation of the epistolary novel's multiple points of view into
the omniscient narrative of a third person provided a perspective
that began to be called objectivity; this perspective promised to
defeat scepticism, egoism, and solipsism in the service of a broader
view of the human condition.[61] However, if the nineteenth-century
novel aims to open up multiple subjectivities and points of view to
the reader, if in Eliot's hands it wants to teach the reader to enter
into the sentiments of others, it must end by acknowledging that it,
too, has placed the reader outside of its characters. If the dramatic
novel is meant to present its characters without the mediating presence of a narrator, it also must cast its reader in the role of impartial

spectator, or in Eliot's phrase, "indifferent outsider." As in *Daniel Deronda*, two versions of theater must compete: one that denies and one that insists upon our positions as spectators in the world. The more the "inward experience" of characters seems to become accessible to us, the more we are reminded that we must *read* characters in order to know them.

We have seen that Eliot looks back to the concerns of the eighteenth-century novel, as she explores the problematic conditions of theatricality, the possibility of sympathy, the interpretation of the self, the relations between narrative fiction, painting, and theater. Her last novel also looks forward to the epistemological crisis at which the nineteenth-century novel will arrive in the hands of one of her most attentive readers, Henry James. By the time we reach the late novels of James, the possibility of access to the inner experience of others is increasingly undermined by epistemological detective stories in which knowing itself is the object of doubt and suspense. The sort of confrontation enacted between a literally blind and veiled woman and a figuratively blind and masked narrator in *The Aspern Papers* (in which the narrator imagines how a conversation with Juliana would "have seemed to a spectator of the scene"[62]) gives way to novels in which both the reader and the narrator are increasingly like spectators who have suddenly stumbled into a room. The most exquisite accounts of sensibilities—of moments of perception that occur or might have occurred or will take place only in retrospect—seem to reveal that the characters can hardly imagine, let alone know, what is passing inside each other's minds. In *The Wings of the Dove*, the narrator introduces Merton Densher by describing how he would have appeared to a beholder who knew no more than seeing and read his aspect in a public park; Densher, we are told, "would have failed to play straight into an observer's hands."[63] In the preface to *The Golden Bowl*, James tries to explain his departure from his preference for "'seeing my story', through the opportunity and the sensibility of some more or less detached, some not strictly involved, though thoroughly interested and intelligent, witness or reporter."[64] However, in addition to the strangely refracted point of view James describes himself dividing between the Prince and Maggie, the reader of the novel also encounters such perspectives as what "a spectator sufficiently detached"[65] might have seen; or how Adam Verver "might have been observed to open the door of the billiard-room with a certain freedom—might have been observed, that is, had there been a spectator in the field."[66] More and more, the reader is like that hypothetical spectator in the field, who knows no more than the wisest beholder who knows no more than seeing. Characters are described as if "sitting for their photograph or even enacting a *tableau-vivant*"—an image which is immediately followed by the authorial gloss, "The spectator of whom they would thus well have been worthy might have read meanings of his own into the intensity of their communion."[67] We are left as spectators to a *tableau vivant*, left to construe our own interpretations of signs that seem to grow more and more meaningful and more and more difficult to read. We are left in the dark, so to speak, like an audience in a theater, until the modernist twentieth-century novel once again tries to throw open the gates of subjectivity, reinventing the interior monologue and reestablishing the novel's ties to the eighteenth century.[68]

Hugh Kenner has suggested Joyce's debts to Swift, Sterne, and Defoe.[69] If Robinson Crusoe can be seen as an ancestor of Bloom—according to Frank Budgen, Joyce called *Robinson Crusoe* the English *Ulysses*[70]—then Molly may lead us back to *Moll Flanders*. (Thinking of her name, Molly reflects: "I dont like books with a Molly in them like that one he brought me about the one from Flanders a whore always shoplifting anything she could cloth and stuff and yards of it."[71]) The first-person monologue spoken by Molly at the end of *Ulysses*—breathlessly unfolding without punctuation or stops in the way that Defoe's narratives flowed without chapters, books, or sections—can be read as Joyce's acknowledgment and reincarnation of the autobiographical fictions with which Defoe portrayed the minds of men and women.

Ulysses, of course, does not leave the theater. Its characters, like *polytropos* Odysseus, transform themselves and play roles—only some of which they are aware of; at one point, an entire chapter turns into the text of a play. If we do not leave the theater, however, it is also because we still find ourselves in the theater after we close the cover of a book. The stories we read in the texts of Shaftesbury, Defoe, Smith, Eliot, and others teach us about the way we look at each other in the world. This is not so much because they represent life in a traditionally mimetic or realistic sense, although they do show us characters in the act of beholding, reading, and interpreting each other. These texts require acts of beholding, reading, and interpreting that are analogous to those modes of understanding that are required as we face the *tableaux*, texts, and acts of other people. Such books teach us how to read their own narratives by dramatizing the characters and theater of the world; and they teach us to negotiate the theatrical relations in which the world casts us. Theater not only describes the scenes and positions we must enact when we enter books of fiction or philosophy. It represents the ways that we know and do not know ourselves and each other. Theater faces us with the risks of knowing and not knowing. It reveals the risks involved in either being, or being seen by, even the wisest beholder.

Notes

Introduction

1. Cf. Laura Brown, *English Dramatic Form 1660–1760: An Essay in Generic History* (New Haven: Yale University Press, 1981); Ian Watt, *The Rise of the Novel: Studies in Defoe, Richardson, and Fielding* (Harmondsworth: Penguin Books, 1966); Alexandre Beljame, *Men of Letters and the English Public in the Eighteenth Century, 1660–1744: Dryden, Addison, and Pope*, trans. E. O. Lorimer, ed. Bonamy Dobrée (London: K. Paul, Trench, Trubner, 1948), p. 151; M. C. Bradbrook, *English Dramatic Form: A History of its Development* (New York: Barnes and Noble, 1965), p. 16; Henry William Pedicord, *The Theatrical Public in the Time of Garrick* (New York: King's Crown Press, 1954), pp. 14–17; Raymond Williams, *The Sociology of Culture* (New York: Schocken, 1982), p. 156.

2. Cf. Margaret Anne Doody, *A Natural Passion: A Study of the Novels of Samuel Richardson* (Oxford: Oxford University Press, 1974); Ira Konigsberg, *Samuel Richardson and the Dramatic Novel* (Lexington: University of Kentucky Press, 1968); Leo Hughes, "Theatrical Convention in Richardson: Some Observations on a Novelist's Technique," in Carol Camden, ed., *Restoration and 18th-Century Literature: Essays in Honor of Alan Dugald McKillop* (Chicago: University of Chicago Press, 1963), pp. 239–250; Ronald Paulson, "The Pictorial Circuit & Related Structures in 18th-Century England," in Peter Hughes and David Williams, eds., *The Varied Pattern: Studies in the 18th Century* (Toronto: A. M. Hakkert, 1971), pp. 165–187, and "Life as Journey and as Theater: Two Eighteenth-Century Structures," *New Literary History* (1976) 7:43–58, and *Satire and the Novel in Eighteenth-Century England* (New Haven: Yale University Press, 1967), pp. 85–99.

3. Jonas Barish, *The Antitheatrical Prejudice* (Berkeley: University of California Press, 1981).

4. Cf. Michael Fried, *Absorption and Theatricality: Painting and Beholder in the Age of Diderot* (Berkeley: University of California Press, 1980); "Art and Objecthood" in Gregory Battcock, ed., *Minimal Art: A Critical Anthology* (New York: E. P. Dutton, 1968); "Manet's Sources: Aspects of His Art, 1859–65," *Artforum* (1969), vol. 7; "Thomas Couture and the Theatricalization of Action in 19th-Century Painting," *Artforum* (1970), vol. 8; and "Two Sculptures by Anthony Caro" and "Caro's Abstractness" in Richard Whelan, ed., *Anthony Caro* (New York: Dutton, 1975), pp. 95–110.

5. Cf. Stanley Cavell, *Must We Mean What We Say?* (New York: Scribners, 1969); *The World Viewed: Reflections on the Ontology of Film* (Cambridge: Harvard University Press, 1979); *The Claim of Reason: Wittgenstein, Skepticism, Morality, and Tragedy* (New York: Oxford University Press, 1979).

6. In addition to the works cited above, there is a rich and growing body of studies which focuses on theater, theatricality, role-playing, play, and related topics in a variety of

disciplines and historical periods. Questions about the theatrical conditions of the self and its relation to others are addressed throughout the works of Jean-Paul Sartre and Kenneth Burke. Maurice Merleau-Ponty discusses "le spectacle du monde," "le théâtre de l'imaginaire," and the other as "spectateur étranger" in *Phénoménologie de la perception* (Paris: Gallimard, 1945), (pp. iii, v, vii). In sociology, Erving Goffman's work (especially *The Presentation of Self in Everyday Life* [Garden City, New York: Doubleday, 1959]) is concerned with role-playing and the theatrical relations of everyday life; while in anthropology, Clifford Geertz has presented important analyses of theatrical dynamics in Balinese culture. (See "Deep Play: Notes on the Balinese Cockfight" in *The Interpretation of Cultures: Selected Essays* [New York: Basic Books, 1973], pp. 412–453, and *Negara: The Theater State in Nineteenth-Century Bali* [Princeton: Princeton University Press, 1980], pp. 98–136.) Richard Sennett discusses roles, actors and spectators, and the theaters of public and private life in *The Rise of Public Man* (New York: Vintage, 1978). Relevant discussions of play include D. W. Winnicott, *Playing and Reality* (London: Tavistock, 1982); Gregory Bateson, "A Theory of Play and Fantasy," *Steps to an Ecology of Mind* (New York: Ballantine Books, 1972), pp. 177–193; Hans-Georg Gadamer, *Truth and Method* (New York: The Seabury Press, 1975), pp. 91–150; and Johan Huizinga, *Homo Ludens: A Study of the Play-Element in Culture* (Boston: The Beacon Press, 1955). The significance of role-playing and spectator–spectacle dynamics in the Renaissance is discussed in Stephen Orgel, *The Illusion of Power: Political Theater in the English Renaissance* (Berkeley: University of California Press, 1975); Stephen Greenblatt, *Sir Walter Raleigh: The Renaissance Man and His Roles* (New Haven: Yale University Press, 1973) and *Renaissance Self-Fashioning: From More to Shakespeare* (Chicago: University of Chicago Press, 1980); Margaret Ferguson, "Nashe's *The Unfortunate Traveller*: The 'News of the Maker' Game," *English Literary Renaissance* (1981), 11(2):165–182; Thomas Greene, "The Flexibility of the Self in Renaissance Literature," and A. Bartlett Giamatti, "Proteus Unbound: Some Versions of the Sea God in the Renaissance," in Peter Demetz et al., eds. *The Disciplines of Criticism: Essays in Literary Theory, Interpretation, and History* (New Haven: Yale University Press, 1968), pp. 241–264 and 437–476. Peter Brooks discusses the importance of melodrama for the nineteenth-century novel in *The Melodramatic Imagination: Balzac, Henry James, Melodrama, and the Mode of Excess* (New Haven: Yale University Press, 1976). Norton Batkin analyzes the problem of theatricality in the work of Paul Strand (see *Photography and Philosophy*, Diss. Harvard 1981). Finally, in *Worlds Apart: Market and Theater in Anglo-American Thought, 1550–1750* (Cambridge: Cambridge University Press, 1986), a work which treats some of the same issues and authors considered in this book, Jean-Christophe Agnew traces the history of the relation between theater and the marketplace. I cite these various studies both to map some of the territory that forms a context and a background for my own work and to suggest some of the many roads that (inevitably) I have not taken.

Prologue to Part I

1. Joseph Addison and Richard Steele, *The Spectator*, 4 vols., ed. Gregory Smith (London: J. M. Dent, 1970), 1:5.

2. Addison, 1:5.

3. Addison, *The Spectator*, No. 10, 1:31–32.

4. Addison, 1:31.

5. Addison, *The Spectator*, No. 1, 1:3–5.

6. Anthony Ashley Cooper, Earl of Shaftesbury, *Characteristics of Men, Manners, Opinions, Times, etc.*, ed. John M. Robertson (Gloucester, Mass.: Peter Smith, 1963), 1:109. All further citations from the *Characteristics* will refer to this edition. I also have consulted the third edition (1723) of the *Characteristics* and in a few cases I have restored the eighteenth-century punctuation or typography where I thought that Shaftesbury's emphasis was lost in modernization.

7. *Characteristics*, 1:197.

8. For an account of this transition, see the works cited above in "Preface," note 1. On the rise of publishing and its consequences, see: Ian Watt, "The Consequences of Literacy," *Comparative Studies in Society and History* (1963), 5:304–345, and "Publishers and Sinners: The Augustan View," *Studies in Bibliography* (1959), 12:3–20; Q. D. Leavis, *Fiction and the Reading Public* (Norwood, Pa.: Norwood Editions, 1977); Elizabeth L. Eisenstein, *The Printing Press as An Agent of Change: Communications and Cultural Transformations in Early Modern Europe* (New York: Cambridge University Press, 1979); Terry Belanger, "Publishers and Writers in Eighteenth-Century England," in *Books and their Readers in Eighteenth-Century England* (New York: St. Martin's Press, 1982), pp. 1–25; A. S. Collins, *Authorship in the Days of Johnson, Being a Study of the Relation Between Author, Patron, Publisher, and Public, 1726–1780* (London: Robert Holden, 1927); J. H. Plumb, "The Public, Literature, and the Arts in the 18th Century" in Paul Fritz and David Williams, eds., *The Triumph of Culture: 18th-Century Perspectives* (Toronto: A. M. Hakkert, 1972), pp. 27–48; Lennard J. Davis, *Factual Fictions: The Origins of the English Novel* (New York: Columbia University Press, 1983); and Michael Shinagel, *Daniel Defoe and Middle Class Gentility* (Cambridge: Harvard University Press, 1968), pp. 107–121.

9. Henry Home, Lord Kames, *Elements of Criticism*, 3d ed., 2 vols. (Edinburgh, 1765), 2:347. For background on the *ut pictura poesis* tradition, see: Rensselaer W. Lee, *Ut Pictura Poesis: The Humanistic Theory of Painting* (New York: W. W. Norton, 1967); William G. Howard, "'Ut Pictura Poesis,'" *PMLA* (1909), 24:40–123; Rémy G. Saisselin, "Ut Pictura Poesis: Du Bos to Diderot," *Journal of Aesthetics and Art Criticism* (1961–62), 20:145–156; Jean H. Hagstrum, *The Sister Arts: The Tradition of Literary Pictorialism and English Poetry from Dryden to Gray* (Chicago: University of Chicago Press, 1958); John B. Bender, *Spenser and Literary Pictorialism* (Princeton: Princeton University Press, 1972); Cicely Davis, "Ut Pictura Poesis," *MLR* (1935), 30:159–169; and Hugh Witemeyer, *George Eliot and the Visual Arts* (New Haven: Yale University Press, 1979).

10. Samuel Johnson, *A Dictionary of the English Language* (London, 1783).

11. Henry Fielding, *The History of Tom Jones, A Foundling* (New York: The Modern Library, 1950), p. 1.

1. *The Characters of Books and Readers*

1. My characterizations of the book are indebted to Hugh Kenner's discussions of "the book as book" in chapter 2 of *The Stoic Comedians: Flaubert, Joyce, and Beckett* (Berkeley: University of California Press, 1962), pp. 30–67. For a related discussion of the status of the published book for Swift, see Neil Saccamano, "Authority and Publication: The Works of 'Swift,'" *The Eighteenth Century* (1984), 25(3):241–262. John Hayman relates Shaftesbury's use of the letter form to the problem of finding an appropriate *persona*. (See

"Shaftesbury and the Search for a Persona," *Studies in English Literature 1500–1900* [1970], 10:491–504.) A. O. Aldridge writes that Shaftesbury uses "a distinction between private and public works" to remove his works from the jurisdiction of classical rules. ("Lord Shaftesbury's Literary Theories," *Philological Quarterly* [January 1945], 24:53).

2. The French reviews to which Shaftesbury refers are: Jean le Clerc, *Bibliothèque Choisie, pour servir de suite la Bibliothèque Universelle* (Amsterdam, 1709), vol. 19; Monrs. ***, *Histoire des Ouvrages des Scavans* (Rotterdam, 1708); Octobre, Novembre, Decembre; Anon., *Le Journal des Scavans pour l'année* 1709 (Paris, 1709), 25 Mars; Jacques Bernard, *Nouvelles de la Republique des Lettres*, March, 1710.

3. Daniel Defoe, *The Fortunes and Misfortunes of the Famous Moll Flanders* (New York: Norton, 1973), p. 3.

4. Shaftesbury, *The Life, Unpublished Letters, and Philosophical Regimen of Anthony, Earl of Shaftesbury*, ed. Benjamin Rand (London: Swan Sonnenschein and Co., 1900), pp. 526–527 (November 22, 1712). Further citations followed by PR will refer to this edition.

5. Shaftesbury, *Second Characters; or, The Language of Forms*, ed. Benjamin Rand (Cambridge: Cambridge University Press, 1914), p. xviii. All further citations followed by SC will refer to this text.

6. For other accounts of the use of the dialogue form by Shaftesbury, see A. O. Aldridge, "Lord Shaftesbury's Literary Theories," *Philosophical Quarterly* (1945), 24:46–64; Carol Sherman, "In Defense of the Dialogue: Diderot, Shaftesbury, and Galiani," *Romance Notes* (1973), 15:268–273; E. R. Purpus, "The 'Plain, Easy, and Familiar Way': The Dialogue in English Literature, 1660–1725," *ELH* (1950), 17:47–58; Thomas Fowler, *Shaftesbury and Hutcheson* (London: Sampson Low, *et al.*, 1882), p. 54; Robert Marsh, *Four Dialectical Theories of Poetry: An Aspect of English Neoclassical Criticism* (Chicago: University of Chicago Press, 1965), pp. 22–47; Martin Price, *To The Palace of Wisdom: Studies in Order and Energy from Dryden to Blake* (Carbondale, Ill.: Southern Illinois University Press, 1970), pp. 86–87; James W. Davidson, "Criticism and Self-Knowledge in Shaftesbury's *Soliloquy*," *Enlightenment Essays* (1974), 5(2):50–61.

7. Émile Benveniste, *Problèmes de linguistique générale* (Paris: Gallimard, 1966), 1:239–241. In general, Benveniste's discussions of the situation of *énonciation* and the characteristics and positions of discourse are relevant here. Discourse, for Benveniste, is necessarily spoken by a person to a person. It takes the form of an address which has an aim and object as well as a source. Benveniste writes that the structure of *énonciation* and discourse is built around the dialogic relation between a *je* and a *tu*; it occurs necessarily between partners. The "locuteur," "dès qu'il se déclare locuteur et assume la langue, il implante l'*autre* en face de lui, quel que soit le degré de présence qu'il attribue à cet autre. Toute énonciation est, explicite ou implicite, une allocution, elle postule un allocutaire." ("L'Appareil formel de l'énonciation," *Langages* [1970], 17:14.) Thus, the dialogue is the fundamental scene and enactment of discourse. Benveniste asserts that there is no dialogue outside of *énonciation* and no *énonciation* without dialogue. There are passages in Shaftesbury, as there are in Diderot, that are uncannily close to Benveniste's terms and concerns; and passages in Benveniste that seem to be describing one or both of those eighteenth-century philosophers. Consider this passage: "Le 'monologue' est un dialogue intériorisé, formulé en 'langage intérieur,' entre un moi locuteur et en moi écouteur. Parfois le moi locuteur est seul à parler; le moi écouteur reste néanmoins présent; sa présence est nécessaire et suffisante pour rendre signifiante l'énonciation du moi locuteur. Parfois aussi le moi écouteur intervient par une

objection, une question, un doute, une insulte. La forme linguistique que prend cette intervention diffère selon les idiomes, mais c'est toujours une forme 'personnelle.' Tantôt le moi écouteur se substitue au moi locuteur et s'énonce donc comme 'première personne'; . . . Tantôt le moi écouteur interpelle à la 'deuxième personne' le moi locuteur . . . Cette transposition du dialogue en 'monologue' où EGO tantôt se scinde en deux, tantôt assume deux rôles, prête à des figurations ou transpositions psychodramatiques: conflicts du '*moi* profound' et de la 'conscience,' dédoublements provoqués par l'inspiration, etc." ("L'Appareil formel," pp. 16–17.)

　　8. "Homer, admirable as he is in every other respect, is especially so in this, that he alone among epic poets is not unaware of the part to be played by the poet himself in the poem. The poet should say very little *in propria persona*, as he is no imitator when doing that. Whereas the other poets are perpetually coming forward in person, and say but little, and that only here and there, as imitators, Homer after a brief preface brings in forthwith a man, a woman, or some other Character—no one of them characterless, but each with different characteristics." Aristotle, *Poetics*, chapter 24, 1460a, translated by W. Rhys Roberts (New York, 1954), p. 258.

　　9. Denis Diderot, *Le Fils naturel et les Entretiens sur le Fils Naturel* (Paris: Larousse, 1970), p. 106. For a discussion of the problem of theatricality in the context of Diderot's art criticism and dramatic theory, see Michael Fried, *Absorption and Theatricality: Painting and Beholder in the Age of Diderot* (Berkeley: University of California Press, 1981). It is worth noting that Diderot read and translated Shaftesbury. In a forthcoming work I will argue that Shaftesbury was very much on Diderot's mind when he wrote the *Entretiens sur le Fils Naturel*.

　　10. Diderot, *Oeuvres Esthétiques*, ed. Paul Vernière (Paris: Garnier, 1959), p. 792.

　　11. Diderot, *Salons*, III, ed. Jean Seznec and Jean Adhémar (Oxford: Clarendon Press, 1963), p. 94.

　　12. Diderot, *Discours de la poésie dramatique* (Paris: Larousse, 1970), p. 66.

2. The Characters of Philosophy

　　1. Paul de Man discusses the rhetoric of crisis as it is used by both literary criticism and modernist texts in "Criticism and Crisis" and "Literary History and Literary Modernity" in *Blindness and Insight* (New York: Oxford University Press, 1971). See also: Daniel Brewer, "The Philosophical Dialogue and the Forcing of Truth," *MLN* (December 1983), 98(5):1241–1243, and Maurice Roelens, "Le Dialogue philosophique, genre impossible? L'Opinion des siècles classiques," *Cahiers de l'Association Internationale des Études Françaises*" (Mai 1972), no. 24, pp. 43–58.

　　2. This characterization of the actor/character who engages himself in dialogic soliloquy suggests the importance of Hamlet as a model for Shaftesbury's soliloquist. For a discussion of Shaftesbury's reading of *Hamlet*, and its place in the history of Shakespeare criticism, see Ernest Tuveson, "The Importance of Shaftesbury," *ELH* (1953), 20:267–299. (A. D. McKillop reviews this article in *Philological Quarterly* [1954], 33:296–297.) A general discussion of Shaftesbury's relation to the tradition of literary theory appears in R. L. Brett, *The Third Earl of Shaftesbury, A Study in Eighteenth-Century Literary Theory* (London: Hutchinson's University Library, 1951). The influence of Shaftesbury's ideas about self-

knowledge and introspection are suggested in R. D. Havens, "Unusual Opinions in 1725 and 1726," *Philological Quarterly* (1951), 30:447–448. Cf. Tuveson, p. 290, note 41. See also Wallace Jackson, *Immediacy: The Development of a Critical Concept from Addison to Coleridge* (Amsterdam: Rodopi, 1973), and Jerome Stolnitz, "On the Origins of 'Aesthetic Disinterestedness,'" *Journal of Aesthetics and Art Criticism* (1961–62), 20:131–143.

3. Cf. Price, p. 89: "Just as the poet creates a character, so each of us must create our own." Stanley Grean alludes to but minimizes Shaftesbury's treatment of "the problem of the identity and continuity of the self" (*Shaftesbury's Philosophy of Religion and Ethics: A Study in Enthusiasm* [Athens: Ohio University Press, 1967], p. 146). For background on the tradition of character-books, see Benjamin Boyce (with the assistance of notes by Chester Noyes Greenough), *The Theophrastan Character in England to 1642* (Cambridge: Harvard University Press, 1947), and Boyce, *The Polemic Character, 1640–1661: A Chapter in English Literary History* (Lincoln, Nebraska: University of Nebraska Press, 1955). Joseph W. Donohue discusses changes in the concept of dramatic character in *Dramatic Character in the English Romantic Age* (Princeton: Princeton University Press, 1970). Cf. also Amelie Oksenberg Rorty, "A Literary Postscript: Characters, Persons, Selves, Individuals," in Rorty, ed., *The Identities of Persons* (Berkeley: University of California Press, 1976), pp. 301–323.

4. Shaftesbury, *Soliloquy, or Advice to an Author* (London: John Morphew, 1710), pp. iii–iv.

3. Reading Characters

1. Cf. Epictetus, *Encheiridion*, 33, 2: "And be silent for the most part, or else make only the most necessary remarks, and express these in a few words. But rarely, when occasion requires you to talk, talk indeed, but about no ordinary topics." Cited in F. H. Heineman, "The Philosopher of Enthusiasm," *Revue Internationale de Philosophie* (1952), 6:306. For an argument about the Stoic foundations of both the *Characteristics* and the *Philosophical Regimen*, see Esther C. Tiffany, "Shaftesbury as Stoic," *PMLA* (1923), 38:175–195.

2. On the difficulty of reading Shaftesbury's ironic tone, see A. O. Aldridge, "Shaftesbury and the Test of Truth," *PMLA* (1945), 60:130.

3. David Fate Norton argues that Shaftesbury advocates an epistemological but not an ethical scepticism. See *Shaftesbury and the Two Scepticisms* (Torino: Edizioni di'Filosofia, 1968).

4. My reading of Shaftesbury has not focused on his ideas about religion or ethics. For accounts of these aspects of his work, see Grean; A. O. Aldridge, "Shaftesbury and the Deist Manifesto," *Transactions of the American Philosophical Society* (1951), new ser., 41, part 2, pp. 297–385.

5. Jeremy Taylor, *A Discourse of the Liberty of Prophesying. Shewing the Unreasonableness of prescribing to other men Faith, and the Inequity of persecuting differing opinions* (London: 1648), p. 69.

Prologue to Part II

1. Daniel Defoe, *The Storm, or, a Collection of the most Remarkable Casualties and Disasters which happen'd in the late Dreadful Tempest, both by Sea and Land in The*

Novels and Miscellaneous Works of Daniel Defoe (London: Bell and Daldy, 1869), p. 251.

2. Daniel Defoe, *A Review of the Affairs of France: and of all Europe, As Influenced by that Nation: Being, Historical Observations, on the Publick Transactions of the World; Purg'd from the Errors and Partiality of News-Writers, and Petty-Statesmen of all Sides* (London, 1705), preface, reproduced in the facsimile edition of Defoe's *Review*, ed. Arthur Wellesly Secord (New York: Facsimile Text Society, Columbia University Press, 1938), 1, n.p.

3. *The Storm*, p. 251.

4. Daniel Defoe, *The History and Remarkable Life of the Truly Honourable Col. Jacque, Commonly Call'd Col. Jack* (London: Oxford University Press, 1970), p. 184.

5. *The Storm*, p. 255.

6. Daniel Defoe, *The Review*, June 20, 1706, in *Robinson Crusoe and Other Writings*, ed. James Sutherland (Boston: Houghton Mifflin Company, 1968), pp. 308–309.

7. Quoted in Maximillian E. Novak, "Defoe's Use of Irony," in Novak and Herbert J. Davis, eds., *The Uses of Irony* (Los Angeles: William Andrews Clark Memorial Library, University of California, 1966), p. 11.

8. Daniel Defoe, *A System of Magick; or, a History of The Black Art* (London: J. Roberts, 1727), p. 336.

9. Maximillian E. Novak, *Economics and the Fiction of Daniel Defoe* (Berkeley: University of California Press, 1962), p. 1.

10. John Robert Moore, "Defoe's Persona as Author: *The Quaker's Sermon*," *Studies in English Literature 1500–1900* (1971), 11:507.

11. Moore, p. 509.

12. E. Anthony James, *Daniel Defoe's Many Voices: A Rhetorical Study of Prose Style and Literary Method* (Amsterdam: Rodopi Nv, 1972), p. 21.

13. Charles Gildon, *The Life and Strange Surprizing Adventures of Mr. D... De F... of London, Hosier* (London, 1719), reprinted in Paul Dottin, ed., *Robinson Crusoe Examin'd and Criticis'd* (London: J. M. Dent & Sons, 1923), p. 65–66.

14. In addition to Novak, Moore, and James (cited above) see: Arnold Weinstein, *Fictions of the Self, 1550–1800* (Princeton: Princeton University Press, 1981); Leopold Damrosch, Jr., "Defoe as Ambiguous Impersonator," *Modern Philology* (1973), 71:153–159; Frederick R. Karl, "Moll's Many-Colored Coat: Veil and Disguise in the Fiction of Defoe," *Studies in the Novel* (1973), 5:86–97; David Blewett, *Defoe's Art of Fiction: Robinson Crusoe, Moll Flanders, Colonel Jack, and Roxana* (Toronto: University of Toronto Press, 1979); Maximillian E. Novak, "Defoe's *Shortest Way With the Dissenters*: Hoax, Parody, Paradox, Fiction, Irony, and Satire," *Modern Language Quarterly* (1966), 27:402–417, and Intro., *English Literature in the Age of Disguise* (Berkeley: University of California Press, 1977), pp. 1–14; Leo Braudy, "Daniel Defoe and the Anxieties of Autobiography," *Genre* (1973), 6:76–97; Irvin Ehrenpreis, "Personae," in Carroll Camden, ed., *Restoration and 18th-Century Literature: Essays in Honor of Alan Dugald McKillop* (Chicago: University of Chicago Press, 1963), pp. 25–37.

15. Quoted in Maximillian E. Novak, "Defoe's Theory of Fiction," *Studies in Philology* (1964), 61:666.

16. Edmund Gosse, *A History of Eighteenth-Century Literature* (London: Macmillan, 1889), p. 184.

17. Quoted in Gosse, p. 180.

18. *Read's Journal*, November 1, 1718, cited in William Lee, *Daniel Defoe: His Life and Recently Discovered Writings* (New York: Burt Franklin, 1969), 1:282.

19. Novak, *Economics and the Fiction of Daniel Defoe*, p. 5.

20. Novak, *Economics*, preface, p. viii.

21. Gildon, p. 66. For an account of Defoe's works as examples of socialist realism, see the entry, "Daniel Defoe," in the *Great Soviet Encyclopedia: A Translation of the Third Edition* (New York: Macmillan, Inc., 1975), 8:89.

22. Daniel Defoe, *A Letter to Mr. Bisset, Eldest Brother of the Collegiate Church of St. Catherines; in Answer to his Remarks on Dr. Sacheverell's Sermon* (London: J. Baker, 1709), p. 10.

23. Hugh Kenner, *The Counterfeiters* (Garden City, New York: Anchor Books, 1973), p. 71. Professor Kenner inadvertently attributes the inscription of the footprint to Friday, an answer that the reader is never given.

24. See preface, note 1, and Shaftesbury prologue, note 8.

4. Fictions and Impersonations: The Double Imposture

1. Daniel Defoe, *Robinson Crusoe*, ed. Michael Shinagel (New York: W. W. Norton & Co., 1975), p. 208. Further citations followed by *RC* will refer to this edition.

2. For discussions of the relation between self and other in *Robinson Crusoe*, see Homer O. Brown, "The Displaced Self in the Novels of Daniel Defoe," *ELH* (1971), 38:562–590; and Thomas M. Kavanaugh, "Unraveling Robinson: The Divided Self in Defoe's *Robinson Crusoe*," *Texas Studies in Literature and Language* (1978), 20:416–432.

3. Daniel Defoe, *A Journal of the Plague Year*, eds. Anthony Burgess and Christopher Bristow (Harmondsworth: Penguin Books, 1966), p. 256. Further citations followed by PY will refer to this text.

4. Cf. E. K. Chambers, *The Elizabethan Stage* (Oxford: Clarendon Press, 1923). I am grateful to Neil C. Saccamano for letting me read an unpublished essay, "Some Notes on the Theatrical Indictment."

5. Kenner, *The Counterfeiters*, p. 73.

6. Cf. Mikhail Bakhtin, *Rabelais and His World*, trans. Helene Iswolsky (Cambridge: MIT Press, 1969), esp. ch. 3, "Popular-Festive Forms and Images in Rabelais."

7. Daniel Defoe, *Moll Flanders*, ed. Edward Kelly (New York: Norton, 1973), p. 3.

8. Daniel Defoe, *The Farther Adventures of Robinson Crusoe* in *The Life and Strange Adventures of Robinson Crusoe* (New York: The Jenson Society, 1907), 2:vii.

9. For an excellent account of the blurring of fact and fiction in the eighteenth century, see Lennard J. Davis, *Factual Fictions: The Origins of the English Novel* (New York: Columbia University Press, 1983). See also Arthur Jerrold Tieje, "A Peculiar Phase of the Theory of Realism in pre-Richardsonian Fiction," *PMLA* (1913), 28:213–252, and William Nelson, "The Boundaries of Fiction in the Renaissance: A Treaty Between Truth and Falsehood," *ELH* (1969), 36:30–58.

10. For background on Puritan antagonism to literature and the theater, see David Leverenz, *The Language of Puritan Feeling: An Exploration in Literature, Psychology, and Social History* (New Brunswick: Rutgers University Press, 1980); Jonas Barish, *The Anti-theatrical Prejudice* (Berkeley: University of California Press, 1981); Edmund S. Morgan, "Puritan Hostility to the Theatre," *Proceedings of the American Philosophical Society* (1966), 110:340–347; Elbert N. S. Thompson, *The Controversy Between the Puritans and the Stage* (New York: Holt, 1903); Russell Fraser, *The War Against Poetry* (Princeton: Princeton Univer-

sity Press, 1970); and John T. Taylor, *Early Opposition to the English Novel: The Popular Reaction from 1760 to 1830* (New York: King's Crown Press, 1943). For accounts of Defoe's relation to Puritan doctrine, see: George A. Starr, *Defoe and Spiritual Autobiography* (Princeton: Princeton University Press, 1965); J. Paul Hunter, *The Reluctant Pilgrim: Defoe's Emblematic Method and Quest for Form in Robinson Crusoe* (Baltimore: The John Hopkins University Press, 1966); Robert W. Ayers, "*Robinson Crusoe*: Allusive Allegorick History," *PMLA* (1967), 82:399–407; Rudolf G. Stamm: "Daniel Defoe: An Artist in the Puritan Tradition," *Philological Quarterly* (1936), 15:225–246. For more general discussions about Defoe's ambivalent relation to fiction, see: Blewett, *Defoe's Art of Fiction*; Novak, "Defoe's Use of Irony"; Novak, "Defoe's *Shortest Way with the Dissenters*"; Novak, "Defoe's Theory of Fiction," *Studies in Philology* (1964), 61:650–668; George A. Starr, *Defoe and Casuistry* (Princeton: Princeton University Press, 1971); Niels Jørgen Skydsgaard, "Defoe on the Art of Fiction" in Michael Chesnutt et al., eds., *Essays Presented to Knud Schibsbye on his 75th Birthday* (Copenhagen: Akademisk Forlag, 1979), pp. 164–171; Dieter Schulz, "'Novel,' 'Romance,' and Popular Fiction in the First Half of the Eighteenth Century," *Studies in Philology* (1973), 70:77–91; Alan Dugald McKillop, *The Early Masters of English Fiction* (Lawrence: University of Kansas Press, 1956); Walter Allen, *Six Great Novelists* (London: H. Hamilton, 1955).

    11. Hunter, p. 115.

    12. McKillop, p. 42.

    13. Cf. Stamm and Ayers.

    14. Gildon, p. 113.

    15. Most notably by Starr and Hunter.

    16. Novak, "Defoe's Use of Irony," p. 35.

    17. Blewett, pp. 15–18.

    18. Michael Shinagel, *Daniel Defoe and Middle-Class Gentility* (Cambridge: Harvard University Press, 1968), pp. 144–197. James Sutherland argues that fiction is present in Defoe's pre-1719 and post-1724 "non-fictional" writings as well as in his romances. Cf. "The Relation of Defoe's Fiction to his Non-Fictional Writings" in Maynard Mack and Ian Gregor, eds., *Imagined Worlds: Essays on Some English Novels and Novelists in Honour of John Butt* (London: Methuen, 1968). This question will be discussed further in my chapter on *Roxana*.

    19. *The Storm*, p. 252.

    20. *The Storm*, p. 253.

    21. *The Storm*, pp. 251–252.

    22. *The Storm*, p. 253.

    23. *The Storm*, p. 252.

    24. *The Storm*, p. 258.

    25. *The Storm*, p. 252.

    26. Cf. James Sutherland, *Defoe* (Philadelphia: J. B. Lippincott, 1938), pp. 219–220, and Novak, "Defoe's Theory of Fiction," p. 666.

    27. *Moll Flanders*, p. 4.

    28. James T. Boulton argues Defoe's preference for a 'plain style' in his introduction to his selection of Defoe's writings, *Daniel Defoe* (New York: Schocken Books, 1965), pp. 1–22. See also George A. Starr, "Defoe's Prose Style: 1. The Language of Interpretation," *Modern Philology* (1974), 71:277–294. For discussions of Defoe's use of irony, see Novak, "Defoe's Use of Irony" and "Defoe's *Shortest Way with the Dissenters*" and Damrosch, "Defoe

as Ambiguous Impersonator," cited above; and Michael M. Boardman, "Defoe's Political Rhetoric and the Problem of Irony," *Tulane Studies in English* (1977), 22:87–102. There is a well-known critical controversy about irony in *Moll Flanders* which focuses more on point of view and narrative technique in the presentation of an "autobiographical" character. See Ian Watt, *The Rise of the Novel* (Harmondsworth: Penguin Books, 1957); Wayne C. Booth, *The Rhetoric of Fiction* (Chicago: The University of Chicago Press, 1961); Dorothy Van Ghent, *The English Novel: Form and Function* (New York: Harper and Row, 1953); Maximillian E. Novak, "Conscious Irony in *Moll Flanders*: Facts and Problems," *College English* (1964), 26:198–204; Howard L. Koonce, "Moll's Muddle: Defoe's Use of Irony in *Moll Flanders*," *ELH* (1963), 30:377–394.

29. Daniel Defoe, *The Complete English Tradesman in Familiar Letters* (New York: Augustus M. Kelley, 1969), 1:26 (reprint of 1727 edition).

30. Quoted in Novak, "Defoe's Use of Irony," p. 16.

31. Novak, "Defoe's Theory of Fiction," pp. 658–659.

32. Stamm, "Daniel Defoe: An Artist in the Puritan Tradition," p. 245.

33. Cf. the appendix to *Defoe and Casuistry*, "Fiction and Mendacity," pp. 190–211.

34. *The Letters of Daniel Defoe*, ed. George Harris Healey (Oxford: Clarendon Press, 1955), p. 42; quoted also by Starr, p. 195.

35. Daniel Defoe, *A New Family Instructor* (London, 1742), p. 52.

36. *A New Family Instructor*, p. 55.

37. *A New Family Instructor*, pp. 52-53.

38. Cf. Hunter, pp. 93–124.

39. For background on the history and theory of the defense of fiction, particularly in the Renaissance, see Margaret W. Ferguson, *Trials of Desire: Renaissance Defenses of Poetry* (New Haven: Yale University Press, 1983). Margaret Ferguson has contributed to my understanding of the rhetoric and psychology of the defense.

40. Hunter, pp. 116–117.

41. For a discussion of Dante's theory of the historical and allegorical levels of the *Divine Comedy*, see Charles Singleton, "Allegory," in Mark Musa, ed., *Essays on Dante* (Bloomington: Indiana University Press, 1964), pp. 48–75.

42. Cf. Aristotle, *Poetics*, trans. Ingram Bywater in *Rhetoric and Poetics* (New York: Modern Library, 1959), ch. 8, 1451, pp. 234–235.

43. *Farther Adventures*, pp. vii–viii.

44. Daniel Defoe, *Serious Reflections During the Life and Surprising Adventures of Robinson Crusoe with His Vision of the Angelic World* in *The Life and Strange Adventures of Robinson Crusoe*, 3 vols. (New York: The Jenson Society, 1907), 3:ix. Further citations followed by *SR* will refer to this text.

45. Cf. Braudy, "Daniel Defoe and the Anxieties of Autobiography," p. 84.

46. Hunter, p. 121.

47. J. L. Austin, *Philosophical Papers*, ed. J. O. Urmson and G. J. Warnock (New York: Oxford University Press, 1979), p. 176.

48. *The Storm*, pp. 251–252.

49. *The Storm*, p. 257.

5. Moll Flanders: *Portrait of the Artist as a Play-Actor*

1. Defoe, *Moll Flanders*, pp. 4–5. All further citations in this chapter will refer to this text, unless otherwise noted. J. Paul Hunter notes: "Many objections to novels were

analogous to the traditional Puritan distrust of the stage, and warnings about the evils of playhouses are often recast slightly to become warnings about '*the Reading of vain Books, Play-books, Romances and feigned Histories.*'" ("The Loneliness of the Long Distance Reader," *Genre* [Winter 1977], 10:460.)

2. This bibliography appears in Sister Rose Anthony, *The Jeremy Collier Stage Controversy, 1698–1726* (Milwaukee: Marquette University Press, 1937), pp. 303–307 and is cited by Jonas Barish in *The Antitheatrical Prejudice*, p. 221. See Barish's own discussion of Collier, *The Antitheatrical Tradition*, pp. 221–235.

3. Jeremy Collier, *A Short View of the Immorality and Profaneness of the English Stage* (New York: Garland, 1972), p. 1.

4. For summaries of Defoe's *Review* articles on theater, see: J. A. Downie, "Defoe's *Review,* The Theatre, and Anti-High Church Propaganda," *Restoration and 18-Century Theatre Research* (1976), 15: 24–32 and Edward G. Fletcher, "Defoe and the Theatre," *Philological Quarterly* (1934), 13:382–389.

5. John Robert Moore, *Daniel Defoe: Citizen of the Modern World* (Chicago: University of Chicago Press, 1958), p. 230. See also: Moore, "*The Tempest* and *Robinson Crusoe*," *Review of English Studies* (1945), 21: 52–56, and Moore, "Defoe and Shakespeare," *Shakespeare Quarterly* (1968), 19: 71–80.

6. All references to *The Review* are taken from the facsimile edition edited by Arthur Wellesly Secord (New York: Facsimile Text Society, Columbia University Press, 1938).

7. Defoe, *The Family Instructor,* Seventh Dialogue, in *The Versatile Defoe*, ed. Laura Ann Curtis (Totowa, New Jersey: Rowman and Littlefield, 1979), p. 428.

8. See, for example, the end of the Fourth Dialogue: "The Author leaves these Dialogues therefore without particular Remarks, and leaves room for abler Hands to Annotate upon them hereafter, when the Persons concern'd may be gone off the Stage. . . ." (Boulton, p. 207).

9. William Prynne, *Histrio-mastix, the Players Scourge, etc.* reprinted in Arthur Freeman, ed., *The English Stage: Attack and Defense 1577–1730* (New York: Garland, 1974), p. 325.

10. Prynne, p. 515.

11. Prynne, p. 376 ff.

12. "Notorious whores" is an entry under the heading of "Women-Actors" in Prynne's index.

13. This phrase appears in Barish's article, "The Antitheatrical Prejudice," *Critical Quarterly* (1966), 8:331.

14. Barish, pp. 48–49.

15. Barish, p. 92.

16. Prynne, p. 159. Cf. Barish, pp. 91-94.

17. Prynne, p. 158.

18. Stephen Gosson, *Playes Confuted in Five Actions*, ed. Arthur Freeman (New York: Garland, 1972), n.p. The citation is from the Third Action.

19. In a provocative chapter entitled "Identity in Fact and Fiction" in *Imagining A Self: Autobiography and Novel in Eighteenth-Century England* (Cambridge: Harvard University Press, 1976), Patricia Meyer Spacks argues that although a "novelistic view of identity may reflect a nervousness resembling that of the philosophers about the possible implications of change," characters in eighteenth-century novels "testify their stability far more eloquently than their flexibility" (p. 8). Contrasting such characters with Hume's account of the imaginary status of the self, Spacks states that "the novelists of the eighteenth century insist on the ease with which Hume's doubts can be refuted" (p. 11). I will argue in this chapter that Defoe, at least, is in important ways an exception to Spacks' claims, that he follows Shaftesbury's and

anticipates Hume's meditations about the instability of the self. Defoe's differ, however, because he does not appear to be anxious about the protean character of the self; indeed, for Defoe's characters—who flee their origins, change their names, and constantly change identities—stability or fixity of self is to be feared. I will suggest that if Moll Flanders can be seen to "remain essentially the same" (Spacks, p. 8) in any sense, this is because she is portrayed as an actress: a constant identity that subverts notions of the self as stable and reliable. (For another view similar to Spacks', see Weinstein, *Fictions of the Self*, pp. 87–99.)

    Martin Price discusses characters and roles in "The Other Self: Thoughts about Character in the Novel" in Maynard Mack and Ian Gregor, eds., *Imagined Worlds: Essays on Some English Novels and Novelists in Honor of John Butt* (London: Methuen, 1968), pp. 279–299. See also Price's *Forms of Life: Character and Moral Imagination in the Novel* (New Haven: Yale University Press, 1983). Also relevant here are Lionel Trilling's discussion of the self in *Sincerity and Authenticity* (Cambridge: Harvard University Press, 1974) and Alexander Gelley's comparison of character as "persona or social role" and character as "person or soul" in "Character and Person: On the Presentation of Self in Some Eighteenth-Century Novels," *The Eighteenth Century: Theory and Interpretation* (1980), 21:109–127. Cf. Patrick Coleman, "Character in An Eighteenth-Century Context," *The Eighteenth Century: Theory and Interpretation* (1983), 24:51–63; Joel Weinsheimer, "Theory of Character: *Emma*," *Poetics Today* (1979), 1(1–2):185–211; W. J. Harvey, *Character and the Novel* (Ithaca: Cornell University Press, 1965); and the works cited above in "The Characters of Philosophy," note 3.

    20. Katherine Eisaman Maus, "'Playhouse Flesh and Blood': Sexual Ideology and the Restoration Actress," *ELH* (1979), 46:603. Cf. Barish's account of seventeenth-century clerical antitheatricalism: "For the reformers, both English and continental, antitheatricalism joins hands with antifeminism as part of the war against pleasure" (p. 203). For discussions of the status of women in Defoe's thought and fiction, see: Nancy K. Miller, *The Heroine's Text: Readings in the French and English Novel, 1722–1782* (New York: Columbia University Press, 1980), pp. 3–20; John J. Richetti, "The Portrayal of Women in Restoration and Eighteenth-Century Literature" in Marlene Springer, ed., *What Manner of Woman: Essays on English and American Life and Literature* (New York: New York University Press, 1977), pp. 65–98; Miriam Lerenbaum, "Moll Flanders: 'A Woman On her own Account,'" in Arlyn Diamond and Lee R. Edwards, eds., *The Authority of Experience: Essays in Feminist Criticism* (Amherst: University of Massachusetts Press, 1977), pp. 101–117; Marsha Bordner, "Defoe's Androgynous Vision in *Moll Flanders* and *Roxana*," *Gypsy Scholar* (1975), 2: 76–93; J. Karen Ray, "The Feminine Role in *Robinson Crusoe, Roxana,* and *Clarissa*," *Emporia State Research Studies* (1976), 24(iii):28–33; Shirlene Mason, *Daniel Defoe and the Status of Women* (St. Albans, Vermont: Eden Press, 1978); Maximillian E. Novak, *Defoe and the Nature of Man* (London: Oxford University Press, 1963).

    21. Gildon, pp. 65–66.

    22. Among those critical works previously cited (note 14, ch. 3) that address Defoe's concern with deception, impersonation, and disguise, David Blewett's *Defoe's Art of Fiction* deals most specifically with Defoe's theatrical imagery and Moll Flanders' "zest for role-playing" (p. 80). In his chapter "Moll as Whore and Thief," Blewett describes a "pattern of disguise and deception" (p. 70) in *Moll Flanders* and he argues that life for Defoe "is like a play" (p. 84) in order to draw the moral that life is filled with uncertainty, duplicity, traps, and changing appearances. "It is because life resembles this kind of drama," writes Blewett, "that life is a cheat" (p. 84). My interpretation of Moll Flanders as an actress will differ from Blewett's account of Defoe's view of a dangerous and deceptive world of tricks and illusions. I

will argue that *Moll Flanders* and *Roxana* represent meditations on the conditions of theater and theatricality — and how those conditions determine the construction of the self, the status of the published book, and Defoe's own activity as an author.

23. Daniel Defoe, *Roxana, The Fortunate Mistress*, ed. Jane Jack (London: Oxford University Press, 1969), p. 1.

24. *Serious Reflections*, p. 102.

25. Braudy, p. 80.

26. *The Complete English Tradesman*, 1:28–29.

27. Daniel Defoe, *Street-Robberies, Consider'd: The Reason of their being so Frequent*, reprint of 1728 edition, ed. Geoffrey M. Sill (Stockton, New Jersey: Caroligian Press, 1973), pp. 30–35.

28. Quoted in Dale B. J. Randall, *Jonson's Gypsies Unmasked: Background and Theme of The Gypsies Metamorphos'd* (Durham, N.C.: Duke University Press, 1975), p. 51.

29. Randall, p. 57.

30. Cf. Edwin Nungezer, A *Dictionary of Actors and Of Other Persons Associated with the Public Presentation of Plays in England Before 1642* (New Haven: Yale University Press, 1929). Jonson's duel with Spencer was well-known since Jonson was not prosecuted because he claimed benefit of the clergy; that is, he demonstrated he could write.

31. Cf. Edward B. Partridge, introduction to *Bartholomew Fair* (Lincoln: University of Nebraska Press, 1969), p. xv.

32. Jonson, *Bartholomew Fair*, V, v, 90–97.

33. Braudy, p. 81.

34. Brown, "The Displaced Self," p. 563. Brown's discussion of the problem of concealment in Defoe's work (particularly in *Robinson Crusoe*) is enlightening and very helpful.

35. Brown, "The Displaced Self," pp. 570–571.

36. Defoe, *Roxana*, p. 326.

37. For another account of Moll's relationship with her Governess, see Robert A. Erickson, "Moll's Fate: 'Mother Midnight' and *Moll Flanders*," *Studies in Philology* (1979), 76:75–100.

38. *Roxana*, p. 6.

39. My discussion here about conversion and autobiography is indebted to Professor Neil Hertz. Starr and Hunter discuss other aspects of religious autobiography in *Defoe and Spiritual Autobiography* and *The Reluctant Pilgrim*, respectively.

40. John Freccero, Introduction to *Dante: A Collection of Critical Essays* (Englewood Cliffs, N.J.: Prentice Hall, 1965), p. 5.

41. Gustave Flaubert, *L'Éducation sentimentale* (Paris: Garnier, 1964), p. 77.

42. In this sense Moll Flanders is closer to Rousseau, who undergoes repeated "conversion experiences" in the course of his autobiographical texts, than to Dante, whose autobiography is structured around a single conversion.

6.   Roxana *and the Theater of Reading*

1. Daniel Defoe, *Roxana, The Fortunate Mistress*, ed. Jane Jack (New York: Oxford University Presss, 1969), p. 6. All further citations in this chapter, unless otherwise noted, will refer to this text.

2. "The History of this Beautiful Lady, is to speak for itself," we are told by an editor; yet a "Relator" has dressed up that history in worse clothes than the lady, "whose Words he speaks" (1). Even if we did not know that *Roxana* was a theatrical performance in which Defoe appeared in the person and in the costume of a woman, we would be asked to imagine some version of this situation by the editor—who is, of course, another part or costume used to cover Defoe.

3. As I noted in the last chapter, David Blewett discusses the recurrence of play-acting and disguise in Defoe's narratives. He sees these elements in *Roxana* as "part of the familiar pattern of disguise and dissimulation that in Defoe's fiction creates and supports a vision of human uncertainty and insecurity" (*Defoe's Art of Fiction*, p. 137). John J. Richetti writes of Roxana arranging "a tableau in which she stars, using the props and costumes that social relationships and the extraordinary personal accidents of her career provide. Her delighted self-dramatizing in this scene interacts beautifully with the aristocratic *mise en scène* provided for her" (*Defoe's Narratives: Situations and Structures* [Oxford: Clarendon Press, 1975], p. 216).

4. See, for example, Maximillian E. Novak, "Crime and Punishment in Defoe's *Roxana*," *Journal of English and German Philology* (1966), 65:450. For a psychoanalytic interpretation of Roxana's relation with Amy, see Terry J. Castle, "'Amy, Who Knew My Disease': A Psychosexual Pattern in Defoe's *Roxana*," *ELH* (1979), 46:81–96.

5. Moll Flanders has a similar experience when she sees her Lancashire husband from a window after her marriage to her Gentleman husband (*Moll Flanders*, p. 144).

6. Richetti notes, "Most commentators, in short, have found Roxana an appalling person and concluded with some justice that Defoe's purpose was to satirize her and the Restoration immorality she at times embodies" (pp. 192–193). In "Crime and Punishment in Defoe's *Roxana*," Novak argues that "the plot of *Roxana* revolves about the decline of Roxana's moral character" and that "the course of her career implies the moral decline of the entire society" (p. 459). He writes, "Defoe attacked the masquerade as leading inevitably to the decline of sexual morality" (p. 463). Blewett also argues that "Defoe is concerned in *Roxana* with the decline in social morality *in his own age* which he attacks under the guise of its resemblance to the notorious age of Charles II" (p. 124). He sees "the public immorality of the masquerade party" as "Defoe's vivid example of the moral and social decay of his age" (p. 143). Some critics move from a view of the narrative as a moral condemnation to their own moral condemnation of Roxana. E. Anthony James speaks of Roxana's "unnatural and unwomanly psychology," her "unstated jealous loathing of the male sex," and her "twisted morality and sexual coldness" (p. 242). Novak describes Roxana's "defense of sexual freedom for women" as "unnatural," although it is unclear whether he is simply paraphrasing Defoe's statements about the "natural order" of the sexes (p. 453). Other critics have been more sympathetic toward Roxana. In her introduction to *Roxana*, Jane Jack notes the "tension between sympathy and reprobation which is evident throughout the book" (p. xi). Katharine Rodgers sees *Roxana* as an indictment of the conditions of women in Defoe's time (Afterword, *Roxana* [New York: New American Library, 1979], pp. 287–295). Blewett's Introduction to his edition of *Roxana* ([Harmondsworth: Penguin Books, 1982], pp. 9–25) takes a somewhat more sympathetic approach than his *Defoe's Art of Fiction*, arguing what amounts to an "insanity defense" for Roxana.

Defoe's ability—indeed his propensity—to argue both sides of an issue is, of course, well known. What seems important here is to recognize that regardless of Defoe's possible intentions to write a Puritan condemnation of his society, *Roxana* becomes a psychological arena in which many of Defoe's preoccupations, anxieties, and fears are played out. It is crucial to see Defoe's own investment in the situation and character of Roxana. Richetti notes "Defoe's apparent imaginative participation in his narratives" (p. 193) and cites George Starr's comment that Defoe's "imaginative oneness" with Roxana "often seems virtually complete, and at such times we too may be drawn into a kind of complicity with her" (*Defoe and Casuistry*, p. 165). Jack speaks of Defoe's identification with his heroine (p. vii) and Michael Shinagel writes that "Defoe became involved personally in the career of Roxana" (*Daniel Defoe and Middle-Class Gentility*, p. 193). I will argue that we must read *Roxana* with Defoe's identification and complicity in mind. Novak writes that "disguise and deception are the essence of Roxana's life" (p. 464) but he does not seem to worry that Defoe may have convicted himself of a double imposture—despite Novak's own documentation in an article published in the same year as "Crime and Punishment in Defoe's *Roxana*" that Defoe himself delighted in disguise and deception ("Defoe's Uses of Irony"). See also: Wallace Jackson, "*Roxana* and the Development of Defoe's Fiction," *Studies in the Novel* (1975), 7:181–94; George A. Starr, "Sympathy vs. Judgement in Roxana's First Liaison," in Henry K. Miller, ed., *The Augustan Milieu: Essays Presented to Louis A. Landa* (Oxford: Clarendon Press, 1970); Ralph E. Jenkins, "The Structure of *Roxana*," *Studies in the Novel* (1970), 2:145–158; Richetti, "The Portrayal of Women in Restoration and Eighteenth-Century English Literature"; and Ray, "The Feminine Role in *Robinson Crusoe, Roxana,* and *Clarissa.*"

7. Recall that when Moll Flanders is identified, named, and imprisoned, she says, "I was now fix'd indeed" (*Moll Flanders*, p. 214). In *The Novel of Worldliness* (Princeton: Princeton University Press, 1969), Peter Brooks discusses what it means to be *fixed* by describing the act of beholding for Crébillon: "The glance is used to gain knowledge and control of another; the other can attempt to refuse the act of possession: 'Je la regardai fixement, mais mon attention la gênant sans doute, elle baissa les yeux en rougissant et me quitta.' Crébillon exploits the three related meanings of the verb *fixer*: to attach, to capture in arrest, and to gaze at fixedly. . . . Seeing, knowing, and controlling form the nucleus of a system of values shared by the novelist and his characters" (p. 19).

8. Blewett quotes the following from the *Memoirs of the Life of the Count de Grammont* (1714): "The Earl of Oxford fell in Love with a handsom, graceful Player, belonging to the Duke's Theater, who acted to Perfection, particularly the Part of Roxana in the Rival-Queens, insomuch that she afterwards was call'd by that Name" (*Defoe's Art of Fiction*, p. 123). For more on Roxana's name, see Novak, "Crime and Punishment," pp. 460–462; John Robert Moore, *Defoe in the Pillory and Other Studies* (Bloomington: Indiana University Press, 1939), pp. 39–49.

9. For other comments about Roxana's fear of exposure and desire for concealment, see Richetti, pp. 200–202, 218–222; Blewett, *Defoe's Art of Fiction*, pp. 141–143; Jackson, pp. 184–185; Steven Cohan, "Other Bodies: Roxana's Confession of Guilt," *Studies in the Novel* (1976), 8:410–411; Homer O. Brown, "The Displaced Self in the Novels of Daniel Defoe"; and Leo Braudy, "Daniel Defoe and the Anxieties of Autobiography."

10. *The Life and Strange Surprizing Adventures of Robinson Crusoe* also has a surprisingly nonlinear narrative as Crusoe doubles back to include various versions of his autobiography. Crusoe's Journal recapitulates events that already have been narrated and is strangely interwoven with Crusoe's retrospective narrative. *Roxana* interrupts itself to go back and retrace events, but it does so to introduce material that has been omitted. In addition to the self-censorship and revision that I have described, there are repeated images of accounts being fragmented. The daughter is said to have "a broken Account of things" which came in

"a broken manner" to Roxana's sister-in-law and was passed on in "broken Fragments of Stories" (269). At an uncomfortable moment Roxana seeks an excuse "to break off the Discourse for the present" when speaking with her husband; he responds by picking up a book and starting to read (297). The Captain tells Roxana's husband "a broken Piece of News that he had heard by halves" (299). Roxana's occasional reminders to herself to "go on a little with that Part, in order to bring the subsequent Parts of my Story together" (203) become increasingly necessary as the story becomes more and more fragmented and as it approaches the points where it must break off.

      11. For discussions of the ending of *Roxana*, see: Jenkins, "The Structure of *Roxana*"; Rodgers, "Afterword," p. 293; Richetti, *Defoe's Narratives*, p. 222; Novak, "Crime and Punishment," p. 465; Everett Zimmerman, *Defoe and the Novel* (Berkeley: University of California Press, 1975), p. 189; Robert D. Hume, "The Conclusion of Defoe's *Roxana*: Fiasco or Tour de Force?" *Eighteenth-Century Studies* (1970), 3:475–90; Benjamin Boyce, "The Question of Emotion in Defoe," pp. 54–58; James Sutherland, "The Conclusion of Roxana," in Max Byrd, ed., *Daniel Defoe: A Collection of Critical Essays* (Englewood Cliffs, N.J.: Prentice Hall, 1976), pp. 140–150; Michael Shinagel, *Daniel Defoe and Middle-Class Gentility*, pp. 192–196; Paul Dottin, *Daniel Defoe et ses romans* (Paris: Les Presses Universitaires de France, 1924), p. 731; Alan Dugald McKillop, *The Early Masters of English Fiction*, p. 37; Bonamy Dobrée, *English Literature in the Early Eighteenth Century, 1700–1740* (New York: Oxford University Press, 1964), p. 425; James Sutherland, "The Relation of Defoe's Fiction to his Non-Fictional Writings" in Maynard Mack and Ian Gregor, eds., *Imagined Worlds: Essays on Some English Novels and Novelists in Honor of John Butt* (London: Methuen, 1968).

      12. My discussion here is informed by Cavell's "Knowing and Acknowledging" and "The Avoidance of Love: A Reading of *King Lear*" in *Must We Mean What We Say?*

      13. Daniel Defoe, *The Life, Adventures and Piracies of the Famous Captain Singleton* (London: Dent, 1969), p. 335.

      14. For references to critics who speak of Defoe's identification with Roxana, see note 6.

      15. Shinagel writes: "By 1724 Defoe surely realized that he was, as a devout Puritan, dealing with a difficult and dangerous medium that induced him to give his teeming imagination free play. . . . Defoe no longer was able to control his imagination or his material, and being a good Puritan he decided not to tempt the devil any longer. . . . Defoe was astute enough as a Puritan and as an artist to realize that his fictions were leading him to excesses of the imagination over which he could not exercise the same control as in his other forms of writing, or as in his earlier works of prose fiction" (pp. 193–196). Although I agree with Shinagel that Defoe is worried about losing control, that writing the texts we know as his novels has come to feel dangerous for him, I am not convinced that the problem is really *fiction*. James Sutherland has demonstrated that Defoe continued to write fiction after 1724; in a sense, no work by Defoe can easily be categorized as "nonfiction." (See Sutherland, "The Relation of Defoe's Fiction to his Non-Fictional Writings.") *Street-Robberies, Consider'd*, for example, published in 1728, is a fictive criminal autobiography that reads like a "short story" version of *Moll Flanders* or *Colonel Jack*. As I argue in chapter 4, regardless of Defoe's place in the Puritan tradition, the situation of theater (in the case of *Roxana*, the conditions of theatricality) represents more of a problem to Defoe than the writing of fiction. In the context of my interpretation of *Roxana*, one could also imagine the daughter as a figure for Defoe's text: a creation that rebels against its parent or creator and seems to take on a life of its own. In this sense both the daughter and the book must be murdered by the threatened parents,

Roxana and Defoe. These variations on the Oedipal drama acted out both by parents and children and by authors and books also reveal *Roxana* as a prefiguring of Mary Shelley's *Frankenstein*.

Afterword to Part II

1. *The Storm*, p. 251.

2. *Serious Reflections*, pp. 3–4.

3. See, for example, Brown, "The Displaced Self" and Watt, *The Rise of the Novel*, chapter 3.

4. Rousseau, *Lettre à M. d'Alembert sur les spectacles*, in *Du Contract Social et autres oeuvres politiques* (Paris: Garnier, 1975), p. 134.

5. *Robinson Crusoe*, p. 30.

6. *Robinson Crusoe*, p. 156.

7. *Robinson Crusoe*, p. 90.

8. Brown, "The Displaced Self," p. 567.

9. *Robinson Crusoe*, p. 128.

10. *A Journal of the Plague Year*, p. 123; pp. 189–90.

11. *Plague Year*, p. 127.

12. *Serious Reflections*, p. 6.

13. *Serious Reflections*, pp. 8–9.

14. Defoe, *An Essay upon Literature: or An Enquiry into the Antiquity and Original of Letters; proving that the two Tables, written by the Finger of God in Mount Sinai, was the first Writing in the World* (London, 1726), p. 6.

15. *An Essay upon Literature*, p. 62.

16. *An Essay upon Literature*, p. 7; p. 16.

17. Defoe, *The History of the Life and Adventures of Mr. Duncan Campbell* in *The Novels and Miscellaneous Works of Daniel De Foe*, vol. 6 (London: Henry G. Bohn, 1856).

18. *Serious Reflections*, p. 4.

19. *Serious Reflections*, p. 4.

20. *Roxana*, p. 304.

21. *Roxana*, p. 304.

22. *Roxana*, p. 306.

23. *Moll Flanders*, p. 134.

24. *Plague Year*, p. 125.

25. *Roxana*, p. 308.

26. *Roxana*, p. 302.

27. *Roxana*, p. 277.

28. *Roxana*, p. 277.

7. Adam Smith and the Theatricality of Moral Sentiments

1. See, e.g., T. D. Campbell, *Adam Smith's Science of Morals* (London: George Allen and Unwin, 1971); Andrew S. Skinner, *A System of Social Science: Papers Relating to*

Adam Smith (Oxford: Clarendon Press, 1979); J. Ralph Lindgren, *The Social Philosophy of Adam Smith* (The Hague: Martinus Nijhoff, 1973); D. A. Reisman, *Adam Smith's Sociological Economics* (London: Croom Helm, 1976); Bernard Foley, *The Social Physics of Adam Smith* (West Lafayette, Indiana: Purdue University Press, 1976); A. L. Macfie, *The Individual in Society: Papers on Adam Smith* (London: George Allen and Unwin, 1967); D. D. Raphael, "The Impartial Spectator" in Andrew S. Skinner and Thomas Wilson, eds. *Essays on Adam Smith* (Oxford: Clarendon Press, 1975); Robert Lamb, "Adam Smith's System: Sympathy Not Self-Interest," *Journal of the History of Ideas* (1974), 35:671–82; Norman Fiering, "Irresistible Compassion: An Aspect of 18th-Century Sympathy and Humanitarianism," *Journal of the History of Ideas* (1976), 37:195–218; D. D. Raphael and A. L. Macfie, Introduction, *The Theory of Moral Sentiments* (Oxford: Clarendon Press, 1976), (all further references to this edition of *The Theory of Moral Sentiments* will be included parenthetically in the text); Glenn R. Morrow, "The Significance of the Doctrine of Sympathy in Hume and Adam Smith," *Philosophical Review* (1923), 32:60–78; R. F. Brissenden, "Authority, Guilt, and Anxiety in *The Theory of Moral Sentiments*," *Texas Studies in Literature and Language* (1969), 11:945–962.

2. In addition to the works cited above, see W. L. Taylor, *Francis Hutcheson and David Hume as Predecessors of Adam Smith* (Durham, North Carolina: Duke University Press, 1965).

3. Campbell, *Adam Smith's Science of Morals*, pp. 134–135; 102. I have omitted Campbell's references to Smith's text for each of his citations.

4. Raphael, "The Impartial Spectator," p. 88. Raphael is quoting from a Glasgow University Library Manuscript (ca. 1752), which he identifies as "the latter part of one of Smith's lectures on ethics from which he later composed *The Theory of Moral Sentiments*" (p. 88).

5. Jonas Barish, *The Antitheatrical Prejudice* (Berkeley: University of California Press, 1981), p. 244. Barish calls *The Theory of Moral Sentiments* "an anomaly" and refers to "Smith's view of the moral life as a genteel theater of mutually self-correcting passions." For Barish, Smith turns "the theatricality of society" into "something as innocuous as an invalid's pudding" (pp. 243, 255). In this chapter I will argue that Smith's theatrical perspective can be seen as belonging to a problematic developed by Shaftesbury, Defoe, and other eighteenth-century authors. Although I agree with Barish that Smith sometimes displays a "reluctance to face the implications of his own theatrical scheme" (p. 255), I will argue that Smith's view of theatricality is finally the opposite of "genteel" and "innocuous." Brissenden, in "Authority, Guilt, and Anxiety," writes about guilt and anxiety in *The Theory of Moral Sentiments* but nevertheless concludes that "the general tenor of Smith's work is optimistic" (p. 961). It is my sense that any optimism expressed by Smith is contained within a view of the world severely circumscribed by anxiety about theatrical relations. The close connection between theories of sympathy and theories of acting in the eighteenth century has been discussed by Earl R. Wasserman in "The Sympathetic Imagination in Eighteenth-Century Theories of Acting," *Journal of English and Germanic Philology* (July 1947), 46:264–272. See also Walter Jackson Bate, "The Sympathetic Imagination in Eighteenth-Century English Criticism," *ELH* (1945), 12:144–64.

6. Francis Hutcheson, *Inquiry Concerning Beauty, Order, Harmony, Design, An Inquiry into the Original of our Ideas of Beauty and Virtue*, 5th ed. (London, 1753), p. 103; *An Essay on the Nature and Conduct of the Passions and Affections: With Illustrations upon the Moral Sense* (London, 1728), pp. 63, 77–79.

7. David Hume, *Enquiry concerning the Principles of Morals* in L. A. Selby-Bigge, ed., *Enquiries Concerning Human Understanding and Concerning the Principles of Morals* (Oxford: Oxford University Press, 1975), pp. 178, 251, 221.

8. L'Abbé Batteux, *Principes de la littérature*, 5 vols. (Paris, 1764), 3:2.

9. L'Abbé Du Bos, *Réflexions critiques sur la poésie et sur la peinture*, 3 vols. (Paris, 1740), 1:39.

10. Henry Home, Lord Kames, *Elements of Criticism*, 3d ed., 2 vols. (Edinburgh, 1765), 1:421, 423, 37.

11. Kames, 1:82, 79; 2:326.

12. Hume provides a related description of the mirror effect of sympathy: "In general we may remark that the minds of men are mirrors to one another, not only because they reflect each other's emotions, but because those rays of passions, sentiments and opinions, may be often reverberated, and may decay away by insensible degrees. Thus the pleasure, which a rich man receives from his possessions, being thrown upon the beholder, causes a pleasure and esteem; which sentiments again, being perceived and sympathized with, encrease the pleasure of the possessor; and being once more reflected, become a new foundation for pleasure and esteem in the beholder" (*A Treatise of Human Nature* [New York: Oxford University Press, 1978], p. 365).

13. Joseph Butler, *The Works of Joseph Butler*, 2 vols. (Cambridge, Mass., 1827), 2:52 and see 2:47-65. In *The Individual in Society*, A. L. Macfie notes that no work by Butler is listed in Bonar's *Adam Smith's Library* and that there are no references to Butler in Smith's works. He adds, however, that Smith would have learned his Butler, at the least, from Hutcheson's teaching and writing (p. 99).

14. "By our continual and earnest pursuit of a character, a name, a reputation in the world, we bring our own deportment and conduct frequently in review, and consider how they appear in the eyes of those who approach and regard us. This constant habit of surveying ourselves, as it were, in reflection, keeps alive all the sentiments of right and wrong" (Hume, *Morals*), p. 276.

15. *Characteristics*, 1:121–122; 129.

16. *Characteristics*, 1:110; 113.

17. *Characteristics*, 1:128–129.

18. See, for example, Campbell, *Adam Smith's Science of Morals*, pp. 71, 94; Macfie, *The Individual in Society*, p. 84; Reisman, *Adam Smith's Sociological Economics*, pp. 79, 195; Skinner, *A System of Social Science*, p. 113; and the section "Influence of Contemporary Thinkers" in Raphael and Macfie's introduction to *The Theory of Moral Sentiments*, pp. 10–15. Smith himself seems to ignore his apparent debt to Shaftesbury, whom he belittled in a lecture in 1762. See Smith, *Lectures on Rhetoric and Belles-Lettres Delivered in the University of Glasgow by A.S. Reported by a Student in 1762–1763*, ed. John M. Lothian (London: Thomas Nelson and Sons, 1963), pp. 51–57. See also Smith's lecture on character and character-books, pp. 74–79.

19. Rousseau writes that "un comédien sur la scène, étalant d'autres sentiments que les siens . . . représentant souvent un être chimérique, s'anéantit, pour ainsi dire, s'annule avec son héros." Jean-Jacques Rousseau, *Lettre à M. d'Alembert sur les spectacles* in *Du Contract Social et autres oeuvres politiques* (Paris: Garnier, 1975), p. 187.

20. Hume, *Morals*, p. 234. Butler writes: "When we rejoice in the prosperity of others, and compassionate their distress, we, as it were, substitute them for ourselves, their interest for our own" (*Works*, 2:78). He tries to refute Hobbes by claiming that Hobbes' notion

of a "fiction or imagination of danger to ourselves from the sight of the miseries of others" would "not, indeed, be an example of substituting others for ourselves, but it would be an example of substituting ourselves for others" (*Works*, 2:81). For discussions of Smith's position on "self-interest" see R.H. Coase, "Adam Smith's View of Man," *Journal of Law and Economics* (Oct. 1976) 19:529–546; and Frederick M. Keener, *The Chain of Becoming: The Philosophical Tale, The Novel, and A Neglected Realism of the Enlightenment: Swift, Montesquieu, Voltaire, Johnson, and Austen* (New York: Columbia University Press, 1983), pp. 55–72. See also Samuel Hollander, "Adam's Smith's Approach to Economic Development" in Peter Hughes and David Williams, eds., *The Varied Pattern: Studies in the 18th Century* (Toronto: A.M. Hakkert, 1971), pp. 269–296.

    21. See Raphael and Macfie, Intro. to *The Theory of Moral Sentiments*, pp. 5–10. They note in particular: "In the fresh material added to edition 6 of *TMS*, Smith's elaboration of his account of Stoicism in Part VII is less significant than the clearly stoic tone of much that he wrote for Part III on the sense of duty and for the new Part VI on the character of virtue. Part VI deals with the three virtues of prudence, beneficence, and self-command. The third of these, which also figures in the additions to Part III, is distinctively Stoic" (p. 6). Cf. Plato's discussion in Book 10 of *The Republic* of the need to moderate passions. In speaking of a good man who has suffered misfortunes, Socrates asks: "Will he be more likely to struggle and hold out against his sorrow when he is seen by his equals, or when he is alone in a deserted place?" Glaucon responds: "The fact of being seen will make a great difference." Plato, *The Republic* in *The Dialogues of Plato*, trans. B. Jowett, 4th ed. rev. (Oxford: Clarendon Press, 1953), 604a.

    22. Du Bos, for example, begins his *Réflexions critiques* by reflecting on the paradox that "L'art de la Poësie & l'art de la Peinture ne sont jamais plus applaudis que lorsqu'ils ont réüssi à nous affliger" (p. 1). Cf. Smith's discussion of our "struggle against that sympathetic sorrow" when "we attend the representation of a tragedy" (p. 46). Raphael and Macfie note that Smith is in part responding to an objection by Hume, who raises the problem, in a letter written on July 28, 1759, of how "to account for the Pleasure, receivd from the Tears and Grief and Sympathy of Tragedy"; this would not be a problem, writes Hume, "if all Sympathy was agreeable. An Hospital would be a more entertaining Place than a Ball" (p. 46 n. 2).

    23. Shaftesbury, *Characteristics*, 2:4.

8. Daniel Deronda *and the Wisest Beholder*

    1. George Eliot, *Daniel Deronda*, ed. Barbara Hardy (Harmondsworth: Penguin Books, 1967), p. 35. All further citations in this chapter, unless otherwise noted, will refer to this text.

    2. Horace, *Ars Poetica*, 147–148 in *The Art of Poetry*, trans. Burton Raffel and James Hynd (Albany, New York: State University of New York Press, 1974), p. 35. Tristram writes that he will "go on tracing every thing in" his story "as *Horace* says, *ab Ovo*," neglecting to mention that Horace advises against this method. Later in the novel, he writes of rushing "as I may into the middle of things, as *Horace* advises" (Laurence Sterne, *The Life and Opinions of Tristram Shandy, Gentleman*, ed. Ian Watt [Boston: Houghton Mifflin, 1965], pp. 6, 215). Cf. Marthe Robert, *Roman des origines et origines du roman* (Paris: Gallimard, 1972).

3. Johan Wolfgang Goethe, *Faust: Der Tragödie Erster Tiel* (Stuttgart: Philipp Reclam, 1971), pp. 4–9.

4. Although my argument in this chapter (and in this book in general) does not depend upon the *influence* of Smith on Eliot, I should note that there is no evidence that I know of that can either prove or disprove that Eliot read Smith's *Theory of Moral Sentiments*. I have found no reference to it by name in Eliot's letters, journals, or essays. The book certainly would have been available to Eliot in her wide-ranging and often eccentric readings. *The Theory of Moral Sentiments* appeared in eighteen separate editions between 1800 and 1876, including both complete works of Smith and individual editions which were reprinted at regular intervals throughout the nineteenth century. (See D. D. Raphael and A. L. Macfie, Introduction to Adam Smith, *The Theory of Moral Sentiments* [Oxford: Clarendon Press, 1976], p. 32.) Furthermore, at the very least we know that Eliot had immediate access to extensive summaries of Smith's *Theory*. The library she shared with Lewes included an edition of *The Wealth of Nations* that contains a long summary of *The Theory of Moral Sentiments* by Dugald Stewart. (Cf. Adam Smith, *An Inquiry into the Nature and Causes of The Wealth of Nations*, ed. Edward Gibbon Wakefield, with *Life of the Author* by Dugald Stewart [London: Charles Knight & Co., 1843], 1:xxxiii–liv.) Also in the library was Victor Cousin's *Cours d'Histoire de la Philosophie Morale au dix-huitième siècle* (Brussels: Société Belge de Librarie, 1841). The fifth and sixth lessons of the "Seconde partie—Ecole écossaise" contain a long summary and paraphrase of *The Theory of Moral Sentiments* (pp. 125–172). My source for information about Eliot's library is William Baker's *The George Eliot-George Henry Lewes Library: An Annotated Catalogue of their Books at Dr. William's Library, London* (New York: Garland Publishing, Inc., 1977).

Other connections are possible: we know that Eliot was in contact with Leslie Stephen during the period that she was writing *Daniel Deronda* and he was completing his *History of English Thought in the Eighteenth Century.* (See Haight, p. 476, and Leslie Stephen, *George Eliot* [New York: Macmillan, 1906].) It is possible that she read or they discussed his discussion of Smith's "impartial spectator" in his chapter on Hartley and Smith. (Cf. Stephen, *History of English Thought in the Eighteenth Century* [New York: Harcourt, Brace, and World, 1962], 2:59–68.) Eliot could have been exposed to Smith's terms and ideas in less direct ways as well. Eliot might have read the chapter on "Self-Love and Benevolence" in her and Lewes' copy of William Godwin's *Enquiry Concerning Political Justice and its Influence on Morals and Happiness*; there she would have encountered such paraphrases of Smith as: "We are able in imagination to go out of ourselves, and become impartial spectators of the system of which we are a part" (*Enquiry*, ed. F.E.L. Priestley [Toronto: The University of Toronto Press, 1946], 1:427). See also Priestley's Critical Introduction: "[Godwin] borrows from Adam Smith and the Moral Sense school the 'impartial spectator'" (2:21).

Of course, for positivists in the 1870s, believing that the progress of their knowledge would render past philosophy obsolete, Smith's *Theory of Moral Sentiments* might have seemed rather out of date. However, questions about sympathy, altruism, egoism, social feeling, and society continued to interest Lewes, Spenser, Comte, and, of course, Eliot herself. Eliot praises sympathy in "The Natural History of German Life," calling it "the raw material of moral sentiment" (*Essays of George Eliot*, ed. Thomas Pinney [New York: Columbia University Press, 1963], p. 270). In her translation of Feuerbach's *The Essence of Christianity*, Eliot writes, "Feeling alone is the object of feeling. Feeling is sympathy. . . . In feeling man is related to his fellow man as to himself; he is alive to the sorrows, the joys of another as his own" (Ludwig Feuerbach, *The Essence of Christianity*, trans. Marian Evans

[London: John Chapman, 1854], p. 277). In "Worldliness and Other-Worldliness," Eliot condemns Young for his "deficiency in moral, *i.e.*, in sympathetic emotion" (*Essays*, p. 379). See also: K. K. Collins, "G. H. Lewes Revised: George Eliot and the Moral Sense," *Victorian Studies* (1978), 21:463–492.

    5. Felicia Bonaparte, *Will and Destiny: Morality and Tragedy in George Eliot's Novels* (New York: New York University Press, 1975), pp. 133, 169. See also W. J. Harvey, *The Art of George Eliot* (New York: Oxford University Press, 1969); Barbara Hardy, *The Novels of George Eliot: A Study in Form* (London: The Athlone Press, 1959); K. M. Newton, *George Eliot: Romantic Humanist: A Study of the Philosophical Structure of her Novels* (Totowa, N.J.: Barnes and Noble Books, 1981); Calvin Bedient, *Architects of the Self: George Eliot, D.H. Lawrence, and E.M. Forster* (Berkeley: University of California Press, 1972); Karl Kroeber, *Styles in Fictional Structure: The Art of Jane Austen, Charlotte Brontë, George Eliot* (Princeton: Princeton University Press, 1971); Hugh Witemeyer, *George Eliot and the Visual Arts* (New Haven: Yale University Press, 1979); Deirdre David, *Fictions of Resolution in Three Victorian Novels: North and South, Our Mutual Friend, Daniel Deronda* (New York: Columbia University Press, 1981); Mary Ellen Doyle, *The Sympathetic Response: George Eliot's Fictional Rhetoric* (Rutherford: Fairleigh Dickinson University Press, 1981); Neil Roberts, *George Eliot: Her Beliefs and Her Art* (London: Paul Elek, 1975); P. Bourl'homme, *George Eliot: Essai de biographie intellectuelle et morale, 1819–1854: Influences anglaises et étrangères* (Paris: Librairie Ancienne Honoré Champion, 1933); Steven Marcus, *Representations: Essays in Literature and Society* (New York: Random House, 1975); James D. Benson, "'Sympathetic' Criticism: George Eliot's Response to Contemporary Reviewing," *Nineteenth-Century Fiction* (1975), 29:428–440. For a discussion of the debate about the physiological senses of sympathy in the early nineteenth century, see Ruth Leys, "Background to the Reflex Controversy: William Alison and the Doctrine of Sympathy Before Hall," *Studies in the History of Biology* (1980), 4:1–66.

    6. Doyle, p. 160; David, p. 144; David R. Carroll, "The Unity of 'Daniel Deronda,'" *Essays in Criticism* (October 1959), 9:373.

    7. Gordon S. Haight cites this description of *Daniel Deronda* from George Henry Lewes' diary entry of June 29, 1873, in *George Eliot: A Biography* (New York: Oxford University Press, 1968), p. 471.

    8. F. R. Leavis, *The Great Tradition* (New York: Doubleday, 1954), pp. 101–154. James' dialogue, *"Daniel Deronda: A Conversation,"* is reprinted as an appendix, pp. 300–319.

    9. *Roxana*, p. 73.

    10. The allusion to Goethe is also noted by Hugh Witemeyer in *George Eliot and the Visual Arts*, p. 93. Witemeyer points to this entry from Eliot's Berlin journal: "I was pleased also to recognize among the pictures the one by Jan Steen, which Goethe describes in the 'Wahlverwandtschaften' as the model of a *tableau vivant*, presented by Luciane and her friends. It is the daughter being reproved by her father, while the mother is emptying the wineglass." The passage appears in J. W. Cross, ed., *George Eliot's Life as Related in her Letters and Journals* (Boston: Dana Estes and Co., 1968), 1:279. George Henry Lewes' *The Life of Goethe*, which was being prepared for its third edition while Eliot was writing *Daniel Deronda* (see Hardy, intro., *Daniel Deronda*, p. 885), has a chapter on private theatricals in Goethe's Weimar (New York: E. P. Dutton, 1938), pp. 237–245. For a discussion of Goethe's scene and the painting—which, as Witemeyer notes, is actually by Ter Borch—see Michael Fried, *Absorption and Theatricality*, pp. 171–173. I do not mean to suggest that *Mansfield Park* is not an important backdrop for *Daniel Deronda*. Fanny seems defined by her non-

theatrical and perhaps even antitheatrical sensibilities. She is thrown into a crisis when called upon to participate in the play, crying, "I could not act any thing if you were to give me the world. No, indeed, I cannot act" (Jane Austen, *Mansfield Park* [Harmondsworth: Penguin Books, 1966], p. 168). Fanny is also "shocked to find herself at that moment the only speaker in the room, and to feel that almost every eye was upon her" (pp. 168–169).

    11. Goethe, *Elective Affinities*, trans. Elizabeth Mayer and Louise Bogan (South Bend, Indiana: Gateway Editions, 1963), pp. 171, 187. References to the German text are from *Die Wahlverwandtschaften* (Stuttgart: Reclam, 1977).

    12. Witemeyer, p. 94.

    13. Newton, p. 182. For other discussions of acting or theater in Eliot's work, see Kroeber, pp. 100–107; David, pp. 182–183; Witemeyer, p. 42; Bedient, p. 60; Hardy, p. 109; Harvey, p. 59.

    14. Fried, *Absorption and Theatricality*, ch. 1.

    15. Jean-Jacques Rousseau, *Lettre à M. d'Alembert sur les spectacles* in *Du Contract Social et autres oeuvres politiques* (Paris: Garnier, 1975), p. 195; p. 212.

    16. Bonaparte, p. 104.

    17. Suave, mari magno turbantibus aequora ventis,
       e terra magnum alterius spectare laborem;
       non quia vexari quemquamst iucunda voluptas,
       sed quibus ipse malis careas quia cernere suave est.

T. Lucreti Cari, *De Rerum Natura*, ed. H. A. J. Munro (Cambridge: Deighton Bell and Co., 1866), 1:78. Munro's translation of these lines is: "It is sweet, when on the great sea the winds trouble its waters, to behold from land another's deep distress; not that it is a pleasure and delight that any should be afflicted, but because it is sweet to see from what evils you are yourself exempt" (3:28).

    18. William Shakespeare, *The Tempest* in *The Complete Works*, General Editor, Alfred Harbage (Baltimore: Penguin Books, 1969), I, ii, 26; 5–6; 27. Further citations from Shakespeare will refer to this edition.

    19. Abbé Du Bos, *Réflexions critiques sur la poésie et sur la peinture* (Paris: Pierre-Jean Mariette, 1740), p. 13. Cf. Aristotle, *Poetics*, trans. Ingram Bywater in Friedrich Solmsen, ed., *Rhetoric and Poetics of Aristotle* (New York: The Modern Library, 1954), especially 1448b and 1452b–1453a. Cf. also the appendix on pity and fear in Pierro Pucci, *The Violence of Pity in Euripides' Medea* (Ithaca: Cornell University Press, 1980).

    20. Rousseau writes: "En donnant des pleurs à ces fictions, nous avons satisfait à tous les droits de l'humanité, sans avoir plus rien à mettre du nôtre" (*Lettre à d'Alembert*, p. 141).

    21. Smith, p. 137.

    22. Smith, p. 110.

    23. George Eliot, "Impressions of Theophrastus Such" in *Miscellaneous Essays* (New York: Doubleday, Page, 1901), p. 256.

    24. Smith, p. 131.

    25. Smith, p. 112.

    26. Smith, p. 152.

    27. See, especially, the "Cinquième Promenade" in *Les Rêveries du promeneur solitaire* (Paris: Garnier, 1960).

    28. Rousseau, *Lettre*, p. 187; Smith, p. 152.

    29. Smith, p. 29.

30. David, p. 144.

31. Alan Mintz, *George Eliot and the Novel of Vocation* (Cambridge: Harvard University Press, 1978), p. 161. See also J. B. Schneewind, "Moral Problems and Moral Philosophy in the Victorian Period," *Victorian Studies* (Supplement) (Sept. 1965), 9:29–46, esp. pp. 45–46.

32. Carroll, p. 380.

33. K. M. Newton relates what he calls "assertive egotism" to "actors and role-players" in Eliot's work. "Acting is probably the main symbol in the novel of the ego's desire for power and dominance" (p. 177). I am suggesting that the dynamics of the interplay between power and theatrical relations are somewhat more complicated.

34. The vagueness of Mordecai's reference—"Somewhere in the later *Midrash*, I think, is the story"—makes the parable difficult to identify. A reference to "the later *Midrash*" is in itself somewhat strange. I have been unable to locate this story in one of Eliot's sources, *Parabeln, Legenden und Gedanken aus Thalmud und Midrasch*, trans. Ludwig Seligmann, ed. Giuseppe Levi (Leipzig: Ostar Leiner, 1863); or in Ignaz Ziegler, *Die Königsgleichnisse des Midrash beleuchtet durch die Römische Kaiserzeit* (Breslau, 1903). Although I have not been able to make a complete search, I would not be surprised if it turned out that Eliot invented the story, as she sometimes invents verse for her epigraphs. Its allegorical status in the novel is striking in either case, however. For more information on *Daniel Deronda* and Judaism, see William Baker, *George Eliot and Judaism* (Salzburg: Institut für Englische Sprache und Literatur, 1975) and Avrom Fleishman, *Fiction and the Ways of Knowing* (Austin: University of Texas Press, 1978).

35. Clearly the maiden does not empathize with her rival in our modern sense of sympathy; she acts out the positions and structure of sympathy by taking the other woman's part and place. Perhaps this substitution and exchange of roles should be seen as a parody, or at least a literal rendering of the metaphor of sympathy.

36. Defoe, *Serious Reflections*, pp. 3–4.

37. *The George Eliot Letters*, ed. Gordon S. Haight (New Haven: Yale University Press, 1954), 2:156 (May 19, 1854). Bonaparte also cites this letter in the provocative conclusion to the second chapter of *Will and Destiny*. She writes that Eliot maintains that "every individual is born in complete isolation and in vital respects remains insular throughout his life. Irrevocably bound to the limits of his own consciousness—again, Eliot accepts the empiricist view—each man finds himself unable to participate directly in the equally isolated consciousness of another or to understand, even indirectly, its true nature. Each man sees, as a result, only from his own point of view, and can never know either the point of view of another or the objective fact as it really is" (pp. 102–103).

38. In thinking about the questions about other minds raised in this chapter, I have received instruction, as well as confirmation of the significance of the questions I was taking Smith and Eliot to ask, in parts of Stanley Cavell's *The Claim of Reason: Wittgenstein, Skepticism, Morality, and Tragedy* (New York: Oxford University Press, 1979), especially Part Four, "Skepticism and the Problem of Others."

39. Newton, p. 178.

40. Eliot's use of the terms "sincere acting" and the "conscious representation" of "real" "feeling" may be related to Austen's description of Lady Bertram in *Mansfield Park*. She is described as moving from "playing at being frightened" to writing "in a different style, in the language of real feeling" (p. 417). Earlier, Sir Thomas Bertram is described as exhibiting "a piece of true acting" (p. 198). Although the Bertrams are relatively minor characters in the

novel, the terms of "true acting" and "real feeling" are crucial in the crisis of meaning brought about by the Crawfords' (and others') playing.

41. J. Hillis Miller, "Narrative and History," *ELH* (1974), 41:455–473; and "Optic and Semiotic in *Middlemarch*," in Jerome H. Buckley, ed., *The Worlds of Victorian Fiction* (Cambridge: Harvard University Press, 1975), pp. 125–45; Neil Hertz, "Recognizing Casaubon," *Glyph 6* (Baltimore: The Johns Hopkins University Press, 1979), pp. 24–41.

42. Diderot, *Oeuvres romanesques,* ed. Henri Bénac (Paris: Éditions Garnier Frères, 1962), p. 869.

43. *Miscellaneous Essays,* p. 253.

44. Cf. Haight, p. 51, and for more information about Eliot and physiognomy, see Witemeyer, pp. 46–55.

45. Norton Batkin explores the question of the past and future of a photograph, as well as the relation of photographs to film, in *Photography and Philosophy* (Diss. Harvard, 1981).

46. *Elective Affinities,* pp. 158, 98; *Die Wahlverwandtschaften,* pp. 135, 86.

47. *Moll Flanders,* p. 142.

48. Hugh Kenner, *Joyce's Voices* (Berkeley: University of California Press, 1978), pp. 4–5.

49. Samuel Richardson, *Pamela: Or, Virtue Rewarded* (New York: New American Library, 1980), p. 23.

50. *The Correspondence of Samuel Richardson,* 6 vols., ed. Anna Laetitia Barbauld (London: R. Philips, 1804), 2:104–105 (December 7, 1756).

51. Reported in *Boswell's Life of Johnson,* ed. George Birkbeck Hill and L. F. Powell (Oxford: Clarendon Press, 1934), 2:48–49.

52. Ian Watt, *The Rise of the Novel: Studies in Defoe, Richardson, and Fielding* (Harmondsworth: Penguin Books, 1977), pp. 310–311. See Henry Fielding, *The History of Tom Jones, A Foundling* (New York: The Modern Library, 1950), p. 112.

53. John Locke, *An Essay Concerning Human Understanding,* ed. Alexander Campbell Fraser (New York: Dover, 1959), 2:8, 3, 154.

54. Henry Fielding, "An Essay on the Knowledge of the Characters of Men" in Henry Knight Miller, ed., *Miscellanies by Henry Fielding, Esq.* (Oxford: Clarendon Press, 1972), 1:155, 162.

55. Patricia Meyer Spacks, *Imagining A Self: Autobiography and Novel in Eighteenth-Century England* (Cambridge: Harvard University Press, 1976), pp. 193–226.

56. "An Essay on the Knowledge of the Characters of Men," p. 174; Henry Fielding, *Joseph Andrews and Shamela,* ed. Sheridan Baker (New York: Thomas Y. Crowell, 1972), Preface to *Joseph Andrews,* p. 63.

57. Laurence Sterne, *The Life and Opinions of Tristram Shandy, Gentleman,* ed. Ian Watt (Boston: Houghton Mifflin, 1965), pp. 55–57.

58. Watt, *The Rise of the Novel,* p. 334.

59. Dorrit Cohn, *Transparent Minds: Narrative Modes for Presenting Consciousness in Fiction* (Princeton: Princeton University Press, 1978), p. 115. Cohn writes: "The pattern set by Jane Austen thus unfolds throughout the nineteenth century: precisely those authors who, in their major works, most decisively abandoned first-person narration (Flaubert, Zola, James), instituting instead the norms of the dramatic novel, objective narration, and unobtrusive narrators, were the ones who re-introduced the subjectivity of private experience into the novel: this time not in terms of direct self-narration, but by imperceptibly

integrating mental reactions into the neutral-objective report of actions, scenes, and spoken words."

60. Austen, *Mansfield Park: A Novel*, p. 149.

61. First-person narratives and fictive autobiographies, of course, continued in the nineteenth century. One could argue, however, that some authors were aware that this mode of narrative somehow placed them in a closer relation to their literary forebearers. *Great Expectations*, for example, opens up to include within its autobiography the autobiography of a Newgate rogue who never knew his parents, lived a life ˙of crime and adventure, and was fond of changing his name and appearance; his trial is described as a kind of theatrical representation. I take this narrative excursion to be Dickens' acknowledgement of his debt to—as well as his distance from—the novels of Defoe.   .

62. Henry James, *The Aspern Papers and Other Stories* (Harmondsworth: Penguin Books, 1976), p. 58.

63. Henry James, *The Wings of the Dove* (Harmondsworth: Penguin Books, 1976), p. 34.

64. Henry James, *The Golden Bowl* (Harmondsworth: Penguin Books, 1978), p. 7.

65. *The Golden Bowl*, p. 537.

66. *The Golden Bowl*, p. 111.

67. *The Golden Bowl*, p. 50.

68. For discussions of the development of the interior monologue, see Cohn, *Transparent Minds*; Melvin Friedman, *Stream of Consciousness: A Study in Literary Method* (New Haven: Yale University Press, 1955); Robert Humphrey, *Stream of Consciousness in the Modern Novel* (Berkeley: University of California Press, 1954); Robert Scholes and Robert Kellogg, *The Nature of Narrative* (Oxford: Oxford University Press, 1966), pp. 240–282; Wayne C. Booth, *The Rhetoric of Fiction*, 2d ed. (Chicago: The University of Chicago Press, 1983). See also J. Hillis Miller, "The Narrator as General Consciousness" in *The Form of Victorian Fiction: Thackeray, Dickens, Trollope, George Eliot, Meredith, and Hardy* (Cleveland, Ohio: Arete Press, 1979), pp. 53–90.

69. Hugh Kenner, *The Stoic Comedians: Flaubert, Joyce, and Beckett* (Berkeley: University of California Press, 1974), pp. 48–49; cf. *Joyce's Voices*, pp. 94–95.

70. Frank Budgen, *James Joyce and the Making of Ulysses* (Bloomington: Indiana University Press, 1960), p. 181.

71. James Joyce, *Ulysses* (New York: Random House, 1961), p. 756.

Index